ALSO BY ISHION HUTCHINSON

Far District
House of Lords and Commons
School of Instructions

FUGITIVE TILTS

Farrar, Straus and Giroux
New York

TILTS

FUGITIVE

ESSAYS

ISHION

HUTCHINSON

Farrar, Straus and Giroux
120 Broadway, New York 10271

Owing to limitations of space, all acknowledgments for permission to reprint previously published material can be found on page 365.

Illustration credits can be found on pages 367–368.

Library of Congress Cataloging-in-Publication Data
Names: Hutchinson, Ishion, author.
Title: Fugitive tilts : essays / Ishion Hutchinson.
Description: First edition. | New York : Farrar, Straus and Giroux, 2025.
Identifiers: LCCN 2024038332 | ISBN 9780374600518 (hardcover)
Subjects: LCGFT: Essays.
Classification: LCC PR9265.9.H85 F84 2025 | DDC 811/.6—dc23/eng/20241023
LC record available at https://lccn.loc.gov/2024038332

Designed by Patrice Sheridan

Our books may be purchased in bulk for promotional, educational, or business use. Please contact your local bookseller or the Macmillan Corporate and Premium Sales Department at 1-800-221-7945, extension 5442, or by email at MacmillanSpecialMarkets@macmillan.com.

www.fsgbooks.com
Follow us on social media at @fsgbooks

1 3 5 7 9 10 8 6 4 2

In memory of Professor Edward Baugh
and
for the Chancellors,
Dante Micheaux and Adam Wiedewitsch

CONTENTS

FUGITIVE TILTS

TREASURE ISLAND AND ME

FOUR YEARS AGO, AS I WALKED DOWN VIA GIULIA IN ROME, the sea rose in front of me. It surfaced from the cobblestones, in a blue moment, then gone. Years before, in Berlin, the same thing happened. Before that, it had happened in Marrakech, and years before, recurring many times over, the sea rose from the paved asphalt streets in New York City, especially in Brooklyn, where I was living. It was the sea of home, which far from home it has been my luck to glimpse, the quicksilver flash calming the anxious fit of homesickness that would come over me.

But the first blue moment was at home, in Kingston. I had recently moved there from my hometown, Port Antonio, a small seacoast town in northeast Jamaica, to study at the university in the city. Within weeks, the excitement of Kingston—this was September 2003—began to be replaced by an emotion I couldn't have anticipated: homesickness. Missing home, yes, but not with the intensity associated with homesickness, the longing for home you have while in a foreign country, away from your familiar cultural orientations. But homesickness was the emotion I felt in Kingston, a dreadful longing for Port Antonio and its sea.

The longing drove me one morning into the campus library, of all places. Hours later I emerged to a blue glow trembling before my eyes on the neat row of gray flagstones decorating the lawn in front of the library building. I thought the bright sunlight, after the dimmer light of the library, was having some effect on me. In the same instance, however, the anxiety that drove me into the library lifted clean. I knew then the hallucination, whatever you call the blue disappearing even as it appeared, was the sea of home. When I was reading inside the library the book I had gone in search of, the anxiety had already started to lift, so the sight of the sea outside was like the tangible, ungraspable gift of the book's calming magic. It was still in my hand while I stood on the library steps, Robert Louis Stevenson's *Treasure Island*.

I was eleven when I first opened *Treasure Island*, curled in a chair on the veranda of my grandmother's house. Built sometime in the 1970s, her house stands on a hill overlooking the Caribbean Sea in Port Antonio. I had got it from the public library one evening. The title, new to me, seemed to offer a promising story. But really I chose it no differently from the way I chose other books, to shield me from chores at home, where during the two-week loan period no one bothered me when I was seen reading around the house or the yard. I was a fast reader, so usually half of that time I was only pretending to be reading. It was my odd, strict quirk when I returned to the library to never borrow the same book twice. There was no reason anyway, because I would copy out my favorite passages of books into my notebooks, filling several pages at a time. Since age ten this had been my pattern: one book for two weeks—sometimes copying out passages—followed by the next book for another two weeks.

Then *Treasure Island* arrived and for the next decade I renewed it up to four times each year before eventually I left Port Antonio for university in Kingston. Each successive reading activated something in me, a yearning toward wonder that I had felt before but could neither name nor grasp. This grew intensely during those intervals of two weeks when I was rereading *Treasure Island*, until at some point, long after I had closed the book, there seemed to be hardly any gap between my imagination and reality. My world had become blurred with this sensuously charged, unnamable, ungraspable thing and I wanted nothing else but to both name and grasp that feeling. Only much later, and through different stages of training my imaginative focus, I began to understand that *Treasure Island* was, in my childhood, a three-dimensional map, simultaneously pointing me to myself, by taking me out of myself and literally toward the landscape I knew.

I read other books around the house, in my room or on the veranda, and out in the yard, seated on a flat rock at the side of the house or on a bamboo bench under the ackee tree in the front yard, but rarely ever beyond these places. *Treasure Island* I read all over Port Antonio. I started tentatively, taking it to places near my grandmother's house, like the beach Bryan's Bay just down the hill and the bamboo grove at the riverhead above Rio Grande farther up the hill.

As I grew older, I went farther. I began at the pier, about forty minutes' walk in the middle of town, finding a perch away from but within earshot of the day's bustle—it's a commercial area of town—to read. I started going to the far edges of town, like on the peninsula of Folly Point, an hour's walk from my grandmother's house. There I read on the spiky rock of the bluff, occasionally looking up from the pages across the expansive open sea to the pincer curve of Titchfield Peninsula opposite. Half-hidden in the dense green of that peninsula were the buildings of the high school I attended. I read *Treasure Island* on the grounds of the school, which was founded in 1786 on the ruins of Fort George, which the British built in 1729 to defend the island from invasion by sea, especially from the Spanish, the first colonizers of the island, whom the British had kicked out in 1655. I read it many evenings all over the long reef bordering the west side of the school, circling back afterward into the town by cutting through the Errol

Flynn Marina to arrive on the West Harbour, from where I'd start the steep uphill climb to my grandmother's house.

Why, growing up in Jamaica in the 1990s, did I expend all this ambulatory energy on a sea yarn published in Britain in 1883? It was the yarn itself, set in "the year of grace 17—" (likely the 1750s), according to the opening sentence, that was so arresting.

The adventure moves quickly; a sea-worn buccaneer arrives at an inn in a remote hamlet; for good reason his nerves are raw, his old pirate cronies are after a treasure map stowed in his heavy sea chest; they will stop at nothing to retrieve it; he terrorizes the inn and breaks often into the haunting "Dead Man's Chest" song, his truly glorious contribution to the text: "Fifteen men on the dead man's chest—Yo-ho-ho, and a bottle of rum"; he drinks lots of rum; it is what ultimately kills him, a stroke from rum and fright when pirates start to arrive at the inn; from there, in a series of incidents all hell breaks loose; the hamlet becomes engulfed in a standoff at the inn between the buccaneers and Jim Hawkins; at the last moment, the frightened hamlet folks rally to his help; the pirates flee at their arrival but one, Pew, dies that night—he is the third person to die in the novel's early section—by stampede, horses crushing him into the sand; it is a spectacular scene Stevenson compresses into two sentences: "Down went Pew with a cry that rang high into the night; and the four hoofs trampled and spurned him and passed by. He fell on his side, then gently collapsed upon his face and moved no more."

The night tests young Jim's mettle. Scared, he shows bravery and a great agility to think and act under pressure. On Treasure Island, this agility saves his life and that of his companions—all men much older than him—several times. He navigates the island as if it were second nature to him; it's a studied intimacy because before he departs for the island,

I brooded by the hour together over the map, all the details of which I well remembered. Sitting by the fire in the housekeeper's room, I approached that island in my fancy, from every possible direction; I explored every acre of its surface; I climbed a thousand times to that tall hill they call the Spy-glass, and from the top enjoyed the most wonderful and changing prospects. Sometimes the isle was thick with savages, with whom we fought; sometimes full of dangerous animals that hunted us; but in all my fancies nothing occurred to me so strange and tragic as our actual adventures.

It's not savages or dangerous animals but pirates with gold, blood, and rum on their brains that Jim and his friends battle; there the narrative hurtles between chase scenes ("a little cloud of pirates leaped from the woods"!), shoot-outs, "embassy"—peace—talks going awry (these are some of the funniest parts of the book); there are many little unexpected twists, but the most significant is Jim's discovery of Ben Gunn, a "half-idiot maroon" who becomes integral to the novel's climax, of securing the treasure and finally departing the island, back to Bristol. Back home, the island haunts Jim, the surf seeping into his dreams. The book ends on that note of haunting: "I hear the surf booming about its coasts or start upright in bed with the sharp voice of Captain Flint still ringing in my ears: 'Pieces of eight! Pieces of eight!'"

When I started to read *Treasure Island* far away from home, I began to realize I did so to put myself back in the motion of those early trapezing days, when I read it around the bays, the pier, and the market of Port Antonio. Filtered through the book, the landscape and the sea were mine in a special way. But I read for stillness as the years drifted, too. The stillness of that first read, at age eleven, high in the mast of a hill with the sea beneath me, curled in the lattice chair on the veranda of my grandma's house. The posture of that evening was a kind of fetal position, the original self-curling shell of defense. The farther away I travel from home, the more I turn to *Treasure Island* to put myself in that position, not in the physical way I did in childhood, but holding the text feels that way. It is as if contorting myself around its familiar words, I can feel a sudden burst of sea spume on my face.

For the sea is *Treasure Island*'s true element. Hawkins calls it an "unbroken mirror." There's nothing particularly startling about the phrase. But it is one of the many simple phrases, which on subsequent reading of the novel, I found startling. It lives now in my head as a precise depiction of the sea around me. I cannot "critically" account for why I hear in it the authority of a fresh vernacular force, the force that brings to me the blue moment of home sea and quiets my homesickness in distant foreign streets. It is just there, even though—and only belatedly I began to admit this to myself—the tropical water of the Caribbean Sea is not present in Stevenson's book. For instance, some mornings on the island get so cold that Jim feels "a chill that pierced into [his] marrow." I never felt cold at home, and it was bizarre to associate the sea with cold.

Only in my second or third year in Kingston did I begin to realize Stevenson's sea is a heavily literary sea. To create *Treasure Island*, Stevenson culls his sea from books, most of which are classics of European piracy in the Caribbean, like Captain Charles Johnson's 1724 *General History of the Pyrates*. But what mattered to me as a boy, what pierced into my marrow, was what I intuitively felt, Stevenson's prose magnifying the Caribbean Sea I saw spread out beneath my grandmother's hill, the foam breakers crashing white against the black rock of Titchfield Peninsula.

From my grandmother's veranda, I was the lone surveyor of the open sea and all it touches. Eyeing the sea from above the pages of *Treasure Island*, I wondered longer at it and at the landscape. I wondered—I was about twelve at this time, a full year of reading *Treasure Island*—how the bays, the coves, and the ridges behind our house got their names. Because the book is studded with place-names, relished by Hawkins, I wonder about this. Strange to think, later when I left home, that it was *Treasure Island* that brought on this kind of wondering about inheritance.

Slowly, I began to learn that the names of everything around me derived from the great hurt of colonial subjugation. All these beautiful names—Frenchman's Cove, Blue Lagoon, Fort George, Folly Estate—masked the pain subdued in the sea and landscape. They amount to indexes within a catalog of official robbery. I learned this not from the (official) history taught at my school, much though the lessons taught made clear to me the terror of colonial subjugation. It was something else. It was the indirect, subtle cues in the way people I grew up with talk. They spoke as if the sea were in their mouths. This way of speaking, I came to realize perhaps only when I got to Kingston, was a kind of psychic courage. It was the great effort of sounding, without self-betrayal, these names laden with history's betrayal, the ongoing malaise of colonial pain.

This is one of the reasons why every time I reread the first sentence of *Treasure Island*, my breath catches on what Hawkins declares as his purpose in writing about the island. He does so to set down "from the beginning to the end, keeping nothing back but the bearings of the island," then adds, "because there is still treasure not yet lifted." There is a revelatory tension in the latter phrase; that fettering of "there is" to "not yet" depicts, to my ear, the air of dispossession that never disappears for a Caribbean person, even when they own the title to the land. The phrase expresses the essential—the existential— postcolonial contradiction of my grandmother.

She was a landowner and a baker who sold in Port Antonio's Musgrave Market. The market was named for Sir Anthony Musgrave, a descendant of a powerful slaveholding family who was the governor-general of Jamaica from 1877 to 1883. Decades before I was born, my grandmother made a shaky *X* on the signature line of a property deed, thereby giving her life's work a pirate's marker. She lived after aware she had not named herself fully to what belonged to her. Her *X* was both a placeholder and a legal fiction of ownership, seemingly waiting to be remedied. But by whom? By the current representative of the queen of England in Jamaica, the governor-general, Sir Howard Felix Hanlan Cooke, the man who said, "Jamaica's greatness was entirely due to slavery"?

Or the boy reading in the lattice chair?

My grandmother's eyes held such an injured and assaulted stare whenever we visited the land title and deed section of the Portland Municipal Corporation (PMC), worried the land she had bought long before I was born belonged to someone else. Because I had seen her so the first time we went together to the PMC, the remedying became a point of duty for me. We had to go to other offices, obscure as ever, to find out how to put her name correctly in the land title. And so, for months, a boy of about thirteen and his grandmother trampled from office to office across Portland, going from one justice of the peace to another justice of the peace for years until her name was entered into the property deed. I held her trembling hand that day, not long before I was to leave Port Antonio, as she formed the letters of her name, May Hutchinson. The land finally became ours, and we were the land's. Following that, the kinship I felt with Hawkins as I read and my grandmother passed me by, perhaps with a bushel of my white school shirts, was immense because I knew she was passing with greater peace on her property.

Something else deepened the kinship I felt with Hawkins. Like me as a boy, Jim Hawkins was a pirate of circumstance, an outlaw forced to be "a good, prompt subaltern," up against the torrents of life. Even so, he expressed the long vision that claimed a possibility to come. (He himself was that possibility.) My grandmother saw me in this way, silently affirming in me a future neither of us was able to judge. So, I claimed him.

The claim was moral dignity. Fiction's vision-clearing power allowed me to see through the dim colonial degradation and the leftover poverty of our rural coastal town that can be seen in the long stretches of blighted coconut trees along the coast with—and here was another contradiction—many luxurious tourist oases hidden in the Blue Mountain range behind the coconut trees. Expensive villas with picturesque names nested in the coves near the beaches.

This was the background I brought to *Treasure Island* and found a strange intimacy in the sinew of its language. As I read, I was discovering what Hawkins calls "the joy of exploration" when he arrives on the island. I was learning through him, through the whole flawed enterprise of fantasy, to see my own landscape, the unanticipated possibilities in it, and the people in it, with a certain clarity.

Treasure Island's characters do not resemble the people from my world. Sure, in terms of attitude and psychology, some do. Hawkins's caring, no-nonsense mother, for instance, comes very close to one of my favorite aunts, Auntie Pearl, who I am sure has dismissed men with the same or worse scorn Mrs. Hawkins heaps on the cowardly villagers who first refuse to show at the standoff at the Benbow Inn, as "big, hulking, chicken-hearted men." Ben Gunn is another character who reminded me strongly of so many of the "madmen" I saw in town, from his blackened lips and eyes, which "looked quite startling in so dark a face," to his clothes of "extraordinary patchwork . . . held together by a system of the most various and incongruous fastenings, brass buttons, bits of stick, and loops of tarry gaskin." There is only one tiny moment in the final chapter when black bodies appear, glimpsed among "Mexican Indians and halfbloods selling fruits and vegetables." They're characterized in parentheses: "The sight of so many good-humored faces (especially the blacks) . . ." That is it.

Rereading later in life, I wondered about these caverned-off faces. I knew the touch to be a brush of exotification, that the iron bars of the parentheses contained caricatures. This didn't bother me in my childhood days reading. How could it or why? I saw the parentheses then as a part of the wholeness of the world Stevenson wanted for me to imagine. There was something else, though, that I did not know.

I didn't know *Treasure Island* belonged to what was considered "adventure stories for boys." It is in fact the crowning achievement of these boys' stories. My naïveté didn't prevent me from understanding, again by intuition, that "adventure stories for boys" meant boys across the sea, boys in the U.K. or Europe or America. The reality of that separateness as something more than geographic was already in me. Without my being directly told what it was, that reality of separateness existed in the living presence of history around me. The book helped me to accommodate it, from the first reading at age eleven, something I accommodated and overcame without knowing.

I did so because I adjusted the fiction to my world. Catching my aunt's attitude in Mrs. Hawkins's words—and her essential honesty—was one way. But the deep reason for overcoming the separateness was that, in the first instance, the limits of my world lovingly accommodated me without asking anything of me. My world accommodating me, in the second instance, meant that the dividing sea of racial separateness was bridged. It was bridged without my desiring to change myself, to be one of the boys from across the sea for whom *Treasure Island* was written. My world—from my grandmother's veranda to even our disciplinarian faux-British-style school—protected me from adopting an inferiority complex. The protection was not total; it did not secure me from what history had left behind, its degradation of beautiful names.

By no means was I insulated from the impoverished life immediately around me. Nor was I insulated from what, less immediately, kept life around me impoverished, those very same countries across the sea that had originated these adventure stories for boys, countries from which people come as tourists in scores to Port Antonio. Precisely because of this hard reality of what was immediate and less immediate in my world, my world allowed for illusion, to play with an outside fantasy, and seamlessly, if not raggedly, alter my reality.

Reading *Treasure Island* under these conditions as a child meant

I could release as it pleased me the black figures caught in Stevenson's parentheses. I could take that privilege from the romance because I found it so real. If I focused on these good-humored blacks, I could see them walking Port Antonio town or vanishing into the foothills of the Blue Mountains, going about their business. The page the black faces appeared on is a great passage of resolution; immediately following the parentheses is this: "The taste of the tropical fruits, and above all, the lights that began to shine in the town, made a most charming contrast to our dark and bloody sojourn on the island." It struck in me the serenity of the unbroken mirror, the sea, beneath me in my grandmother's house, that for all its tarnished history was a site of limitless dreaming.

This serenity is a kind of grace note or revelation threading throughout *Treasure Island*. Perhaps it is simply an aspect of the pattern of romance—as it is a trope of history—that serenity follows intensity. But those scenes of highest dramatic intensity in *Treasure Island* that I relished, because of both natural threats—what predators lurk in the bushes?—and artificial ones—the drunk, marauding pirates hunting Hawkins—I relished because they made, as Conrad wrote about romance, "unfamiliar things credible."

The serenity felt very similar to the physical melody I experienced daily when walking the beach inlet of Bryan's Bay, the bay nearest my grandmother's house. In these walks, Hawkins in my head, our islands touched and blurred, and Hawkins and I became, even more, spirit companions. On those walks at Bryan's Bay, whether in heat or in drizzle, the sea loud and close, this was the passage that circled in my head:

> As I continued to thread the tall woods, I could hear from far before me not only the continuous thunder of the surf, but a certain tossing of foliage and grinding of boughs which showed me the sea breeze had set in higher than usual. Soon cool draughts

of air began to reach me, and a few steps farther I came forth
into the open borders of the grove, and saw the sea lying blue
and sunny to the horizon and the surf tumbling and tossing its
foam along the beach.

Supreme serenity, as in a tableau; the revelation of the landscape.
The sea is a self-revelation. Like Hawkins, I also saw the sea breeze,
and the "certain tossing of foliage" I heard was the leaves of the sea
grape trees, groves of which lined Bryan's Bay Beach for miles. They
had none of the blight of the coconut trees. It was under their shade,
a few days after I had first opened *Treasure Island* in a chair on the
veranda of my grandmother's house, that I finished my first reading
of it. I had left the veranda and walked down the hill bearing up her
yellow house above the open sea, which shone a spectral blue green.
There was no one else on the beach: "Not a man, not a sail, upon the
sea; the very largeness of the view increased the sense of solitude." The
sentence encapsulated me. But those are not the final words; the shim-
mery cry "Pieces of eight! Pieces of eight!" haunting Hawkins long
after he leaves the island was the one I read and heard. On that cry
and in deep solitude I finished the novel in front of the sea, perfectly
enclosed in the dateless awe of childhood.

From then to now, Stevenson writes like an eavesdropper on my
heart.

FIRST READING

I WAS IN THE SIXTH FORM AT TITCHFIELD HIGH SCHOOL, IN the parish of Portland, Jamaica, when I had my first public reading. It happened one evening at the Port Antonio Public Library, a two-room concrete building at the back of the Musgrave Market by the pier. There were two other readers. I don't remember why I was the last to read. But however it came about, it was a very bad idea. The first reader was a Rastafarian woman, fiftyish, who had lived many years in Canada, where she had published some chapbooks. (It was in her presence I first heard the word "chapbook"; in fact, she was the first published writer I had ever met.) The second reader was a primary school teacher, I believe, also fiftyish, but he had that look of someone older and younger at the same time. He had two massive hardcover notebooks, the length and girth of which made me think equally of courthouse ledgers and a splintered Domesday Book. They never left his person; he balanced them on his lap when seated; they were at his chest when standing, and at the lectern he alternated shifting each from under his armpits. I was wearing my school uniform of white shirt, purple tie—one of the few occasions I bothered to noose myself—and khaki pants. I sat like a waifish offspring between the two of them, lucky and terrified to be there. After a brief playing of conga drums (a standard at these readings), we were introduced. Immediately I felt no luck but terror.

The Rastafarian woman read first. Her tone was somewhere between chanting and muttering. She read very slowly. With her long locks rivered down both shoulders, she rocked her body as she read from one of her chapbooks, which she held pushed at arm's length in front of her like something menacing. The strange thing was, she didn't return to her seat after she read but vanished through a side door, all eyes following her. I have never seen her again and never found out why she had left that way. I felt a deep abandonment at her departure. The man's style of reading was very different from the woman's: seesawing between his ledgers, he read in a very rapid and dramatic voice. His poems contained beginnings, middles, and ends. The ends—punch lines to narratives filled with folk characters in folk situations with which the room, raised on bawdy country jokes, could easily identify—he landed particularly well. After the end of a poem, the audience clapping loudly, he would slam shut his Domesday Book, then quickly open it and read from that page. The audience loved that action as well and applauded louder.

I sat by myself watching him and eyeing the side door: Which path to follow? Finished, he returned, clutching his impressive tomes and looking significantly like his younger self when he sat down. Automatically, because he sat, I got up. I walked to the lectern. I took a deep breath to settle my nerves and my knees, both rattling, I felt, audibly above the rustle of the audience quieting down. When they were quiet, they seemed to have multiplied. Without planning or meaning to, I closed my eyes, and as soon as the room receded into darkness, I began to recite my poems. Not for a moment of the roughly fifteen minutes that I stood there did I know what was happening in front of me. I kept my eyes tightly closed as I belted out things like "Elysian field," "Nirvana," and "ménage à trois"—all of which I thought, at sixteen, belonged to the delicious and correct language of poetry. How I delivered my poems from memory I had no clue; beyond reading aloud to myself when I would work on them, I had never committed any to memory. Perhaps I was winging it. Whatever it was, I heard from behind the darkness of my eyes a voice nearly like my own addressing either itself or those present.

I opened my eyes to silence. Everybody sat statue-faced under the three or four aluminum ceiling fans. Why were they so quiet? It was not the same quiet at the beginning of my recital; this was heavier, untranslatable. Even as I sat back down, the chair on my right-hand side more abysmally empty, the one on my left filled, but already, I felt the man seated there worlds away. The silence weighed heavy on me. No one stirred, and I looked at no one.

But the evening was over. The crowd broke up and left. Not long after, I found myself outside on the cool, dark pier. An invisible moon made the high, stenciled metal gate sign THE ERROL FLYNN MARINA glint at the end of the pier. It seemed straight out of Dante's *Inferno*. Even the marsh near the sea (the water black and oily) had a Dantesque Malebolge stench. That was what my foul mood made me feel. My friend, who had come along to support me, walked quietly beside me, a sort of shadowy, Virgilian comfort. At least I was not alone. Then at some point in our stroll he told me the audience was not "quiet quiet" but "reverent quiet." Because I didn't remember asking him about the reading or, less, the audience, I cannot imagine how wretched I must have looked for him to have said this. It was an immense kindness, and though I remained quiet, I felt a change, lighter, as we went through the gate. No doubt, ten years later, if I were to really ask my friend the same question, he would have told me the same lie.

AN EXQUISITE SIMULACRUM: REMEMBERING PHILIP LEVINE

IT WAS A LATE EVENING IN THE FALL SEMESTER OF 2007 when I first met Philip Levine. NYU's creative writing program had recently moved out of the literature building on University Place, where the classrooms with their long narrow tables and drab colors seemed to be made for executive board meetings, into a beautiful, labyrinthine brownstone called the Lillian Vernon Creative Writers House on West Tenth Street and Sixth Avenue. I had no quarrel with the move, except that now my two haunts, the Bobst Library and Washington Square Park, were no longer next door; in fact, I was in high spirits, buzzing with the other students sitting under the chandelier about how suitable our new baroque classroom was for writing our magna opera. But the buzz—oh the portraits, oh the stained-glass windows, oh the carpets, oh the books—was a mask for what was truly ticking in our heads: the impending arrival of Philip Levine. None of us, if I am recalling correctly, had worked with him before, but we were not strangers to the mixed rumors of his pedagogical approach—surgical, no anesthesia. We knew we were waiting on someone important, to be owners of his myth, and we were all open for something important to happen to us, a miracle of sorts, which was why, I suppose, when the great mensch opened the door, we all fell silent.

He wore a light, faded jacket, unzipped to show a faded T-shirt, and a peaked cap, also faded, and carried a small dark bag in one hand. Paused on the top of the stairs, he looked, I thought, like a skinnier Clint Eastwood, squinting, I guess, because of the chandelier's glow. Before descending the three or four steps, he smiled, our breaths returned, the chandelier pulsed brighter over our heads, and when he creaked down into his chair at the head of the table, his presence closer, I had the sense that I was one of the twelve at the Last Supper. And so it was, for his opening remarks reminded us that, at eighty years old, this was his last class before retiring, and as if to stem an outbreak of melancholy, wine (I am guessing it came from his bag, but where the cups emerged from, I have no idea) was served as we introduced ourselves.

When my turn came to say my name, I did, and Phil said, "Eh?" So I repeated my name, louder, but he rose up out of his chair not a little bit perturbed, said, "Ah, shit," and walked out of the room. The chandelier exploded in my chest, trampled by wild horses, all the portraits knitted their brows, the other students looked at me, their eyes saying what was ringing in my head: What the hell did you do? Phil, who was out of the room for less than five minutes, eons for us, returned and apologized for his sudden exit. He explained while sitting back down that he had a heart condition of some kind, so he had, at times, to coax back his heart to normal. Taking a sip from his Styrofoam cup, looking now at me—definitely Clint Eastwood—he asked for my name again. Now *my* heart was off-kilter, palpitating at a staggering rate. But somehow I managed to pronounce my name in a measured tone; he nodded, and thus, after almost giving each other heart attacks, we met.

The semester's diastole and systole unfolded many glorious moments. Phil's marvelous giving spirit extended beyond his role as teacher, and we were treated like peers, members of the same tribe, despite our varying capabilities as poets. Direct honesty, that was the outfit of the class; for us the unspoken code was no fences make good poets. Through Phil's voice, as autumn deepened into winter, we got to the bone of what it means to live—and live long—in poetry. His stories were benedictions; they brought, to take a phrase from Donne, "a heart into the room." Listening to Phil, I was enthralled not only with the voice's cadence—a private laugh seems to lurk beneath his words even when he is at his most serious—but with the exactness of details. It was superb the way he fixed recollections with not only dates and time but season and weather, which made all of his tales live, intimate and fresh, leaving us with the impression that they were being told for the first time, and only to us.

I loved to hear those stories so much that I was annoyed whenever we had to get back to a poem at hand. Often watching him talk with his head cocked to one side, I saw the younger Phil's head on the other side, listening, riveted to this bespectacled sage. Typically, a student would read his or her poem, after which the rest of us abused or complimented it according to our cardinal humors while Phil sat listening, doodling on a sheet, waiting for our appraisal to end. It never failed to amaze me, after all the lap we had just run around the poem, the way Phil began his critique with seismographic precision—"You could at least get the grammar right; it is the first line"—and we bowed back our heads to the page, the glaring error mooning us. After that he made other revelations, the poem—lucky bastard!—dwindled in stature, or accelerated in possibility.

Then there would come a moment when he moved off the chart, to a memory. These reminiscences could be considered midrashic the way they distilled a poem by lifting it from the coffin of the page to a living past, Phil's, but—and extraordinarily—all of the literature that came before it, for Phil, was a venerable repository of great literature. Phil's memory reminded us of the primitivity of poetry, and because he taught through telling, with the bare human voice, he took us back to a place where language was consecrated with one fire. (This is not to say Phil's language itself was consecrated; he once said something I repeat every chance I get: "Don't fuck with the muse." Here of course Phil was delighting in a nuanced take on Keats's claim that the poet is "the most unpoetical of all God's Creatures.") If we had closed our eyes—I did a couple of times—it would not have been hard to imagine the chandelier on the floor, stiff flames pointing up, and Phil, our tribe's elder in T-shirt and windbreaker, his voice sparkling from the bulb, animating in us the long love he has carried for the old art. Without being preachy, he made something burn in us and we were willing neophytes, transfigured after each class.

The classroom essentially became a veritable salon, one in which not just the living souls enjoyed the flame but the dead came to warm themselves. Keats was spoken of as if he were making his way down Broadway to class. Edward Thomas entered with his notebooks and mud-caked shoes. Dylan Thomas poured the wine; Hopkins blessed it. Berryman shouted down the furnace at Blake (and at Shadrach, Meshach, and Abednego). Roethke exchanged whispers with Christopher Smart. When Phil spoke of Lorca, Machado, and Neruda ("the pinnacle, the apex, the Alp," to quote what a Spanish tutor said about Machado to Phil once, recorded in Phil's brilliant essay, "Living in Machado"), much as I had read them before, I went home to read them again, and understood what Herbert meant by "the soul in paraphrase, the heart in pilgrimage." It was in Phil's class that I came to realize there were Italians besides Dante and Montale: Pavese soon shoveled his solitude into my head, and Quasimodo, who was still a cathedral bell ringer, only with poems, and not hunchbacked, broke that solitude. (Many other Italians have since followed.)

Almost every week after leaving Phil's class, I headed to the library, my trek slightly longer, to find whatever book he had mentioned in class. So many and diverse were the books that I am certain I have been to every floor of that immense library. There was something validating and exhilarating when I finished reading a line of his recommendation and heard his sprite whispering somewhere in the air, "Isn't that marvelous?" The heart murmured yes. Even now, years after, the heart is murmuring yes.

That semester I was on a pilgrimage for my own kind of tune to fit the vision I had left home in Jamaica with, but having been in New York City for more than a year, I felt the vision going soft. The first time I brought a poem to class, Phil put it properly in its place: "Too grandiose." Another time: "Crane," he said, "not easy to do." How exact, for at the time I was worshipping at the church of Crane and Merrill. I pitched to something else. Though there was no praise, I detected that Phil saw I wasn't wasting his time, and he said incredibly encouraging things to me, inside and outside class. I had something of an epiphany one day when he said to me, "You know, Ishion, humor is one of the great universal conditions your work could benefit from," or some such piece of wisdom. Suddenly forgotten phrases from Henri Bergson's essay on laughter, which I had studied and loved in college, geysered up in my mind—"laughter always implies a kind of secret freemasonry, or even complicity." (Incidentally, the previous year I had received a letter from an old lady in Jamaica imploring me to put "more smiles" in my poetry after she read a poem of mine in a local paper. Clearly, I had not made any progress.)

Diligently, sleeplessly, I worked to better my tone, and toward the end of the semester, the city darker and colder, I felt something freshen in the lines. *Merci*, Phil, for what you aerated. The only way a young poet can express his gratitude to a master is to continue in greater intensity his apprenticeship, so three years after that class I mailed my first book, *Far District*, to him. I remember my accompanying note was a longish apology; I didn't want to provoke another heart condition. When I got Phil's letter, handwritten on a yellow legal pad, my heartbeats pulverized the deserts of Utah, where I was hermitting away in Salt Lake City.

Holding the letter was like holding a warm glass, a bulb from our chandelier; I held tightly and read myself into a sort of lachrymal deficiency. Remembering the letter now, I still experience a small threat of the deficiency, not because of the tremendous kindness Phil showed in it, but because the U.S. Postal Service lost the letter some months later, along with some of my most treasured possessions. On one of the numerous occasions I had to describe to a postal agent the contents of the missing boxes, I wailed to her, "There is a letter from Phil, Philip Levine, in an envelope in a tan notebook, I need it." Both our exasperations clogged the receiver.

The last time I saw Phil at NYU was at my graduate reading wine reception held at the Writers House; the reading itself took place in one of the colossal halls near the library. On that occasion, two of my very good friends, the gifted poets Adam Wiedewitsch and Dante Micheaux, and I decided to attend dapperly dressed in matching outfits, emulating, I suppose, the Rat Pack, though we called our trio the Chancellors. There was no shortage of compliments from everyone about our black vests and black ties and long-sleeved white shirts; we moved singularly, a Hydra amid the wine drinkers in the room. Then we saw Phil, back turned to us, commanding a group. He must have sensed us and turned sharply around: "Hey, Dante, Ishion, Adam"—a pause, then the scalpel—"What are you guys, waiters?" All eyes were on us, laughter charged the room. No doubt, humor is one of the great human conditions, and so is humility, which I feel always, having known Philip Levine. To end, since I have made something both imagined and recalled, please, Marvell, raise my apologia:

Pardon me, mighty Poet, nor despise
My causeless, yet not impious, surmise.

THE SEARCH FOR A FAUN

MY POEM IS CALLED "PRELUDE TO THE AFTERNOON OF A Faun." A famous title, one I am sure most of you will recognize as referring to the name of Stéphane Mallarmé's poem, published in 1876 and subsequently set to music by Claude Debussy, in 1894. Its fame is the reason why I am self-conscious about what I am about to do in this reflection, which is an attempt to give a précis of how I came to write my poem. Doing so amounts partly to betraying the naïveté of my youth. More fatally, it is a betrayal of the poem or, put more correctly, a betrayal of the innocence that made the poem come together.

What I mean by "innocence" is not innocence at all but the many-angled reality confronting innocence. The danger a poet faces in poking back to the genesis of a poem is discovering how far removed the poem seems from the circumstances that issued it, so as to, at worst, deny the circumstances themselves. At best, the poet gets a glimmer of the early effort, the early self in search of language to bring those circumstances together. When the poem happens, reality cedes to myth, and the things felt and lived through can never be recovered. But because the poem exists, things felt and lived through have become eternally subdued presences, awaiting awakening. The poem, at some level, is a vital promissory note of this reawakening, if only the poet has "touched," in Henry James's deathbed dictation, "the large old phrase into the right amplitude." This is why, to me, the poet rather than being a maker—*poiētēs*, maker—is a remaker, someone discovering anew what is already there. Poetry is an honest form of resisting history as the past. In it, history is the living breath that attunes to the special cadences, the private music, a poet finds in fulfilling the poem's promissory note.

As I now try to listen back to how the music of my poem arrived, I will not, as I should, talk about the poem's technique, in particular the pitch and tone of its shape. In lieu, I would like to cite a sentence from a letter Mallarmé wrote to Paul Valéry in 1891. It catches, in retrospect, the creative license I took toward my poem. Mallarmé writes, "Music in the proper sense, which we must pillage, plagiarize, if our own, unspoken, is insufficient, suggests such a poem." "Suggests such a poem" is the watch phrase; its quaint formulation conceals the most agonizing burden before a poet.

One evening in 2003, I heard music coming from the window of a large stucco house on a leafy suburban street near the university campus in Kingston. I assumed, passing these houses daily, it belonged to a professor. Music coming from windows was as common and abundant as there were windows in the city; I was used to hearing the predictable, even banal, sounds coming from these windows and never thought twice of pausing within earshot of one of them. But on that day, the frail, repetitive notes—by one or several flutes?—straining against the vague sunset, seemed different and totally alien. Against my will, I was drawn toward the sound. Kingston, after several months there, was still not much more to me than a name. Its volatile beauty, unpardonable and off-kilter like the reggae songs that defined it, excited me. Still, I was hesitant about the city and chose to return each weekend to Port Antonio, about a two-and-a-half-hour drive away on the coast, to my home by the sea.

And that was what the recurring phrase of the flute seemed to simulate: the sea, waves cresting waves. My body, as if hearing its familiar, elemental calling, leaned in to the alien sound from the window. Fragile and low ebbed, the sound became a breeze moving inside a small cove. I felt I knew the cove, the one at the steep slope of the cliff just outside the village called Hector's River. Listening to the sound, I was transported there. But there was a harder, more immediate fantasy in my mind. I had to imagine, standing in the dusk, hopefully hidden to faces hidden behind curtains, the private, interior moment of the house: Was it a bachelor listening from a sofa, an old lover's letter trembling in his hands? Or was it a family, mother, father, and a daughter of about ten, tiptoeing as they set the dinner table together, the girl, who knows this evening-time music very well, feigning to play the flute with a silver knife. Hushed laughter.

I dreamed neither of those make-believes that night. The memory of the flute melody following me into sleep; I dreamed a boy was running through a garden with high groves, a wall of intense green, green and frightening and narrowing in on him the faster he ran, panting hard. Whoever his invisible pursuers were, they were getting close, and he felt—in all that heat and green—the cold chill of death on his neck, and so he ran straight into one of the groves of the wall, giving up his body for good. But the wall broke like a hole in a cloud; he was saved. Before him in a clearing stood a great tree with a tawny goat's skin stretched and nailed to its massive trunk.

The dream ended there. Except for the walled garden, I've had the dream before. The goatskin nailed on the tree trunk was a sight I grew up with: the pelt of a killed goat hung on a tree for days to be "cured" in the sun. Once cured, it was turned into the surface of a drum and used in a Kumina or Revivalist ceremony. Perhaps the dream was a premonition, because a day or two after the dream ceremony of a more disturbing kind gripped the city. The government, seemingly without warning, hiked the price of gasoline. People took to the streets early in the morning, protesting in a charged, festive excitement that resembled an election rally, lots of banner waving and singing and dancing.

Sometime after noon, however, violence broke out between protesters and the police. In the vigor of the heat, in the waving of banners and cardboard signs, a bloody menace quickly took hold. Singing gave way to screams. Roads were blocked with debris that was then set on fire. Explosions could be heard everywhere. Students who led the protests near the university campus were tear-gassed. The campus was immediately put on lockdown. Sirens blasted throughout the night around the neighborhoods. A national curfew was imposed.

Somehow I figured out a way to get off campus and even more improbably found a lone taxi operator in one of the main depots near campus. I persuaded him to take me all the way to Port Antonio, at great risk and for very little pay. Though the sirens blared, the city at night, as we drove through, shimmered with postapocalyptic vacancy and quiet. I was to remember it that way for a very long time. Back home, I sat on the high veranda in the cool night. The dark sea glittered below me. The calm was immense. It contradicted the terror of the day. In that interval, between tension and serenity, anxiety and repose, the window music returned to me. It did sudden and unbidden, without my thinking about it at all. It came corroborated, blurred with images from the day and the garden dream I had had a night or two before; suspended between reality and dream, at that very moment—at least, so I wished—I started to recall bits of the second stanza of Keats's "Ode on a Grecian Urn," the rapturous unheard melodies, electrified by the ritual of sacrifice. I sat smelling the faint salt breeze, all these things in my head. A poem began, without words, to take shape in me.

Then, for the next ten years, I tried to sound the words, drafts upon drafts, failing at every attempt.

Why was I unable to write the poem? It was the music. I knew nothing about the music I had overheard at that window in Kingston. And yet its primal or primitive force lived incomplete in my inner ear. I needed it again, closer. The ignorance was good only for a momentary reverie. For art, real immersive art, I needed to live more in the music. I needed the music, not because it represented anything, but because it marked (and provoked) a moment of pity and terror my psyche was unable to shake. I began to search for a melody I could barely hum. I began, some weeks after my return to Kingston, by listening to countless catalogs of classical music CDs borrowed from a radio presenter at the university radio station. Exhausting those, a kind professor from one of the leafy homes—the window of the music I never returned to—gave me a few CDs, but the music I heard was not on any of the discs. To this professor, one day in his office on campus, I tried to describe the music I was looking for. He looked so baffled behind his desk that I never tried describing it again.

A few years after Kingston, I moved to New York City in 2006. Soon after the move, I spent hours in the New York Public Library going through endless CDs. I loved handling a CD for the care it required of me; I loved reading liner notes, jealous of the fluidity and compression of the language. This became the game in my search for the music I heard through the window: though I listened to music increasingly more and more online, my search for the window music was more intent whenever I was able to go through CDs available to me. Many times, I thought I came close to hearing that music. But playing back a track, my ears peaked—alert with the faint memory of the window music I had heard—I again didn't find it. The poem remained unwritten. I continued listening through many subsequent moves. New York. Salt Lake City. Baltimore. Ithaca.

Then one morning, in the summer of 2013, in Berlin, the long hiatus, in a moment's serendipity, broke.

Seated in the window of a ground-floor apartment reading, by sheer chance, Mallarmé, a poet I heretofore did not admire—and still don't, really—I turned the page, and certain combinations of phrases—"the glow of them, so nimble in the air . . . did I dream that love? . . . my doubt, the hoard of ancient night . . . then to my native fervor I'll awake . . . burning in the wave"—quickened something in me. I read through the poem again, and again, slower, going back to the title, "L'après-midi d'un faune." Hadn't I seen those words just recently? The apartment belonged to a translator who had a deep passion for music. He had two floor-to-ceiling walls of records and CDs in the living room. On the first day I arrived, he had shown me a few from his collection, laying them out on the dining table with, what I thought, an auctioneer's pride. They were still there. I climbed down from the ledge of the window and picked through the CDs and records on the table. In no time I found the disc, Claude Debussy, conducted by Claudio Abbado. I put it on.

I sat back in the window of the other room and listened to the recording. It came to me hesitantly, intimately as if through the decade-long gap, the harmonic sequence wash of the flutes and harps, their glissandi waves punctuated by the antique cymbals' star twinkles. I heard the postapocalyptic quiet of Kingston; I heard the night around the veranda I sat in, finally calm; I heard the cove outside Hector's River, and I heard the window again, the window of the music, and then the dream of the stretched goatskin: all of this found me in Berlin, listening for the first time in full clarity to Debussy's composition. And after a long repose in the music, I took up my notepad and made the first solid draft of my poem.

Noon ictus cooling the veranda's
fretwork, the child sits after his harp
boning burlesque in the bower, his slit
of gulls' nerves silenced into hydrangea.
Violet and roan, the bridal sun is
opening and closing a window,
filling a clay pot of coins with coins;
candle jars, a crystal globe, cut milk

boxes with horn petals snapping
their iceberg-Golgotha crackle.
The loneliness is terrible, the ice is near,
says the hasp-lipped devil, casting
beatitudes at the castor-oiled pimps
in Parliament; Pray for them, joyfully,
their amazing death! Light seethes
bulging like pipes blown with napalm
from his big golden eyes, turning
the afternoon ten degrees backwards,
then through palm fronds' teething
the bridled air, sprigs of goat hair, fall.

After that initial flush of writing, I spent most of the summer working slowly on the poem. I am certain the poem's atavistic vocabulary arrived thanks to much creative memory, both the lived experience—overhearing Debussy, the turmoil in Kingston, my return to Port Antonio—and the dreams fostered in the poetic imagination that took me years to bring together into words, insufficient perhaps, but still my own unchangeable hoard of ancient night and day.

FAR AWAY:
NAIPAUL AND WALCOTT

IN THE SUMMER OF 2003, JUST BEFORE I ENTERED THE UNI-
versity of the West Indies in Jamaica, I took a weeklong poetry work-
shop with Derek Walcott. It was held not on campus but in a colorless
room of a midtown Kingston hotel. Until then I had only seen his
image in black-and-white photographs, and now I noticed that he
had "sea-green eyes," like his mariner-poet alter ego Shabine in "The
Schooner *Flight*." Also like Shabine, Walcott was at once tender and
pointed about the poet's responsibility to language and craft. In "The
Schooner *Flight*," Shabine cuts a crew member for mocking his poem:
"None of them go fuck with my poetry again."

The week ended. I carried on with university and didn't hear much
about Walcott until two years later, in 2005, when the great Jamaican
scholar and poet Edward Baugh returned to the UWI after a short
spell in the States to teach a seminar on Walcott's work. Though Wal-
cott was revered, he wasn't widely read; few living so-called page poets
were, at least among my generation. Off campus, Jamaican popular
music and theater held sway, and literary matters didn't always capture
the general public's imagination. The country, just forty-three years

independent, was steeped in financial crisis, and an English major was deemed an honorable rather than a practical pursuit. So there was a sense that the twelve of us in Professor Baugh's class, held in a fairly big lecture hall, were in search of a bygone world.

Wonderfully rigorous in his New Critical approach, Professor Baugh was not given to biographical anecdotes. When we fell into stitches over Walcott's couplet from "The Spoiler's Return"—"I see these islands and I feel to bawl / 'area of darkness' with V. S. Nightfall"— Professor Baugh pointed out how the interplay of the Antillean inflection of the lines with the iambic pentameter ensures that the pun on V. S. Naipaul's name isn't just sardonic wordplay. He dwelled on the texture of language and never gave us insider's knowledge of the decades-long feud between Walcott and Naipaul, about which we had heard only the ghostliest of rumors, although, as a slightly younger contemporary of both writers, Professor Baugh was more privy than most to the internecine crack-up between them.

But there was a slip. A couple of weeks into the class we were going through "Laventille," a poem dedicated to Naipaul that dates from the mid-1960s, when some say the feud started. Laventille is an impoverished township in which "the inheritors of the middle passage stewed" above Port of Spain, the capital of Trinidad and Tobago, where Naipaul spent his adolescence and Walcott lived for many years. Rather than damning Naipaul as he did sixteen years later in "The Spoiler's Return," Walcott here uses a paradoxical image—"to go downhill / from here was to ascend"—that seems to praise Naipaul's forbearance in surviving such harsh conditions, or so Professor Baugh explained.

At some point as he took us through the poem, Professor Baugh mentioned "The Garden Path," an essay Walcott had written on Naipaul's ninth novel, *The Enigma of Arrival*. Then he fell quiet, and his gentle, slightly rheumy brown eyes stared over our heads to the wall behind us. He was suddenly a man elsewhere. It was that stare that made me go to the library when class ended to find Walcott's essay and borrow Naipaul's novel, which I hadn't read.

To a few people on campus, borrowing the book would have been heroic; to most, it would have been a kind of heresy. Whereas Walcott was basically respected on campus, Naipaul's politics—politics of citizenship, politics of cultural nationalism, and frankly politics of race—meant that he was considered more or less a pariah. There was general appreciation for his stature as a major international writer from the Caribbean, but he was understood, particularly in his books *The Middle Passage* (1962) and *An Area of Darkness* (1964), to have cast the region aside and become no longer one of us. I hadn't read either of those books; many of my peers hadn't either. Yet speaking about Naipaul in almost any context was problematic, largely due to the quarrels many members of my generation had inherited from the ones before us.

I found "The Garden Path" in Walcott's collection *What the Twilight Says* (1998). The essay had first appeared in *The New Republic* as a review of *The Enigma of Arrival* in 1987. "Press one foot on the soil of England," it begins, "and the phantoms spring. Poets, naturalists, novelists have harrowed and hallowed it for centuries with their furrowing pens as steadily as its yeomen once did with the plough." It then names a cavalcade of those English poets, naturalists, and novelists. I rushed up and down the library stairs in search of Edward Thomas, Ted Hughes, and surnames I dimly recognized: Langland, Spenser, Marvell, Keats. I gave up on finding "the Georgians," stumped by the library's cumbersome card catalog, which dated back to Walcott's time on campus in the 1950s.

In the second paragraph of the essay, Naipaul's book gets its first brush, a kind of schoolboy skewering:

The final essay examination has been submitted, and the marks are in. Gentlemen, we now have among us another elegiac pastoralist, an islander himself, the peer of Clare and Cobbett, not only in style, but in spirit. And if the cost to that spirit has meant virulent contempt towards the island of his origin, then rook, shaw, and hedgerow, tillage and tradition, will soothe him, because although he may reject his own soil, his own phantoms, the earth everywhere is forgiving, even in Trinidad, and rejects no one.

Twisty but clear. A scolding was being handed down, and it spoke to why Naipaul's reputation among my peers was suspect. Walcott's long sentence alleges that Naipaul had turned his back on Trinidad and Tobago, where he was born in 1932, for England. The prevailing spirit on campus—built on the grounds of a former slave plantation, remnants of which could still be seen—was about embracing one's Caribbean heritage, "faults and all" (a phrase found in the fourth and final lines of Walcott's generation-defining poem, "Sea Canes"). To embrace that heritage was to reject Naipaul both for repudiating his Caribbean heritage and for the far worse crime of self-pityingly working within the circumscribed bounds of empire. By this view, Naipaul's "virulent contempt"—Walcott uses pathological language freely throughout the essay—was not just ungrateful. It was vicious.

The intensity builds. Walcott characterizes Naipaul's contempt in two more ways. First, it is thinly veiled by egotistical mythmaking. "The myth of Naipaul as a phenomenon, as a singular, contradictory genius who survived the cane fields and the bush at great cost, has long been a farce." I know the cane fields. They were littered across eastern Jamaica, where I spent parts of my childhood. Next to them were the shanties and barracks in which generations of people of African and Indian descent have endured horrible conditions. With hardly any other income-generating work available to them, eventually they succumb to the cane, working themselves to death in the fields and factories. Some escape, but into conditions only a little better than the spirit-killing life of cane labor. In my notebook I scribbled a naive question: *How can it be a farce to survive the cane fields?*

The second aspect of the contempt for which Walcott indicts

Naipaul is the hatred and racial prejudice in his travel writing. Not having read Naipaul's travel books or any criticism of Naipaul, I found Walcott's charge hard to tally with the stories in *Miguel Street* and the novel *A House for Mr. Biswas*, the only two books of Naipaul's that I had read by then. I loved their portrayal of Indians and black and mixed-race characters in Port of Spain, all done with a generous calypsonian irony, as humans with human flaws and possibilities. When, years later, I read those travel writings and some of Naipaul's interviews (he told *The New York Times* in 1980, "I can't see a Monkey—you can use a capital M, that's an affectionate word for the generality—reading my work"), I came to sympathize with Walcott's charge that Naipaul is "unfair and unjust at an obscene cost, at the cost of those who do not have his eloquence, his style."

For Walcott, Naipaul's writing displays a profound "self-disfigurement." It "is scarred by scrofula." It was my first time coming across that word, and ever the diligent student I jotted it in my notebook: "scrofula," or "the king's evil," a disease supposedly curable by the touch of a royal. I inferred from Walcott's phrase that Naipaul's attitudes amounted to a longing for monarchy. And in the Caribbean, where enslavement, colonialism, and indentureship are all entangled with the British crown, to long for monarchy is the ultimate form of self-betrayal. "Joyce, Shakespeare, Dante, for all their clear hatreds, are beyond this self-disfigurement," Walcott writes, but Naipaul suffers it incurably. The essay carries on this way, with biting eloquence and style, "handing Naipaul his ass," to use a phrase often heard in Trinidad.

There are some exceptional moments of praise. "Tempered and delicate," Walcott writes of *The New Yorker*'s excerpts from *The Enigma of Arrival*, "the mood of these pieces had the subdued subtleties of the weather their pliant sentences celebrated." Walcott admits that "the best leaves of this book are touched by grace." At the end of one of these cited passages, freshly arrived in England and wrestling to express what his Trinidadian origin means to him, Naipaul writes that "the island had given me the world as a writer." I turned to a new leaf in my notebook and wrote that phrase down. It impressed me with the image of a child, perhaps a little sullen but filled with wonder about the things around him. To me the phrase seemed summoned from the turmoil of slavery and indentureship, like old wisdom made new. It quickened in me, an islander and an aspiring writer, something that felt irrevocable.

And yet right after quoting Naipaul's phrase, Walcott mangles it. Naipaul should "more honestly" have written, Walcott suggests, that the island "had given the world me as a writer." The human dignity I had found in Naipaul's phrase was disfigured by Walcott's simple displacement of two words. In Naipaul's phrase, the island is not just the writer's natural habitat but the launchpad of his imagination, the ground, present even when invisible, from which he sees the world. In Walcott's version, the writer has only his bland, naked ego: no island, no land, no ground for his imagination or place from which to make sense of the world. It made me picture the writer as a man-child floating in empty space, a homeless, wandering Caliban. Walcott's next sentence is a blunt "nothing wrong with that." I couldn't make sense of it. It saddened me.

Still, following a moment's pause, I wrote Walcott's rendering in my notebook. I looked at the two phrases in my handwriting, Naipaul's above darkly mirrored by Walcott's below. It was as if the small blank space between them were opening, distant islands pushed permanently apart by a turbulent sea. In the narrow left margin beside Walcott's rendering of Naipaul's phrase, I wrote, "A hit, a very palpable hit!" I finished reading the essay and went home. I had forgotten to check out the novel.

A year later, in 2006, I was studying poetry at New York University. That first autumn of my MFA program I found a well-thumbed paperback of *The Enigma of Arrival* on a bookseller's table near Washington Square Park. It was a late printing of the American edition by Knopf. On its muted turquoise-and-white cover Giorgio de Chirico's titular painting was a small inset above Naipaul's name. That autumn—for many days on benches, in the park, and on subway rides back and forth between Brooklyn, where I lived, and Manhattan—I read the novel in a slow, dreamlike haze. It was "hypnotic," as Naipaul reported his French translator called it.

Trancelike, too, in the word's original sense of "going across," *The Enigma of Arrival* is a book about traversing and blurring the boundaries between the New and the Old Worlds. The narrator's life is the book's unstable center. His physical exile begins when he flies from Trinidad and Tobago to New York City, en route to England. It is 1950, and he is a few weeks short of his eighteenth birthday. He has left home for the same reason I left home, to become a writer, and in the same fashion I did, to attend university abroad. His overnight stay in New York occurs on a day "unseasonably cool and grey for the end of July." The "hideous anxiety" it sets off in him becomes the novel's motif and motivating force.

The narrator remembers the city's "tall buildings, which, with some shame, I stopped to look up at," as being "curiously softly colored"; he remembers the paradoxical gray daytime light outside the Wellington Hotel, where he spent the night, how it shone "without glare" and "suggested a canopied, protected world"; he remembers the city he had landed in the night before, full of bright buildings and dazzling light but also congested. When I arrived in New York City, I also felt the strangeness, the excitement, the shame, and the narrator's "terrible solitude."

The narrator journeys from New York by ship for a little more than a month to Southampton, England. Though the Atlantic crossing is long and he is full of fear ("I feared being assaulted; I feared attracting someone's malevolence"), it is not that journey he recalls when he arrives in England but his time in New York, where "the separation of man from writer" became "complete." The hideous anxiety of New York follows him from his two-month stay at a boarding-house in Earls Court (an "enclave in London") to four years of dreary student life at Oxford. It follows him back to London for a year in which, "very slowly, man and writer came together again." In his sixth year in England he can finally visit Trinidad, penniless but a writer. He stays only six weeks before returning to London in what Naipaul, recounting his own biography, once called "a state of psychological destitution." There he lives for some years before moving to Wiltshire, the end of his wanderings and, in many respects, his true post of exile.

I understand that conundrum of geographic change, its psychic blow. I reeled from it even after I got used to living and working in the city. The anxiety the narrator experiences in New York flitters into his partial pastoral serenity in Wiltshire. After fifteen years there, concentrating on the landscape and on himself, he sees precisely what that anxiety was and is: "I lost a faculty that had been part of me and precious to me for years. I lost the gift of fantasy, the dream of the future, the far-off place where I was going." In this way of looking, he admits his loss of innocence, not as something to be honored, but as a simple, brutal fact. "I lost a faculty"; "the far-off place": how many times, tramping about the West Village in my peacoat that first autumn, did I repeat those phrases under my breath? *The Enigma of Arrival* became part of my internal rhythm of resistance in the city, my bulwark against losing the gift of fantasy my island had given to me—the gift the narrator felt he had lost after his arrival in England. I was hopeful: the narrator regains his gift.

But he regains it with huge losses. By the time his first books are published, his father, who inspired his writing ambition, has died in Trinidad. He is unable to return home for the funeral. A few years later, in his early thirties and much more secure in his writing career, he develops "exploding head syndrome." The illness, which begins in a dream, starts to take over his daily life. The exploding head passages are among Naipaul's most acute and clinical, a vivid blend of realism and the fantastical:

> In this dream there occurred always, at a critical moment in the dream narrative, what I can only describe as an explosion in my head. It was how every dream ended, with this explosion that threw me flat on my back, in the presence of people, in a street, a crowded room, or wherever, threw me into this degraded posture in the midst of standing people, threw me into the posture of sleep in which I found myself when I awakened. The explosion was so loud, so reverberating and slow in my head that I felt, with the part of my brain that miraculously could still think and draw conclusions, that I couldn't possibly survive, that I was in fact dying, that the explosion this time, in this dream, regardless of the other dreams that had revealed themselves at the end as dreams, would kill, that I was consciously living through, or witnessing, my own death. And when I awoke my head felt queer, shaken up, exhausted; as though some discharge in my brain had in fact occurred.

Healing follows, but another illness does "away with whatever remained of youthfulness in me." He is exhausted. Still, he finds himself, middle-aged, in a long period of peace. Then grief strikes again. This time his younger sister Sati dies in Trinidad from a brain hemorrhage. The narrator returns to his island for the religious rites after her cremation. Titled "The Ceremony of Farewell," the novel's brief, luminous epilogue brings the writer's task into relief: performing the hard process of mourning, which underscores that both the individual and the community survive.

I finished *The Enigma of Arrival* that winter of 2006 in my apartment on Macon Street in Bed-Stuy. I hadn't noticed the washed-out gray of morning or felt the space heater nearly burning my feet when I came to the final page, sealed with the dates "*October 1984–April 1986.*" I wiped my face and returned to the book's opening passage:

> For the first four days it rained. I could hardly see where I was. Then it stopped raining and beyond the lawn and outbuildings in front of my cottage I saw fields with stripped trees on the boundaries of each field; and far away, depending on the light, glints of a little river, glints which sometimes appeared, oddly, to be above the level of the land.

The entire novel is there, not as a summary, but as an awakening and reawakening, those double glints that will expand into a single vision of the narrator's journey. The purpose of his journey is to become a writer. It is marked, from the start, with many instances of humiliation. Success comes much later. In the span of a decade in Wiltshire the narrator undergoes what he calls "my second childhood of seeing and learning, my second life, so far away from my first." Repetition is the novel's main harmonic device, and the echo of "second" here, like that of "glints" in the opening scene, reaffirms an experience, makes the experience an indelible memory.

I read the opening sentences again and caught their exhilarating sadness and blessed unease. I felt that they were Naipaul's regained *Paradiso*. I could, like an illustrator drawing from dictation, sketch the scene easily: lawn, outbuildings, trees, fields, a river, and vaguely, at the edge, as if about to disappear, the outline of a man brooding on what he sees in the landscape and what he imagines he can see beyond it. The scene seemed to do what Tarkovsky wrote cinema did: "juxtaposing a person with an environment that is boundless, collating him with a countless number of people passing by close to him and far away, relating a person to the whole world."

I knew I was far away from home. A look at the gray and snow outside my window affirmed it. But the novel affirmed it in another way. In it I could see glints of myself in the distance, a stranger in a strange place, searching for a future. "To go abroad," the narrator muses in "The Ceremony of Farewell," "could be to fracture one's life." The conditional tense attempts to conceal the straightforward pain it confesses. Yet this very strategy makes the emotion all the more raw, an existential cry rather than a pathetic whine of despair by a former colonial subject. Those words rang in me and were to stay ringing during my time in the city and beyond.

Two years later, in 2008, packing to leave New York City to do a PhD in Salt Lake City, I came across my notebook from that evening in the university campus library in Jamaica. Opening it, I noticed, next to my jotted lines by Walcott, my transcription of Osric's line from the fencing scene in *Hamlet*: "A hit, a very palpable hit!" Now the quotation looked mean. Why did I write it? Had I succumbed to the schoolboy jousting implicit in Walcott's essay? Indeed, in the paragraph following his anagramming of Naipaul's phrase, Walcott writes that if Naipaul "doesn't want to play, like the peevish sixth-grader still contained in an almost great writer, he can go and play by himself." It is a threat of banishment I've heard issued by an exam room invigilator or a schoolhouse bully.

Something struck me now about Walcott's decision to change the syntax of Naipaul's phrase "the island had given me the world as a writer" to the almost agrammatic "had given the world me as a writer." It seemed to undermine—in meaning and cadence—the exaltation and wonder of the child awakening to his island, his only vantage from which to see and imagine a world beyond the cane. Further, it undermined Naipaul's ultimate attempt at writing against that threat of self-annihilation brought on by the "hideous anxiety" of leaving home. By writing a confessional autobiography in the form of a novel, and perhaps at times with what Walcott described as a sixth grader's peevishness, Naipaul was writing against the original displacement of colonialism and indentureship. The writing was done to prove the gift the island had given the writer and not, as Walcott's twisting of the phrase would have it, the writer's egotism. Naipaul's phrase is about the writer's capacity to record the child's wonder, making that wonder into a language of vigilant and personal articulacy.

Such articulation is susceptible to easy ridicule. It exposes how often the writer from a colonized country depends on going abroad to fulfill his ambition. When he was eleven, Naipaul witnessed his father's self-published novella of 1942, *The Adventures of Gurudeva*, never gain a readership outside Trinidad and Tobago. This and what Naipaul calls "the pain of his early life" left Seepersad Naipaul a broken man. At the same time, his Caribbean contemporaries like Samuel Selvon and Edgar Mittelholzer, who had their books published abroad, principally in England, enjoyed some level of success. Abroad, then, was where success lay.

But to go abroad oneself—where success isn't guaranteed—is to enter a state of total deracination. Ever on the road, you become victim of a double vulnerability. Elsewhere, Naipaul calls this "colonial schizophrenia." It puts the writer in a dilemma similar to the "three impossibilities" that Franz Kafka described in a letter to Max Brod: "the impossibility of not writing, the impossibility of writing German, the impossibility of writing differently." To which "one might also add," he went on, "a fourth impossibility, the impossibility of writing." In the adamantine plainness of *The Enigma of Arrival*, Naipaul opts for the impossibility of writing differently—a choice that cements him, in style and in substance, as the greatest Caribbean-born writer of Kafkan dread.

* * *

Walcott's essay ends with a blessing. "*Shantih* to his pen, though," Walcott writes, "and a benediction on the peace that has come to him after the exhaustions of a world whose features he has still described more honestly than most." The Sanskrit I recognized from the end of T. S. Eliot's *Waste Land*. Why that word? It cuts close to patronizing. "In a small hillside hotel," Walcott goes on, with "a view of the Caribbean," he finds an old issue of *National Geographic* and takes an "appropriate blessing" for Naipaul from the caption "under the photograph of a sadhu." He does so because he prefers "to cherish the narrator of *The Enigma of Arrival*, not as an enigmatic English squire who has finally arrived, but as the sadhu that he might have become."

There is much that is inappropriate about this *shantih*, not least that it reduces Naipaul to a kind of glossy anthropological spectacle. If Walcott wanted to impose an Eliotic blessing on Naipaul, why not "Home is where one starts from" from *Four Quartets*? Both in its symphonic design and in its theme of consolation in the aftermath of great suffering, *The Enigma of Arrival* resembles Eliot's great postwar poems set in a "nowhere" England.

As I considered Walcott's *shantih*, I thought back to Professor Baugh's face, his elsewhere gaze in the classroom at the UWI when he had mentioned Walcott's essay on Naipaul. That gaze was left unexplained, the way Professor Baugh left much of the Walcott-Naipaul feud unexplained during our discussion of "The Spoiler's Return" and "Laventille." Those poems and "The Garden Path" are not the only times Walcott mentions Naipaul in print. Between 1961 and 1967, he wrote up to ten articles on Naipaul (including an interview with him) for the *Trinidad Guardian*. In the earliest, he argued that Naipaul "has been accused of calling the West Indies 'philistine' and 'hostile,' but whatever his outbursts of anger may stem from, they are not present in his novels, which are full of the pathos of understanding."

Naipaul, for his part, wrote at length about Walcott only once, in a 2007 essay called "The Worm in the Bud." In it he recalls as a

sixteen-year-old schoolboy in Trinidad in 1949 hearing "news" about a
pamphlet Walcott had self-published the year before called *25 Poems*.
Naipaul didn't read the book then, only six years later, when he'd al-
ready been in England four years. Near the end of the essay, he writes
that the grown-up Walcott had become "the man who had stayed
behind and found beauty in the emptiness from which other writers
had fled: a kind of model, in the eyes of people far away."

The last time Walcott mentioned Naipaul was in a poem called
"The Mongoose," which he recited at the 2008 Calabash International
Literary Festival in Jamaica. Walcott never printed "The Mongoose";
the audio of his reading of it exists on various sources online. ("I de-
bated whether to read this here for the first time in public," he said. "I
think you'll recognize Mr. Naipaul.") You can hear not only his voice
but also the breeze and the surf—Calabash is an outdoor festival—
and, louder, the bursts of laughter from the audience after he reads
each couplet: "I have been bitten. I must avoid infection, / or else I'll
be as dead as Naipaul's fiction." The laughs are anonymous. Among
them is my own.

I don't pretend to know what Professor Baugh's gaze meant. But
in the years since I have come to feel as though it led me indirectly to
Walcott's essay and Naipaul's book—a book I read when I needed it
most. It was as if Professor Baugh were encouraging an aspiring Carib-
bean writer to read these two great Caribbean writers without needing
to side with one against the other. With time I came to see—almost
equally—some of Naipaul's views as deplorable, as well as some of
Walcott's. In the final sentence in "The Garden Path," his irony less
barbed, Walcott concludes, "Peace to the traveller, and calm to the
mind growing nearer to that radiance, to the vision that sees all earth
as sacred, including his birthplace, and all people as valuable, includ-
ing Trinidadians."

The word "sacred" recurs in *The Enigma of Arrival*. It appears
seven times in the novel's short final sequence alone, when the narra-

tor observes the religious ceremony that follows his sister's cremation in Trinidad. There he sees her younger son bravely take part in the Hindu final rites of cremation. The boy is brave for carrying out his duty well in the complicated ceremony, but also for asking the pundit in charge of the ceremony a serious question: How had his mother's past "dictated the cruelty of her death"? The pundit does not or cannot answer. The narrator, at this occasion of death and return, sees the sanctity of his island home: "We were immemorially people of the countryside, far from the courts of princes, living according to rituals we didn't always understand and yet were unwilling to dishonor because that would cut us off from the past, the sacred earth, the gods."

IN MY ROOM

MY PLACE OF FRET IS NOT A NARROW ROOM, BUT ONE THAT is short and sort of wide. It is poor in natural light: a bulb's perpetual yellowish wash makes it feel like a cellar, homogeneous, belonging to neither night nor day. This is not a bad thing. The illusion that time is at a standstill helps, somewhat, when I come there to write. But the romance stops there. My desk—solid, coffee black—is directly in front of the only window. Outside is a big green yard with three apple trees at the far end of the fence. The occasional delight is the family of deer that come, some evenings, to graze. If inside the room it is a jaundiced and motionless hour, the sight of the deer outside casts it into a pre-strife world of flux, enacted in the fluid stride of their bodies crossing the yard. My focus lifts often from the desk to the yard in hopes of catching them. But there are long moments when I do not break from the desk, not even for the deer when I sense they are there, not for their Hesiodic world, not for nothing. For the desk, littered with books and notebooks, is my place of second thoughts, where I come to labor through whatever has gestated elsewhere. I must make myself an anchorite here until something is made. It is a good desk, too, strong enough for a heavy dreamer.

Books lie on the floor. I let them stay there, much for their play of titles, which I like to scan whenever I first enter the room, or when I am stuck and nothing can be seen outside, I call out their titles under my breath. But the books, in fact, remain on the floor more for their play of colors and sizes than their titles: dull, big; small, bright, and some blend directly into the pastel carpet on the floor—Wallace Stevens's *The Palm at the End of the Mind* comes to mind—sprouting as if from the floor. (Walter Benjamin once said that books not yet on the shelves are "not yet touched by the mild boredom of order.") This elliptical order is comforting. But it is not intentional: there are no bookshelves here (the library is upstairs).

The only thing on the floor consciously "placed"—near the middle of the room—is a John Coltrane poster. Still in its plastic cover, it has never been hung since I got it in New York City in 2006, the first autumn of my move to the States from Jamaica. For six years the poster followed me everywhere I have lived, from Salt Lake City to Baltimore, and now Ithaca, in upstate New York, where deer come to visit the stranger in his den. When I placed the poster on the floor in the autumn of 2012, three deer ran across the yard just as I did. I took that for a sign, that through this votive act of deliberately placing Coltrane on the ground, a good sign came, and I even joked to myself, "There goes ELATION-ELEGANCE-EXALTATION," the three words forming the antepenultimate line of Coltrane's poem "A Love Supreme."

Coltrane's poem I discovered about the time I got the poster in New York City. I had come to cherish it, even its heavily didactic parts, as much as I cherish the titular album, *A Love Supreme*, which I have long loved. Two years after, in another city, I discovered Coltrane had included his poem in the album's original liner notes. That surprised and moved me, like finding a hidden P.S. in an old love letter. But even more staggering was finding out that Coltrane would place the handwritten poem on his music stand and play it like a score. This latter discovery, for some reason, helped me to better bear my time in the city's no-man's-land bleakness. The city is nestled in a half desert valley, terrifyingly landlocked. Homesick for home sea, I thought of Coltrane's handwritten poem as a shield held up in front of his music. A shield that reflected like a mirror what I thought, or rather hoped, my own handwritten poems reflected, the sea of home, and the greater desire of the eighth line of Coltrane's poem, to find the means to "help [us to] resolve our fears and weaknesses." Its didacticism, which I had doubted, had in that no-man's-land city become luminous.

On the poster, Coltrane's right arm is up and goes behind him to cradle his head; his left hand is at his mouth, index finger on his bottom lip. He looks down, not out, and in that fixed gaze—you can see his dark pupils clearly—is a serious contemplation the camera flash cannot penetrate and so cannot disturb. His eyes on the ground abolish any idea of an audience; his contemplation is without vanity; he does not know or care if I am there.

Yet I have lived with the sense that at a "moment's notice" (to borrow one of the titles of a track on the album *Blue Train*, for which the poster is the cover) he will look up and say, "Okay, you got it." Since this is a validation that will never come, I seek it even more.

Behind my desk are two double-door closets of a light maroon color. The door to the right is closed, and the one to the left is half-open. The right side is empty, not even a bulb in the socket, but jammed on the two shelves of the left are things, odd and conventional, that go back to childhood: books, photographs, my grandmother's torn saffron scarf. On the second shelf sits the great treasure: the 1896 first English printing of the great three-volume Bulfinch Press edition of *The Complete Letters of Vincent van Gogh*. Unlike Coltrane's fixed, elsewhere gaze on the poster on the floor, the *Letters* gazes out from its aperture with godlike scrutiny on my secular (and slow) work.

In this space of fret where I come daily, Van Gogh's tone in some of his letters, urgent, restless, and hectoring, seeps into me. Occasionally, too, his golden solace—"instead of giving in to despair, I chose the part of active melancholy"—brings a holy peace to the room's yellow glare. The holy peace of the sea.

At least so I imagine, but as I write now, I look up through the window and see a deer halt, alert. It is a young buck with horns just starting. Mere months ago, in summer, it had no horns to speak of and its body was only a faint reddish blaze. Now, at the end of autumn, its pelt is almost fully ash, and the pronounced muscles as it moves off make its body appear one lean ripple, the very meaning of mass and majesty.

I know I will need a mind as agile as such a body to write through the coming winter. Slowly the deer is vanishing through the fence. There the romance begins.

CATCH A FIRE:
JAMAICA AT FIFTY IN TORONTO

∎

IN THE GAME OF CRICKET, WHEN A BATSMAN MAKES A HALF century, he raises his bat like a scepter and slowly twirls it to the four corners of the field. His audience watching from the stands promptly stands and cheers until he is done with his papal gesture. They sit back, blessed. And like people who've just received a blessing, they lapse into a silence broken by modest chatter in praise of what has brought the batsman to his moment of triumph. That triumph, consecrated by the mock-heroic twirls of his bat, is carried off with a nonchalance that borders on the joyless. Not joyless, but as if joy were held in abeyance by a studied, artful reticence. It is theater, this act of reticence. It is in part the art of the game, and the emotion of cricket, careless of place and time, remains rigidly British. But the reticence also speaks of what is waiting in the wings, something that may or may not come: the next fifty runs. To raise his bat like that again, he'll have to make another fifty runs. This could take hours or even days in, as usual, grueling heat. The chance that the batsman is bowled out is only a ball away. This is on his mind during the momentary stirring of the air with his bat. No wonder the pause is so brief before he gets back to the infernal business of the pitch. Just imagine leaving the pitch, bowled out, seconds after making such a gesture.

The image of the celebratory raised bat is a very West Indian image to me. Even when I watch other cricket teams doing it—Sri Lanka or Australia, for example—the gesture strikes in my mind the indelible image of the West Indies of the 1960s, the generation making that final wave goodbye to British rule. Growing up, I knew many people of that generation, and they talk a lot about cricket. By the time I came of age to watch and understand the game on my own, I did so through their eyes. I could see how they saw the raised bat in the hand of a West Indian cricketer—and a cricketer from the Caribbean is always referred to as West Indian—as a polite middle finger to the British Empire. There is another potent side to the gesture. C. L. R. James in his magisterial book on cricket and West Indian society, *Beyond a Boundary*, calls it simply "promise and possibility." These are the things offered by cricket heroes from the islands, according to James, especially when their bat is raised in the short-lived moment of triumph.

It was this Jamesian sense of the image that came to my mind two years ago during the night's literary event to celebrate Jamaica's fiftieth anniversary of independence from Britain.

It took place in September 2012 at the Harbourfront Centre in Toronto, Canada. Toronto has an old and large immigrant Jamaican community, currently numbering more than three hundred thousand. For this reason, it was one of the more important cities across the world playing host to Jamaica's independence celebration. Toronto was auspicious, some of us present half joked, for one reason other than the old and large immigrant Jamaican community: dried cod.

Dried cod, which Jamaicans call salt fish, is the second key ingredient of Jamaica's national dish of ackee and salt fish, and its source is Canada. First imported by slave masters in the seventeenth century to supplement the diet of the island's enslaved Africans, salt fish continued coming from Canada throughout the centuries and until independence in 1962.

The gathering was small for this momentous half-a-century event. Only four Jamaican writers were onstage. Their number reflected how young the nation was and how fresh its severance from Britain. Three of the writers were born a few years before independence on August 6, 1962—though one, Kwame Dawes, was born on the very cusp, July 28, in another country, Ghana. I was the youngest, born the year independent Jamaica became of legal drinking age. The other two, Afua Cooper and Honor Ford-Smith, are residents of Toronto. The event's aim was not to show Britain how far Jamaica's literature has progressed since the Union Jack went down fifty years ago; festive as the mood was, we were there to attend to the business of the pitch, the next half century and beyond.

It happened in a large, darkened conference room. The audience was seated, about five to a group, at little round tables with fluttering candles. They paid full attention to the bright, spotlighted stage. The atmosphere felt a little like a late-night Revival prayer meeting in the Jamaican countryside, though much more somber, in which we talked at ease about the complexities of post-independent Jamaican literature. Cooper, elegant in a soft yellow head tie, moderated. Her first question dominated the evening: whether a writer writing about home away from home did so at the cost of a fatal compromise; whether such a writer operated, at all times, at a crossroads of disconnection. Toronto being already frigid in early September, her question reminded us that even among ourselves, away from home, we were fugitives colonizing in reverse and wrestling with—to riff on George Lamming's title—the displeasures of exile.

Old anxieties lurked behind the question. It chiefly concerned not so much authenticity as betrayal. The betrayal goes beyond selling out and becoming, in that biting Jamaican phrase, "foreign-minded" (which no one cares about seriously): claiming West Indian origin with one hand and denying it with the other, subjecting home to footnote status. V. S. Naipaul is most famously accused of this: of Trinidad in 1962, its year of independence, he wrote, "I knew Trinidad to be unimportant, uncreative, cynical." But it was the same Naipaul, a year later, in 1963, who would write praising his countryman C. L. R. James's *Beyond a Boundary* as "one of the finest and most finished books to come out of the West Indies, important to the West Indies," summing up: "[*Beyond a Boundary*] gives a base and solidity to West Indian literary endeavor." James and Naipaul are great Trinidadian writers, great West Indian writers, and great Caribbean writers in English. They are colonials, complex and complicated in their various individual ways. Our varied responses to Cooper's question honored the greatness of these two pioneering writers (and many more), but from the vantage of our own postindependence complexities. Even so, our direct answer to her question about any disconnection from home caused by exile was a resounding no.

Our no was not a denial of the physical or psychological disconnect of exile. We all, after all, lived outside Jamaica, which we embraced as both a choice and a compromise. Rather, our no emphasized that writing—conscientious writing—away from home was at once an act of always returning home and extending home. Such a dual condition, return and extension, was the beginning of our literary modernism, going back to pre-independent writers like Claude McKay (1889–1948). McKay made it to the United States, largely unaided, in 1912. He was never to see Jamaica again, but after eight years of a peripatetic and menial life in various states, he was able to publish his first poetry volume in America, which he called *Spring in New Hampshire*. (Spring of all seasons! New Hampshire of all places! By a Jamaican stalwart of the Harlem Renaissance!) McKay's journey away from home—like James's, like Naipaul's, like ours—was primarily to find publishing opportunities. (True, McKay published two volumes of verse in Jamaica—written in Jamaican patois—the same year he left for America, but this was more or less a novelty act, greatly supported by his British patron, Walter Jekyll.) McKay's reality, the lack of viable publishing opportunities at home, has not changed significantly fifty years into Jamaica's independence.

Our talk circled this persistent reality, its implications in light of our past, our present, and our future. Present work, we agreed, was future work. The past, whether we made good of it or not, was secured. It was secured in spite of or perhaps—and this is a cruel fact—because of all the suffering the Jamaican writers of McKay's generation and those who followed had to endure in order to publish. They were the generation that lost their homeland and created a Jamaican literary tradition. This point lent a grave solidity to our event. Cooper wanted to know how the cycle was being broken, at least its most vicious aspect. And it was here that Ford-Smith and Dawes spoke at length about the tremendous work they have been doing, outside and inside Jamaica, to see to the production of Jamaican literature in Jamaica, though more often than not that production is centered on places outside, like Toronto.

Production, a theater word, is apt when it comes to Ford-Smith. She co-founded the Sistren Theatre Collective in Kingston in 1977. Sistren, along with staging plays and mentoring playwrights, actors, and directors for thirty-five years, has been involved with working-class community ventures, primarily manufacturing textiles and screen printing, for financial support. The latter—an ethos of self-reliance— echoed the Michael Manley–era brand of socialism, coinciding with the rise of reggae and the Rasta movement: the 1970s was the era, too, when the West Indies cricket team came into full form, winning the first Cricket World Cup, in 1975, beating Australia in England. In England! (Prime Minister Manley, incidentally, wrote *A History of West Indies Cricket* in 1988, the year that some say marked the beginning of the decline of the W.I. team and Manley. As to the former I disagree; from the late 1980s into the early 1990s the W.I. cricket squad was a formidable force.) The era's euphoria waned; promises became more promises and possibilities became less probable. It was these unsustainable changes that partly led Ford-Smith to migrate to Canada. Sistren remained on the ground in Kingston, working under her aegis from abroad.

Dawes's role in publishing is far more wide reaching. To a great extent, he has almost single-handedly altered the usual leave-home-to-publish cycle for Caribbean poets through his involvement as associate poetry editor of the Leeds-based Peepal Tree Press. Founded in 1985 by Jeremy Poynting on a sugar estate on the east coast of Demerara in Guyana, Peepal Tree issues books by black British and Caribbean writers living anywhere in the world. Dawes has edited, since the 1990s, an astonishing number of its poetry collections. He has shepherded at least two generations of Caribbean poets, some of whom have never left their island. Handsome in his cream-colored Nehru jacket, he held up the most recent work, *Jubilation! Poems Celebrating 50 Years of Jamaican Independence*, specially published for the occasion. Dawes then spoke about his role as program director for the annual Calabash International Literary Festival in Jamaica. Founded in 2001 by the novelist and poet Colin Channer with the support of Dawes and the producer Justine Henzell, Calabash is the veritable Woodstock of Jamaican—and Caribbean—literature. Every major Jamaican writer and poet since its inception has been touched by it, either directly through its writers' workshop series and publishing seminars or indirectly in ways nearly impossible to measure through the yearly presence of international writers gathering in the small fishing village where it is held annually on the hard-to-get-to southern coast of Jamaica.

The final phase of the conversation, the most exciting for me, was about the relationship between language, that is, writing, and Jamaica's popular music. To an extent, the relationship took us back to our opening question, the conundrum of exile. The framing was less whether writing can express song lyrics and more whether the pitch and tone of a poem or a novel could capture the texture and dimension of rocksteady or ska. If writing could capture the texture and dimension of rocksteady or ska, could it do so in "standard" language or only in "dialect"? The question implied Jamaican music was the truly national, truly independent Jamaican form, and writing, whether standard or dialect, was secondary entertainment. We each in turn dismantled this politics of authenticity.

Our writing is not an adjunct of our music; in fact, our writing (when good) subsumes our music and pushes against the notion, in some quarters, that our music is a mere cultural pastime. Though present in all forms of post-independent Jamaican writing, this notion finds its furthest radical utterance in dub poetry, a form of oral performance poetry based primarily on reggae baseline and Rasta drumming. When dub emerged in the 1970s, it became possible to synthesize our lived experiences with the violent erasures of our historical experiences. The synthesis itself was not new, but how the ineffable found urgent voicing was utterly new. The effect of such a voicing reminded me of James's beautiful, pained description of the effect of cricket, what he calls the ethics of cricket, on a pre-independent West Indian: "There is a whole generation of us, and perhaps two generations, who have been formed by cricket, not only in social attitudes but in our innermost personal lives, in fact there more than anywhere else. The social attitudes we could to some degree alter if we wished. For the inner self the die was cast." James's second sentence gets to the heart of the tragic colonial weight, but his first and second sentences transfigure that weight close to the way the aesthetics of dub subsumes, with intimacy, the Caribbean's ethics of resistance and survival.

The conversation dwelled longer on the voicing released by dub. Because it is a voicing often limited to performance poetry, its effect on fiction writing, for instance, is sometimes missed. But even in this,

Dawes stressed, many dub poetry pioneers—and he cited examples from Linton Kwesi Johnson to Mikey Smith—cared deeply and strove to make sure their poems worked off as well as on the page. The basic principle of dub voicing demands simultaneously layering multiple registers of sounds while disassembling, as they unfold, all new sonic layers before they can be settled into too fixed a pattern. In this way, to oversimplify, dub constantly shatters the core of our "innermost personal lives" into shards of remembrances, and in the layers we hear across the void of time the cry of an ancestor whose language we do not speak and whose face we cannot see but who is seen, we said, looking at the audience, wherever a Jamaican is present, at home or away from home.

It was sometime during this line of talk that Dawes began to half hum the opening words of the first verse of Bob Marley and the Wailers' song "Slave Driver": "Every time I hear the crack of a whip / My blood runs cold / I remember . . ." The audience sang back to him, ". . . on the slave ship, / How they brutalize our very soul." Dawes sang back to the low flame of the candlelit table, "Today they say that we are free," then some in the audience slapped the tabletops, making the flame jerk as if to say back to us, "There can be music without language, but there can be no language without music," to which we would have said, "Amen!" as they began to rise, laughing and clapping for what felt like forever, much to the great frustration of the man responsible for locking up the conference room, who soon began to realize, to his horror, that the audience was going to stay back and chat, taking liberty with their writers and poets.

Indeed, the night was great West Indian cricket theater and a most delightful rendezvous beyond the boundary.

WOMEN SWEEPING

■

Édouard Vuillard (French, 1868–1940), *Woman Sweeping*, c. 1899–1900,
oil on cardboard

THE WOMAN IN ÉDOUARD VUILLARD'S *WOMAN SWEEPING*, painted between 1899 and 1900, is Marie Michaud Vuillard, the painter's mother. She is tall and stocky, her posture—that slight give of the back to the broom, without bending—marking a nonchalant style of carrying out a chore that routine hasn't made any less complex. As Madame Vuillard sweeps, her gaze seems to fall on the broom or the floor. We might detect deference or humility in such a pose, but the turn of her head, her face ringed with a whitish glow as if lit by an inner ardor, conveys ease. We cannot see her gaze; we are given only the black slash of her eyelashes, which suggests an almost closed-eye intensity. Madame Vuillard is invested in her work and in herself, though perhaps in this moment she does allow herself to be mildly flattered by her painter son's attention. The slash also conveys a quiet authority; you know that she need not look up to be heeded.

The glow that illuminates Madame Vuillard's face is also visible on the middle section of the broomstick, where her left hand holds it. There, the brushwork reveals something elemental: her power to enliven the inanimate through the intimacy of work. Her grasp has not turned the broom into a light saber; nothing supernatural has occurred. It is simply that through perpetual use the wood has come to appear less lifeless.

This change permeates the room. It is there in Madame Vuillard's clothing, well chosen and cared for: the neatness of her rich damask housecoat of rust and black, the snowy ruffle of her blouse poking through the housecoat's neck and sleeves. It is there in that hard-to-make-out black leather shoe that peeks from under her hem, and in her French braid with not a strand of silvery-brown hair out of place. The room's embellishments—the wallpaper, the framed paintings, even that little elegant brass doorknob on the richly grained brown door—suggest a space that has evolved with keen, artisanal patience over years.

Every crevice is bursting with her life. The interior does not simply belong to her; it is her. Everything therein sensuously affirms it. The wallpaper's heavy reddish brown, ocher, and black seem to culminate in the swell of her striped housecoat. The bed, the chest of drawers, and the open door reflect the expansive gentleness of her presence. Camouflaged by her possessions, she can disappear into her task without relinquishing her personality, because her home, designed so completely in her own image, will always reassert it.

It is as though all the work done by her hands—the sweeping, the dusting, the polishing, the arranging and rearranging of decorations and heavy furniture, day in and day out—is a sort of kindling, a lovingness that these things absorb.

My father's mother, with whom I lived half the time while growing up, did not at all resemble Madame Vuillard, and yet the first time I encountered Vuillard's painting, in the library of the university in Mona, Jamaica, where I was a student, I found in it an intimate portrait: of her strict, indefatigable regime of daily sweeping, and much else of what I know and do not know about her. I saw my grandmother every morning with her broom in hand. The swish it made often woke me as she went throughout her four-room house with its polished red floor, from her bedroom at the very back to the veranda. In the evenings she worked in the reverse order. She did not sing or hum as she swept, nor did she break off sweeping to talk or wield the broom to raise me from the bed or the sofa where I watched her.

My grandmother was short and solidly built. She was energetic about the house, and doubly so in the kitchen, because her profession was baking. She baked on Thursdays and Fridays, mostly unaided, for the Saturday market. On baking days, the usual quiet of the house gave way to the oven's ferocious heat; out of its roar and crackle and the shushed hiss when it opened, above the clatter of pans and metal mixing basins, I would sometimes hear my grandmother's voice bubbling with sounds of jubilation. She beamed whenever a batch of dense black cake or a sheet of coconut drops came out perfectly. In that mood she would call me to the kitchen for scraped handfuls of "bun bun," the bits stuck to the bottom of a baking tin; I would take them back to the veranda or the flat stone I liked to sit on by the side of the house and eat, with gusto, the burnt sweetness. Whenever a cascade of tins fell on the kitchen's battered butcher-block table, it seemed to rattle the building's foundation. But in every other way the house was serene, for my grandmother was a serene woman.

Her presence imbued every object. Whatever she brought into the house, the useless or the useful, was there to stay. Better to say that the useless was transformed into a useful, durable part of the household over time: tin cans of condensed milk, once emptied, their Betty or Carnation labels stripped off, became the utensils for scooping flour or sugar out of the big pails in the kitchen to make cake batter. The shapes and sizes of these cans, along with the free measurements of her hand, decided the amounts of the ingredients that went into a cake mix (for a batch of rock bun, "two Betty scoops of flour, one Carnation scoop of sugar").

The basins in which she mixed the batter were repurposed metal or plastic washtubs no longer suitable for laundry, likely because of slow leaks, but fine for holding the thick cake mixture. These tubs, scoured to a wispy silver, remained stacked in her kitchen long after her death. You could not throw them out, just as you would not throw out a precious china teacup of the sort she stored, untouched, in the floor-to-ceiling cabinet in the living room.

I cannot recall this cabinet ever being opened. I used to stare at the things behind its glass panels, trying to calculate exactly how many crystal-looking wineglasses belonged to the wide-spout decanter, how many plates were stacked there in similar shades of white. These things were kept pristine, as were her overused plastic mugs, washed and turned upside down to dry on the dish rack. They, too, were given such devotion that you could never discard them. There were in fact two dish racks by the sink, the second completely buried under a large, many-colored hump of plastic dishes and bowls.

We ate from these dishes and bowls throughout the day: cornmeal porridge; *gungo* (pigeon pea) soup; the unflagging mixture of boiled yam, banana, and potato, which was always served with a "meat kind" (anything from shredded bits of salted fish to, though I did not eat it, layers of stewed oxtail). Sometimes we allowed a large pile of unwashed dishes and bowls to grow in the sink for one big wash in the evening. No matter how high that pile grew, I never saw what the dish rack looked like, a fact that puzzled me. Equally frustrating in their mystery were my grandmother's long cast-aluminum "Mercury dime" forks, spoons, and ladles, which hung from a strip of wood nailed to the wall above the dish racks. Their uniformity dazzled me—they seem to have come out of the same foundry at the same time—but it appeared to be a kind of trick, for they either grew or shrank in number each time I went in and out of the kitchen. I stood before them on every visit, counting and recounting and never getting the same tally.

Immediately adjacent to these forks, spoons, and ladles were the two shelves above my grandmother's oven, laden with blackened "Dutchies"—cooking pots also made of heavy cast aluminum. These stockpots, frying pans, sauté pans, and saucepans were routinely rubbed with charcoal ash and left to season out in the yard.

The same devotion was given to the oven, the pride of the house, which stood at the entrance to the kitchen. Dark grayish blue, of unknown age and undeterminable brand, it reached my grandmother's waistline and was about twice her width. Once a week my uncle cleaned it with baking soda and a steel-wool Scotch-Brite. He was the only one of my grandmother's six children to have remained at home; he lived a few yards down the hill in a one-room shanty my father had built in 1982.

My uncle was about an inch taller than my grandmother, and the muscles of his arms bulged as he scrubbed the six-burner stovetop, the exertion making him sweat profusely. He would go out to the backyard to wash the burner grates and the oven's racks, which had been left there to soak in a basin of soapy water, before returning to kneel and scour the oven, the top half of his body swallowed into its black hole. On cleaning days, wherever I was in the house, I could hear his long exhalations as he sudsed off bake splatter in the unseen-to-me parts of the oven. My grandmother would come into the kitchen as he scrubbed. My uncle would look out at her, waiting for the glance that meant his work was done. It was not always quick to be given.

Sometimes, while my uncle was Scotch-Briting the oven, my grandmother swept the other rooms. The broom, which was kept, as if on display, in the V-crook of the wall between the cabinet and the entrance to the kitchen, was summoned to her. I would rise to fetch it, poppy-showing on my way to her, twirling it around in my hands as if it were a javelin or spear. It had a lithe feel, which I loved. The worn wood felt glassy, maybe from a wash of varnish applied years ago. I knew it was older than me. I felt the fragile strength in it as I spun it around, cutting down my invisible enemies.

After my grandmother took her broom from my hand, there was always an infinitesimal pause before she began to sweep. Something had arrived to her that she had called for; now it was in her palm, a reality clicked into place. My role as broom bearer deserved no notice (broom bearing was one of many non-errand errands I was called to do). My grandmother's pause did. It marked what, in retrospect, I would call, using the words of William Morris, "the natural solace of . . . labour." The labor Morris is speaking of is art.

Making a home would have been strenuous for Madame Vuillard, a widowed mother of three and a seamstress born in 1839 in Cuiseaux, in the Burgundy region of France. For my grandmother, a black woman born in 1930 in Portland, a rural parish in northeastern Jamaica, the difficulty must have been near insurmountable. To this day, it is unclear how my grandmother built her house, or even when exactly the construction began and ended. With the exception of one of my aunts, her firstborn, all her children grew up in that four-room house. By the time they were grown, her husband, my grandfather, whom I never knew, was long gone. He had hardly been around before he finally disappeared. He seemed, by all accounts, to have been a prolonged incident in my grandmother's life. He was first a name and then a shadow and then nothing.

When she was asked how she had built her house, my grandmother's answer was simple and final: "Through baking." No details, no stories of the countless sorrows and troubles she must have endured. She was thirty-two by the time Jamaica gained its independence from Britain, in 1962—too old and too far from the center of power to have benefited from the short-lived prosperity that followed.

During the plantation period, property ownership, even for freed blacks, was more or less illegal, and in the era afterward the majority of Jamaicans still did not own property, thanks to all manner of delegitimizing practices. For a brutally disenfranchised people, owning a house was an unassailable achievement, perhaps the only signifier of true independence.

The question of when my grandmother acquired her land should have been easy to answer. But the original document of purchase was "lost," a trope of bureaucracy in rural Jamaica, where business often began in thoroughly unofficial ways—on a veranda, in a rum bar—before slowly creeping into bewildering officialdom in places known by their initialisms rather than their functions. The PMC (Portland Municipal Corporation) was one such place. Under its aegis fell the land registry and deeds for the parish of Portland. When I first visited with my grandmother in the IBM-crazed 1990s, dressed in my khaki school uniform, I sat sweating on a bench in the overheated filing room, staring at wall-to-wall shelves of unsorted land documents, some of the coiled and yellowing papers certainly dating back to the muddle of Jamaica's pre-independent period. I was struck with an unnamed revulsion, as if someone, out of sheer spite, had broken up a jigsaw puzzle right in front of me.

The land around our house was indeed like a jigsaw, one shattered by an even more disconsolate reality. Officially referred to as Crown Land or Queen's Land, it was known to the locals, with commonsense honesty, as Capture Land—"captcha," in the Jamaican pronunciation—where people who wished to own property but could not afford to would seize a plot on which to build a shanty. The governmental authorities could show up at any time, and often did, mowing the dwellings down. By this method, people were booted out of the only homes they'd ever known.

The unsanctioned settling of the territory caused ugly disputes among family members. Strangers sometimes arrived to claim the properties, raising the specter of an "original owner," some ancestor dead for several generations. Of course, documents rarely existed to prove such claims, and so other methods were frequently employed to uproot the "trespassers."

"There can be no title in bush," V. S. Naipaul once coldly wrote,

and on Capture Land this was borne out violently. It was not unusual to see men circling each other with machetes during flare-ups over ownership. It was not unusual to see entire households from different factions, grandparents down to toddlers, cheering on these machete-wielding men. Sometimes blood was spilled over a patch of ground as if in a grotesque sacrificial rite. These confrontations were passed down through generations and became known as "tribal wars," a term that itself compounds the dehumanizing legacy of colonialism with the tinderbox politics of postindependence Jamaica.

Our family never had to experience any such displacement or strife. In this mad milieu of protracted imperial confusion, my grandmother legally owned property. How? "Through baking."

The threads of what I knew about her life were so few. Of her start in baking I had only the faintest outline. When she was not yet quite a teenager, so ran the family lore, she apprenticed herself to the second-largest bakery in Port Antonio. CC Bakery, still located across from the marina on West Palm Avenue, was owned by a family rumored to have recently immigrated to the island from China. CC's slogan—"Taste the goodness! Home of the holey bulla!"—was known across the island, its legend only enhanced by the fact that no one knew exactly what "CC" stood for. To a good many, the slogan was a mantra of industriousness, tied to the vision of Jamaica's folk creativity that emerged with the tourism industry in Port Antonio in the late nineteenth century.

The holey bullas, sweet, dry, gingery cakes with a hole in the middle, were sometimes still warm from CC's when they reached my hands in the playground of my first school, Boundbrook Basic, only a few blocks away from CC's brightly colored concrete building. I ate several for my snack or lunch. The hole in the holey bulla made me feel cheated; I took umbrage at that, and by the time I was in high school, CC's was no longer just the innocuous place I walked past almost daily. How could I not have complicated feelings about eating pastries from the same kitchen my grandmother had sweated in as a girl?

My grandmother, certain of her value as a worker, would never have spoken of struggle or of a system set against her. To her, progress meant doing something for and by oneself; anything else was, like my grandfather, incidental to her survival.

"Through baking." History will not hear her saying that phrase, the "through" in her accent, which is to say in her rebellion, cutting the ears like "true."

My grandmother's house brought her immeasurable joy. The twice-daily sweeping of all four rooms gave her a sixth sense of its every nook and cranny. Countless times I saw her stare at a ray of sunlight streaming through a rip in one of the lattice windows of the living room. The light always seemed to rest on the wall above the mauve wool sofa, where an undulating string of Hallmark Christmas cards hung.

These winged cards came from her children in the States and in England, and some dated back to when I was a toddler. But the

majority of them were from later, from a time when I could read, and I did read them to my grandmother, along with the many bundles of letters in thin white airmail envelopes. Even before I had gone more than a few miles outside our hometown, I knew well the addresses of a few streets in England and the States. An itinerant uncle was a waiter with the Royal Caribbean Cruise Line and sometimes sent letters or cards from places with strange, intoxicating names. The foreign postal codes especially mesmerized me. It was from the envelopes, too, that I first discovered that Jamaica was located in some place called the West Indies.

My grandmother would request a certain card from the line, or a letter, as if it contained the words to ward off any oncoming terror. I was summoned to read them in the same way I was summoned to bring her the broom. Even after a landline was installed in our house, sometime in the late 1990s, she continued to ask me to read them aloud, though her children now simply called to talk to her. More rarely, I would dial the phone operator, someone I pictured as a dubious but efficient stranger to whom I must speak "properly" in order for my grandmother to be connected.

Our house was one of the first on Stony Hill Road to have a phone. It was like a slab of white marble with pressed digits, on top of a frilly white runner. The phone meant that people now showed up at our house to receive calls from relatives abroad, just as two decades earlier, apparently, they had stopped by for ice, because my grandmother's house was one of the few with a fridge back then. Such were the things that made my grandmother into someone—"inna somebody," in the Jamaican saying, which has more to do with an upright character than upward mobility.

After a few years with the phone, the readings grew rarer. Almost no new letters or cards came from those foreign addresses; slowly, country area codes and the accents of the dubious operators began to supplant the postal and zip codes in my head, and certainly, before long, the word "Caribbean" came to supplant "West Indies," making me, in that improbable phrase, "a modern." Within a couple of years, my grandmother had stopped selling at the market, so her baking slowed to orders from customers, some of which were phoned in. I took them down, adopting a phone operator's voice, and in this way the phone nearly replaced her oven as the pride of the house.

Our home was respectable, with the additional appeal, surprisingly scarce in our coastal region, of being built on a steep hill with a large veranda facing the Caribbean Sea. Stony Hill was above a dense green valley. Behind us, an even higher hill, Shotover Hill, descended along a trail of the Rio Grande at the foothills of the Blue Mountains, which led east back out to Norwich. We were haunted in more senses than one by English names. My high school, also visible, in the distance, from our veranda, was called Titchfield—a name that appears in the Domesday Book. The position of the veranda meant that there was constant

airflow throughout all four rooms during the day. We never had an electric fan, on account of the breeze from the trade winds—something my grandmother, who loved to "take air," was quite proud of.

The hedges of croton trees planted in front of the veranda were also not typical of poorer rural households like ours. They ran the span of the house, reaching as far back as the unused old pit latrine by the chicken coop at the farthest west boundary of the plot, beyond which lay woodland. The multicolored crotons with their leaves of different shapes and sizes, especially the Joseph's coat, which my grandmother loved, added to the pleasure of sitting on the veranda, with her or alone, watching the sea. They were "bushed"—that is, hemmed into a rough evenness—by my uncle, some flat enough for my grandmother to spread out her laundry on. These crotons mystified me. I often asked my grandmother to tell me when they were planted. I got her usual silence.

We both loved the two Adirondack-style chairs we sat in. Their slats, made of blue mahoe wood, were painted alternately blue and white. I was astonished that the slender slats could endure so much of my now and again insane rocking. Our neighbor, the carpenter Mr. Bell, had told me the name of the wood after I asked him one day how the chairs were so strong. Mr. Bell had not made the chairs himself—his thing was cabinets and coffins—but he worked, he told me, with the same wood. He spoke the name of the tree as if handing off a shibboleth regarding the strength in all things. "Is because a blue mahoe." It was that ordinary.

No such secrets were passed to me from my grandmother's corner of the veranda, where she sat beside me, not close, but not far away either, looking down at the long vista of the Titchfield Peninsula straggling out into the Caribbean Sea. Beneath us, a bamboo bench was nailed to the ackee tree in front of the house, a tree presumably older even than she was. When I asked, "Is who plant the trees them here?" or tried to glean something of what she'd been like as a girl, she didn't dismiss my questions outright. "Me never creamed my hair," she said. "I come see that ackee tree here." But she never gave a sustained story about her past. From the right-hand chair I questioned her like a bailiff's understudy.

I asked her about CC's all the time. And when did she leave to bake on her own? When did she set up her stall at the back of the Musgrave Market next to West Harbour, in the heart of Port Antonio? I used to visit her there on Saturdays as a boy, falling asleep on layers of cardboard under her unlabeled stall when the heat knocked me out. Was it true that for years she used to sell at the very front of Musgrave, by one of the giant iron gates, out of a stall labeled HOME OF AUNT MAY'S BAKERY AND THINGS?

It was utterly mind-boggling to me how she had navigated that life for forty-odd years. My grandmother was not the "higgler" market-woman type, and when I saw her those Saturdays, she made no attempt to sell her "bakes and things." She sat calmly on her stool, her entire disposition the same as when she was at home. Yet her market days produced a stunning career. Out of it she built her house and raised her children.

"How you make your house, Grandma?" "Me? Through baking." She sat, taking her air, implacable, silent, and secret.

"Mysterious," not "secret," would be the right word. Mystery can be shared even when not communicated. Not speaking of a mystery can be its own unique form of communication. The house, painted yellow on the outside and a faded cherry peach inside, was intricately bound up with our communication. When we talked indoors, it often felt as if in some profound sense we were talking with the house.

At night, this sense deepened, and the bond of our communication was like a thaumaturgic scene out of a lost Apocrypha. Every night before sleep I read her verses from the King James Bible, lying in my bed one room over from hers. As if to match the deep quiet of the house, I read in a low voice that carried through the concrete walls to her ears.

She was nearing seventy, her hearing growing dim. Still, she heard me clearly, and I heard her breath clearly, too: the metronome my voice adjusted to as I read. As I listened to her breathing, I felt I could see where she lay on her back, a kerosene lamp placed on the little table by her bed. The light from the lamp was a bronze haze. Her head, covered in a nylon-stocking cap, was raised on the pillow.

Her wardrobe; her chest of drawers with several old leather suitcases on top; her two brown barrels, which, like the suitcases, were sent to her by her children overseas; her enamel chamber pot and washbasin—they all seemed to levitate in the bronze haze. The smaller items—her pill bottles and vials filled with herbal brews or a home remedy of rum, pimento berries, and nutmeg bark—gleamed with a healing force.

One night, after reading the Bible to her, I turned off the light and went to bed. Some time after that I heard her calling my name. I was certain I was asleep. The call could not truly be coming from her bedroom. Her voice sounded very close to my ear. She called again, angrily, and I bolted up in bed.

"Yes, Grandma?"

I could tell that she was sitting up. "What wrong, Grandma?"

"Someone in the house."

I paused and listened to the house. I heard her breathing, and the night insects, but nothing else.

"No, Grandma. Me lock up the place. Everything all right." She insisted, "Him in the living room there."

I could picture her pointing with her mouth to the living room.

But the house was quiet.

"I don't hear nothing," I heard myself say. I wondered if a malignant spirit had overtaken her or the house. Late nights in rural Jamaica, people took extra precaution with what they said, lest they upset an evil spirit, a duppy, or a troublesome "rolling calf."

I opened the door that led from my bedroom to hers, so rarely used that it was more or less forgotten. Even before I held her, I knew she was shaking.

"It all right. Nobody not here. I don't hear nobody, Grandma." "Him in the kitchen now. Him there in me kitchen." Her voice sounded like tears, but she was not crying. She held my wrist. I stayed an endless moment.

Without saying anything, I got up, walked past her wardrobe to the curtain dividing her room from the living room, and drew it back on one side. I looked into the living room, toward the front door: the door I had locked and bolted a few hours ago was opened wide. A clear night sky shone on the veranda. Terror cramped my belly.

I passed the V-crook of the wall with the broom by the cabinet next to the kitchen entrance. I looked through the strings of hundreds of plastic beads that separated the kitchen from the living room. No one, not even somebody with the greatest catlike stealth, could ever get through them without triggering a gnashing windmill—not even me, and I had practiced trying to part them without a sound for years. But there I saw the back door of the kitchen, wide open. I looked both ways, to the veranda and back to the kitchen, again and again, in disbelief. The two doors, front and back, stood open.

My mind raced through a barrage of questions, a million actions to take, including, to my horror, killing the intruder.

Then I heard my grandmother's voice, almost returned to its usual calm. "Him gone already."

My grandmother was illiterate. Such was common among women of her generation, especially those from the rural areas of Jamaica. My grandmother's mother, Lillian Renford, would have been born only three or at most four generations after the end of slavery in Jamaica in 1834. She was married several times and lived in Bellevue, a district in the rugged Rio Grande valley of Portland, which was often flooded out by the river. She died there in 1988, when my grandmother was fifty-nine or sixty and I was five years old, but I never met her. It was probably my great-grandmother who brought her firstborn daughter to CC's to learn the trade of baking. I do not know, and no one seems to know. What I do know is that working at the bakery meant my grandmother did not attend school. The scant bit of literacy she got came from attending church. She was able to write her name, though, curiously, she marked an X for her signature on certain documents. She had worked out a letter system for cake orders: *R* for rock cakes, *G* for gizzadas, and so on.

In the living room of our house was a low center table of an obsidian color. On top of it was a big off-white faux-ceramic bowl in which were piled exotic plastic fruits: purple grapes, green pears, figs, and some others I could not identify. As if guarding this horn of plenty were two collie figurines, the breed we knew from the old American TV show *Lassie*, which was popular on Jamaican television. The left collie had no ears, the right no tail. Beneath them, on the base of the table, were the four books of the house: the King James Bible (which I returned there every morning from my room after the nightly reading); a Church of God hymnal (most certainly given to my grandmother by her denomination of the same name); the Jamaican phone directory (called, with distinct civic pomp, the Island of Jamaica Directory, the crisp copy changing yearly); and, last, a worn, illustrated copy of John Steinbeck's story *The Pearl*.

The first three made absolute sense. They were typical for any respectable rural household. *The Pearl* needed justification. Steinbeck! How did my grandmother come to own this book? It did not belong to my father or to any of his siblings, some of whom had gone to school and others not. No, *The Pearl* had the imprimatur of another of my grandmother's own possessions, acquired for herself and for her household.

When I was a boy of about ten, a visitor, perhaps there to pick up a cake order, pointed to *The Pearl* from the doorway of the living room.

His face lined with more concern than curiosity, he asked, "What that 'bout?"

I blundered the plot to him: "This man him name Kino with him woman name Juana and them boy name Coyotito . . ." The consternation on the man's face worsened. I plowed on, oblivious to the social anxieties behind his question, which in a few years would trouble me, too. ("Yea, for real, what actually 'bout, star?")

My grandmother, of course, never told me how she came to own *The Pearl*. It existed and that was all. Its existence, for me, was, like the house, another enigma of her life, which I came to accept as part of my natural inheritance.

If I'd had the words then, I might have said that my grandmother fused the archetypes of Kino and Juana. Like Juana, she would have tried to cast back the pearl into the sea. Like Kino, she would have taken a chance at keeping the pearl if it meant that she could get her fair share without compromising her integrity. And me? I was Coyotito, through and through. But I would not be stung by a scorpion, though a scorpion's sting, a good one, was bound to develop in me. *The Pearl*, however it came into my grandmother's possession, made her worldly, and it demanded that I, too, become worldly. I read it around the age my grandmother would have been working as an apprentice at CC's. Reading it for myself, and the Bible for her at nights, demystified all of literature for me.

There is a peculiar spirit level at play in *Woman Sweeping*. Vuillard violates the expected horizontal and vertical angles and leaves us with the uncanny sense of having entered the miniature of a vast world. The effect is like experiencing music or light in a small space, their properties widening the environment to mythic proportions. Here everything verges on a kind of Euclidean relation, in which the largest items are nearly equal to the smallest. He paints with an incorruptible intimacy, allowing the stories implicit in every object to decide the form and line. It is an aesthetic that, in Elaine Scarry's words on what art can do, "ignites the desire for truth by giving us . . . the experience of conviction and the experience, as well, of error."

The truth is that, for all its neatness, the room has its disorder: every bit of space is taken up by something. Paintings, perhaps Vuillard's early efforts, hang awkwardly on the wall; the bottom of the large frame on the left is forcing the small one beneath it off its hook. Behind the door, a black chair is rammed against the wall and the chest of drawers, with a crumpled stole, a touch of elegance, lying on it like a snake's discarded skin. There is a sinuous quality to the thick, muted pastel hues of browns and ocher, which makes the atmosphere of the interior slightly gaudy, even gauche. Madame Vuillard seems to be spreading these dominant colors into a dark patch on the floor, making the pale bristles of the broom appear all the more luminous. Her sweeping—that mixing of dark and light to create order and intimacy—has an ineluctable connection with her son's vocation. "Maman is my muse," Vuillard once wrote.

According to his journals, not so long before making this work, he had given up using models to paint from memory. This is significant: *Woman Sweeping* is not strictly a record of Madame Vuillard holding a broom, which would have made it nostalgic at best. Its power is that Vuillard, working from memory, so thoroughly infuses the interior with his mother's subjectivity as to create a new and more comprehensive memory of her.

The urn on the top of the chest of drawers offers another key.

Like the gleaming pill bottles and herbal medicine vials by my grandmother's bed, it is a small, constant reminder of mortality. But the urn is not really so small. Its plump shape closely mirrors Madame Vuillard's ample body: the two bold stripes at its base and middle are multiplied on her housecoat, and the band that circles the urn reverberates, even more boldly, in the French braid around her head.

The placement of the urn as the crowning object on top of the interior's centerpiece leaves us with little doubt that Madame Vuillard herself values the act of remembrance above all else. Why? Because it is the imperishable gift she will pass on to her son.

Vuillard lived with his mother until her death, at age eighty-nine, when he was sixty-one. By then, material inheritance might have held less value to him. A childless lifelong bachelor, he had become a fully entrenched member of the haute bourgeoisie, moving in circles that included his former schoolmate Marcel Proust. Julian Barnes has written that on seeing *Woman Sweeping* at the Phillips Collection in Washington, D.C., he felt it was "a wise painting, filled with the tenderness of age." He was shocked to learn that, in fact, Vuillard was just a young man when he made it. At the time, Madame Vuillard was a year or two retired from her seamstress business. Knowing this, one might ask why Vuillard has not depicted her in the more conventional posture of the retiree, reclining with her feet off the ground. What is clear is that this painting, like his confession—"Maman is my muse"—is not a solemn tribute to his mother's kindness and help but an attestation to the intrinsic value of artistry. In *Woman Sweeping*, Vuillard had discovered his subject, and was embarking on a lifetime of striving toward her example. The result is an astonishing corpus—more than five hundred paintings and countless drawings, prints, and photographs—memorializing her and confirming work as the supreme earthly ethic. It is the concentration on the task at hand that gives the broomstick—the brush—its life-giving glow.

The painting, countering any gloom that the urn's presence might cast, remains undiminished in its human warmth. That warmth resonates most powerfully in the amber gold and brown of the door, a chunky slice of honeycomb. Perhaps the midday sun is on the other side of it, illuminating her hand and her face. But the true source of the radiance is Madame Vuillard herself.

Thinking of that radiance, I recall the one time my grandmother, taking out a cake or putting one in the oven, gave words to its meaning while I stood holding the hanging beads on the threshold: "Work is worship." That was all.

Behind Madame Vuillard's buttocks, almost imperceptible, is a built-in shelf with a sparse few books. What kinds of books? Knowing would tell us much about her—too much. Their presence allows us to imagine her sitting in the black chair with the brown stole over her lap, reading them. Picturing her this way, I think of a passage in Gertrude Stein's *Tender Buttons*, "A Chair":

> A widow in a wise veil and more garments shows that shadows are even. It addresses no more, it shadows the stage and learning. A regular arrangement, the severest and the most preserved is that which has the arrangement not more than always authorised.
>
> A suitable establishment, well housed, practical, patient and staring, a suitable bedding, very suitable and not more particularly than complaining, anything suitable is so necessary.

That is one of her pleasures. Another, we can also imagine, is being read to: one of her children seated in the black chair, Madame Vuillard dozing on the bed nearby.

As we move counterclockwise from her posterior, we encounter the three objects in the room that are larger than Madame Vuillard: the bed, the door, and—oddly—the chest of drawers. Certainly, we expect the chest to be broader than her, but for its height to be exactly equal to hers? We are asked to consider the chest and the woman, at least superficially, together—to wonder what those drawers might contain, besides her oversize striped housecoats, her white blouses, and perhaps bolts of cloth from her workshop. What could be tucked between and underneath these garments, locked in this varnished brown vault?

While my grandmother was living, no one, not even her beloved grandson, was allowed to open her chest of drawers. It stood in a corner at the head of her bed, the only forbidden area in the house. Most, if not all, Jamaican households have such spaces, inner sanctums in plain sight. You see them and you let them alone.

The summer before my grandmother died, she was allowed to come home after a stay in the hospital. In her bed, she went in and out of a kind of delirium—"traveling," my aunt called it, giving the word its old usage, which goes back to the time of slavery, meaning that my grandmother was leaving this life to go "back" to Africa. One day when I visited, my grandmother drew herself up in bed and looked around. And for an hour or so I talked with her nonstop, the lucid look on her face growing into a grin.

The grin widened when I told her that a minister had recently officiated a groundbreaking at the old harbor, a block away from the Musgrave Market, for the first Kentucky Fried Chicken in the parish.

"Him did pray?" she asked.

"Yes, for the holy, holy fowl them!" I said. She cracked up laughing.

When she died the following October, her bed was pulled away from the wall. The suitcases were taken down, and the drawers were opened. The expected things were found inside: the clothing sent by her children from Kingston or the States or England, including dresses, many of them never worn, and several multicolored silk scarves, which she loved and always wore, sometimes rakishly, anytime she went into town, in place of the faded and torn "yard scarf" of orange, blue, and white that she had on every day as she swept.

In between the clothes, in little plastic bags, were letters from some of her children. In large manila envelopes were the various iterations of the deed and land-survey documents, riddled with stamps, that we had acquired after many trips to the PMC. Then there were several little swaths of paper money tied with threads, and stashes of religious tracts, undoubtedly given to her by the Jehovah's Witnesses or the Mormon missionaries who frequently came to our veranda. Scattered throughout were heaps of notebook papers.

Covering these, in large, shaky handwriting, were hundreds of looping letters, incessantly forming a web of shapes, as if there were something she was trying to write, over and over. It seems she had been doing it most of her life. Whatever she was wrestling with, she hid, and yet she did not succumb to resignation.

These writings, in all their mystery, were an inventory of her survival. What I have saved of them, along with her yard scarf, are the most precious things I own.

LEVIATHAN IN THE SUN:
ON LES MURRAY

I FIRST READ *HAMLET* IN JAMAICA. THE BLEAK DAYLIGHT surrounding my high school, Happy Grove, was like the faded glow of an old photograph. Rain was expected; it never came. There might have been thunder, or that could just have been the pages turning in unison.

This was 1998, the beginning of truly reading for me. Thereafter, when I read certain poets, I did so against the light in which Shakespeare first fascinated me. Something else happened, though, when I opened Les Murray's *Learning Human: Selected Poems* eight years later, in autumn, on a high floor of New York University's colossal Bobst Library.

A leviathan tore through the innocence of that first light, right to the very sun, with an almost magical force. I experienced a luminous return and a conversion in its wake. The unaccustomed season, autumn (my first), was abolished, and I felt the world I knew and loved scorching in my palms. I was outside again, playing in the voracious sunlight by Bryan's Bay or any of my other haunts in the rural district of my childhood.

The strange part of the excitement was that Murray's sensory evocation of my world—"the sea's lucent linoleum, / the near trees with green-ants' nests / square-folded out of living leaves"—radiated, as if by sonar, from another world of the commonwealth so that a subtle, estranged quality accompanied my discovery. My conversion was complete, without nostalgia. I got to know Murray with a physical thrill like memories of plunging into the bright sea at home.

Murray's solar power is his religious elevation of his native landscape. When reading his work, I fall helplessly homesick, both for the lived place—the pier, veranda nights, sugarcane—and for the place of the imagination.

My climate is in his tone, the raw energy of heat in my hometown, Port Antonio, where everything would appear cleansed of shadows. There is my sea in his paddocks, translucent as ice. Every sound I hear is distinct, acute with pain or delight, marking a presence larger than the town's smallness. I take refuge in his vernacular republic, which he describes as "that 'folk' Australia, part imaginary and part historical, which is the real matrix of any distinctiveness we possess as a nation."

The vernacular republic, therefore, is more than the expressive forms his local habitation flashes out of: it is, in the original sense of the word "matrix," the mother of imagination itself that speaks the vulgar language with the tongue of the common people.

In Murray's particular temperament as the poet-genius of this vernacular republic, he balances, like Dante, an undisguised love and hurt for his country with the resilience and grace inherent in all great art.

I love his passionate eye-catching reality as it happens. The great poems are like the rush of an invasive species to the horizon, flushed with surprise. Murray's word for this condition is "sprawl."

Sprawl is an ungainly way of being at ease with authority; it is colloquial, the original outlaw. Sprawl contains Whitman's democratic vista, that antiphonal width, but at a severely contorted pitch. In Murray's poetry, sprawl enacts the delirium of history by colliding with modernity's overwhelming despair, as one way to withstand the despair: "It is the rococo of being your own still centre."

The rococo?

Yes, I know it from childhood: sun and salt and a blessed breeze would levitate the hills through the fretwork grille of my grandmother's veranda. The poverty and squalor were so near they seemed far. Then, as always, the blaze of poverty in Murray strikes me with a recognition that is "shockingly voluptuous," to use a phrase Charles Rosen once applied to the effect of suffering and terror in Mozart's music. The blaze is so unabashed in its intimacy I often come down with tears, hearing,

> Dank poverty, rank poverty,
> it hums with a grim fidelity
> like wood-rot with a hint of orifice,
> wet newspaper jammed in the gaps of artifice,
> and disgusts us into fierce loyalty.

If Murray is Mozartian (he once gave Mozart this pruning praise: "I plough the face of Mozart"), it is only in the amplitude of his language and not in the sense of being classical or highly formal. There is an intentional poverty of rhymes happening here: "orifice-artifice"; "poverty-fidelity-loyalty," the rhythm jamming no wider than the limits of the constricting world the language hammers out.

The triumph of Murray is that he takes the classical music—meter and rhyme—out into the open, back into the environment, and exposes it to the tumult of sun. Not as a nature poet or a shaman-farmer—big machineries quake frequently in his poems, none greater than the scudding, luxuriant "Machine Portraits with Pendant Spaceman"—but simply by being the leviathan within that word-hoard of "life-enhancing sprawl / that require[s] style."

His style is the outsider's music; he is the bard from the rough heath, which is never decorous. It is, though, magisterial, ruminative, exhaustive, caustic, simple, irreducible, torqued, equanimous, tourbillion, epical, and dramatic, all "to the glory of God"—as he insists on the dedication page of most of his books—and, for us, he brings out the tears in things.

The tears live in his volumes as elemental as rain, though never dissolving into pity. Pity is lukewarm compassion, much too benign and self-regarding for a poet who has said, "I want my poems to be more than just national parks of sentimental preservation." I read that as an admonishment to, as it were, pull down thy vanity.

His capacity to reveal the reader, without vanity, to himself and to the spirit of the time is visionary. A young poet, driven out of a mixture of vanity and fear, overdosing on the former and weeping artificially in poems, does not understand the courage of true emotional gravity.

Murray is the twenty-first-century bedrock that paves a way for—this courage. I live in awe of his gift to transmute tears with a biting clarity that magnifies the poverty and the landscape of his poems into an art that supersedes the conceit of theme. To me, there is no theme in his poetry. There is only that supreme vision in which, dimly visible, I find myself.

"What I am after," he has further written, regarding his poems, "is a spiritual change that would make them unnecessary." This is a vow of tremendous humility.

More than any aesthetic principle or guidance, he offers me a kind of self-esteem, a backbone to bend and plow, shoveling through immense dross to the marvels of my own world. Sometimes he allows the dross to stay, but taken as a whole, dross in his work is like the abundance of thought. "This country is my mind," he says in one of his most tender poems, "Evening Alone at Bunyah."

The mind has become the poetry of the country he already knows by heart. And in his depth of compassion for those disenfranchised from their humanity throughout the cruel annals of history and left spiritually marooned, he is not unlike an earlier love, César Vallejo, that other catholic poet whose fierce dignity in the face of intolerable suffering makes bright, like the sun, the dark night of the soul.

In Murray's long vocation, the light has not faded. We find "the old book troglodyte," now age seventy-seven, in his newest collection, *Waiting for the Past*, still addressing posterity. Still richly sensed, still divagating into the accumulated moment, the minutiae of everyday life. Only here he is more fine grained, deepening the 52-hertz frequency of earlier work, but still as beautifully resolute as a stranger he sighted once and immortalized "as she paced on, comet-like, face to the sun."

BLOOD AND INK:
ON GEORGE SEFERIS

■

"I BELIEVE THAT THERE IS NO PARTHENOGENESIS IN ART." A poet's statement, once applied to his own work, can appear unrelenting and more wishful than true. "Parthenogenesis" comes from the Greek words for "virgin birth," and here, in the case of George Seferis (1900–1971), the unrelenting and the wishful are indistinguishable. They compound what is enduring and true in his work, an Eliotic desire to intersect the timeless with time, something Eliot, who is a presiding influence over Seferis, says "is an occupation for the saint." Seferis might not have been too happy with the term "saint"—perhaps he would have preferred "angel" (which frequents his poems) or just plain "poet"—but parthenogenetically speaking, since there is nothing original in Seferis (except, fervently, original sin via eternal return). His extraordinary gift occupies that substantial realm beyond originality: the realm of the marvelous real.

Exile and return rule Seferis's poetry. The exilic condition subsumes the latter, making both the same state or act. Here the shade of Odysseus falls acutely, yet only in part. Odysseus's twenty years away from Ithaca are spent, mythical distances accounted for, within the same small geographic location. Compared with Seferis, who had several diplomatic postings abroad, Odysseus is indeed a lost traveler, a military peripatetic who makes a single return, rather than a permanent exile. Their obvious difference, one an ancient and the other modern, matters insofar as the speed of Seferis's many returns underscores the velocity with which home is disappearing, and constitutes the crisis at the heart of his work.

Shuttling back and forth raises the existential dread of homelessness. On every return, from London and Cairo and New York City to various Greek islands, home dims: "After years abroad you've come back / with images you've nourished / under foreign skies / far from your own country" ("The Return of the Exile"). While images are powerful and potentially dangerous, they are mere elusive phantoms within the self. Often in the verse these benign mental images of loss escalate into material dispossession equally painful and disturbing:

> *The houses I had they took away from me. The times*
> *happened to be unpropitious: war, destruction, exile;*
> *sometimes the hunter hits the migratory birds,*
> *sometimes he doesn't hit them. Hunting*
> *was good in my time, many felt the pellet;*
> *the rest circle aimlessly or go mad in the shelters.*
>
> ("THRUSH")

Futility, madness: how harrowing to love a country divided from within! Contempt comes easily, though this is precisely what Seferis resists, and his love for his fractious islands moves with sorrow. "Wherever I travel Greece wounds me": that's the first line of a poem called "In the Manner of G. S." Its self-mocking title widens into the ultimate disillusionment, the horror that is the land itself, both departing and becoming somewhere one cannot depart from, much less return to:

Meanwhile Greece goes on travelling, always travelling
and if we see "the Aegean flower with corpses"
it will be with those who tried to catch the big ship by
  swimming after it
those who got tired of waiting for the ships that cannot move
the ELSI, the SAMOTHRAKI, the AMVRAKIKOS.
The ships hoot now that dusk falls on Piraeus,
hoot and hoot, but no capstan moves,
no chain gleams wet in the vanishing light,
the captain stands like a stone in white and gold.

Even when these desperate swimmers make it on board the ships, as they do, for example, in the great early sequence "Mythistorema," they are presented as "committed to non-existent pilgrimages unwillingly / murmuring broken thoughts from foreign languages." Their journeys, between islands, seem penitential.

Penitential because of a mytho-historical haunting, put this way in section 21 of "Mythistorema": "The ancient dead have escaped the circle and risen again / and smile in a strange silence." A later poem, the celebrated "Helen," amplifies the silence, stretching the deadly defects of the past into the present: "Great suffering had desolated Greece. / So many bodies thrown / into the jaws of the sea, the jaws of the earth / so many souls / fed to the millstones like grain." Rather than an inventory of ruins, or setting up of monuments, this is a poetry of recovery. Seferis achieves this with an uncanny simplicity. The directness of tone feels personal. The pitch works against poetical memory (and memorialization, in a civic sense), toward the difficult, unresolved enigma, that of a collective of individuals, buried in the Greek landscape. By concentrating on these many souls, undifferentiated victims of undifferentiated nature, Seferis raises them up for our sympathy and compassion. This marks another of his departures from Homer (at least the Homer of the *Iliad*), where the focus is on heroic men.

Abroad, pain momentarily softens with nostalgia. Yet, in "Letter to Rex Warner," he finds himself in a world where "everything's television," where he "can't touch things easily at close quarters" due to the alienating powers of modernity. Buildings refract the terror; in New York City, skyscrapers "show their windows gleaming / like the skin of a huge sea monster," and in "Letter of Mathios Paskalis" skyscrapers "will never know the coolness / that comes down on Kifisia." While in Toledo the famous Hospital de Tavera, polluted "with vapours from cars going off / to the country," is merely a large shell "full of crippled children gesturing / at me or at others following me" and a backdrop for trysting lovers ("Tuesday"). Mechanical sounds ratchet his psychic disintegration; in Cairo,

> *Trumpets, trams, cars backfiring, screeching brakes*
> *chloroform his mind in the same way as one counts*
> *so long as one holds out before being lost*
> *in the numbness, at the surgeon's mercy.*

("DAYS OF APRIL '43")

On the streets of London, he hears the broken plangent sounds of accordions played "by well-dressed beggars" who "call on the angels / and their angels are hell" ("Fog"). (Accordion-playing Hells Angels?) Meanwhile, in remote Hampstead, he sees himself in epiphanic terms, like "a dog / forgotten / that barks / alone / and searches for its master / or the Second Coming / or a bone." He aches to return to his Grecian home, to live as a hermit poet in "a hut on a hill," by the sea, where

> *in front of my window*
> *is a sheet immersed in bluing*
> *spread there like the sea*
> *all I want in my vase*
> *is even a false carnation*

red paper wound on wire
so that the wind
the wind can control it easily
as much as it wants to.

The above belongs to "Five Poems of Mr. S. Thalassinos," from a collection called *Mr. Stratis Thalassinos*, the name of Seferis's poetic alter ego, a thoroughgoing Prufrock, who ends his meditation with "I prefer a drop of blood to a glass of ink." Consanguinity, not aesthetics—the fraught pleasures of exile—then, is the poet's epitaph and what calls him back to his home sea. Seferis's poems, in effect, are written in blood.

Once home, however, the pain of the returned exile turns deeper inward. Irrevocable changes everywhere, the landscape unrecognizable. Poems bristle with agon, the raw intensity of the self wrestling against oblivion, hoping to uphold "the depths below memory." He wanders islands, distant and disembodied. On every island, something distorts the beauty. Here, for instance, Santorini:

Naked we found ourselves on the pumice-stone
watching the rising islands
watching the red islands sink
into their sleep, into our sleep.
Here naked we found ourselves, holding
the scales that tilted towards
injustice.

("GYMNOPAIDIA: SANTORINI")

The tilt exacts an Odyssean reversal, the most crucial way Seferis modulates the Homeric shade: Odysseus returns home to restore justice, the opposite happens in Seferis's hands; injustice proliferates, and civilization—all the natural, social, and political life of the islands—stands perpetually violated. Time remains irredeemably out of joint.

Seferis's work recognizes and opposes this lurking oblivion, this tilt. On the one hand, the history of imperial conquest by the Ottoman Empire weighs heavily. On the other, the horrors of the two world wars and British colonization of Cyprus in the twentieth century are double burdens threatening memory. The task to revitalize memory is immense and fatal, and many poems acknowledge so:

> *Whoever raises the great stones sink;*
> *I've raised these stones as long as I was able*
> *I've loved these stones as long as I was able*
> *these stones, my fate.*
> *Wounded by my own soil*
> *tortured by my own shirt*
> *condemned by my own gods,*
> *these stones.*

("GYMNOPAIDIA: MYCENAE")

The dignity of the cry rests on how the laborer—*poiētēs*, maker—purifies self-dramatization into actuality, through the force of the lyric. The cry instances and surpasses Eliot's formulation in "Marina"—"Living to live in a world of time beyond me"—for Seferis *makes* time and self into something beyond, and that beyond is, again, the marvelous real. Because the poet finally is interested not in documentation but in exaltation. And it is through this harmonic pressure (no parthenogenesis!) his archipelago finds a chorus in a single, human voice.

A fresh edition returns the voice always there, invincible as breath, as blood. We are compelled to hear and sing back:

> *Here end the works of the sea, the works of love.*
> *Those who will some day live here where we end—*
> *should the blood happen to darken in their memory and*
> *   overflow—*

let them not forget us, the weak souls among the asphodels,
let them turn the heads of the victims towards Erebus:

We who had nothing will school them in serenity.

("MYTHISTOREMA")

SEE THE BIRDS IN MY MOUTH: REMEMBERING VAUGHN BENJAMIN

■

WITH VAUGHN BENJAMIN'S DEATH ON NOVEMBER 4, 2019, AT age fifty, we mourn a double loss: to reggae music and to poetry, for though in his voice they're indivisible from each other—poetry his gift, music his calling—he mastered both, with unique and varying intensity, as separate art. The intensity is like the seraph's live coal placed on the prophet's lips in Isaiah 6, purifying him to speak.

The fire, an apocalyptic image, abides in Benjamin's work, speaking like Isaiah's voice against injustice, agitating for right cause and greater freedom, warning the merciless of God's wrath. But Benjamin's fire is sublime rather than polemical. Though steeped in biblical and apocryphal prophecy, he neither blames nor condemns (like Isaiah) even as he directly addresses terrible upheavals in the long four hundred years of the African holocaust in the West. "Revenge is not in our plan / We only plan to rebuild a broken man," as expressed in the song "Due Reward," is Benjamin's creed. His insurgency is self-healing. A radical act in the context of colonial history. In another song, "Force and Flames," Benjamin sings, "Please don't try to break the will of the truth / with force and flames." It's for the righteous not to cast blame but to continue to seek atonement.

Benjamin hears the ancient prophets on a similar frequency to how he hears the modern prophets of reggae and Nyabinghi, whether Burning Spear or Ras Michael, the singers I see as most influencing his sound. Even so, the ancient and the modern bond in such a divergent web in Benjamin's sound it's near impossible to make a definitive tracing of his influences. In Benjamin, the original sense of the word "influence," to flow into, finds its richest resonance. His sound flows equally from other domains, inaudible for the most part, which he turns audible: from the sciences and art and literature and above all history, as distinct from literature, where ancestral memories yield words, words he opens and redeems in songs of complex density.

Yet, for all the work's density, "humility" is the core word that stands as epitaph to his life and work. "With humility comes wisdom," the scripture says. Benjamin embodies this principle. Many recognized and are touched by it. Once he expressed that humility to an interviewer not with words but by whistling the sound of the zenaida dove found all over the island of St. Croix. Benjamin was born in Antigua and moved to St. Croix at a young age. His birdcall was in response to the question, what was he currently reading. Neither the scriptures nor secular texts but a whistle. He whistled again, adding, "See the birds here in my mouth." When he whistled again, you could hear the brownish-purple color of the dove of his island.

Later he told the interviewer he was reading the waves, the sand, the trees, and the sky. The whole island, in effect. Its deep tangled roots. Roots that spread and intertwine at a spiritual register everywhere in his music and poetry. Note he said "see" to call attention to hearing the birds in his mouth. That wasn't a mere colloquial turn of speech; he showed a mind moving seamlessly between senses as between worlds. Such a move is the high form of the Antillean imagination, its mode of survival, to flow on the axis of polarities. Ever the median man, Benjamin in his art as well as in his life, sounded out positive contrarieties.

"Without contraries is no progression," writes William Blake. Blake, who hated oppression in all forms, is a poet I believe Benjamin knew well; at least there are many parallels in how their visionary sensibilities of biblical prophecy coincide, each in his own way. When I listen to and read Benjamin, I often think of this superb phrase Blake writes in his prophetic book *Jerusalem*: "the struggles of entanglement with incoherent roots." Benjamin magnifies those struggles and in more than seventy albums and the volume of poetry *Koll Pekude* fused them into if not a logical coherence certainly a lasting harmony against oppression. These works are his labyrinthine *Jerusalem*. Thousands of songs and poems, built with humility. We enter and find good rest.

In that same interview after he whistled the zenaida dove's notes, Benjamin said, "Farming is just paying attention like a little child." The statement is simple and astounding, and I see and hear Benjamin like a child, perhaps not unlike the shepherd David, whistling his psalms from the elements around him as he digs into the earth with sharp-pointed stick.

He has left us the burning coal of his voice that will not go out.

THE TRAUMA OF JOY: WILSON HARRIS'S *GUYANA QUARTET*

THE FOUR YEARS IN WHICH THE NOVELS OF *THE GUYANA Quartet* were published, from 1960 to 1963, remain the anni mirabiles of fiction from the English-speaking Caribbean. The title unites their geographic setting, Guyana, a country on the north Atlantic coast of South America, and their prose style, the music of a fantastical baroque language. They are works of compressed turbulence and beauty, each just over a hundred pages. World wondering as their individual titles—*Palace of the Peacock, The Far Journey of Oudin, The Whole Armour,* and *The Secret Ladder*—the omnibus *Quartet,* issued in 1985, comes to just under five hundred pages.

The length is important for a work usually given the distinction of "epic"; it alerts us to Wilson Harris's gift of crystallization. His fiction is close to Greek tragedy, and as a superb tragedian novelist Harris takes as his central theme evil, specifically the evil of conquest. This evil resides in the fallen Eden of Guyana, a lost paradise in the *Quartet* that its various transplanted inhabitants are trying, and failing, to regain. They cannot regain this lost paradise precisely because they are transplanted and they have no claim, in the biblical sense, of first estate.

Written with the human terror of a Euripides, the novels are cinched by a lyrical apocalypticism. Tormented, characters enter into different kinds of expiation. They end up lost on the river or in the rain forest. Most die, and then die again. Their second death brings them into, to use Harris's wonderful phrase, "the inimitable trauma of joy." The trauma of joy is a mania verging on divine madness. In different registers across the *Quartet*, this trauma is the final release its characters experience. But often there is just trauma without joy, and the novels cleave to the most undivine madness of all: the brutal post-Edenic struggle for survival.

Expulsion takes the form of expeditions in the novels. *Palace* is the expedition upriver, led by the monomaniacal Donne in pursuit of the Amerindian "folk" he wishes to re-enslave; one strand of expedition in *Oudin* is the laborer Oudin and Beti's flight into the rain forest, pursued by Beti's drunken cousin, Mohammed; Cristo, of *Armour*, is likewise on the run from the law in the rain forest, where, at some point during his forty days' and forty nights' run, he is joined by his lover, Sharon; and in *Ladder* "the foolish lovers" Bryant and Catalena also escape into the rain forest after an accidental killing, fleeing from vigilante violence of attempted rape and murder.

These expulsions-as-expeditions underscore the fugitive nature of the books. The landscape itself is fugitive. The rain forest, the sea, the river, are frontiers on the move from the old, undiminished El Dorado looming into modern Guyana. As these expeditions inevitably end in failure, horror, and sadness, just like the quest for El Dorado in the sixteenth and seventeenth centuries, where the *Quartet* opens, a new inner adventure of homecoming breaks forth, traumatic, promising, and joyful.

Palace of the Peacock is set in the European conquistadorial period of Guyana's history. The exact time, like its title, remains vague. Until the very end, it is a novel cast in extreme chiaroscuro. It operates as a dream in which images rise and fall with their own logics of assurance. One could call it poetic logic. And so it begins, unfolding with such assurance:

> A horseman appeared on the road coming at breakneck stride. A shot rang out suddenly, near and yet far as if the wind had been stretched and torn and had started coiling and running in an instant. The horseman stiffened with a devil's smile, and the horse reared, grinning fiendishly and snapping at the reins. The horseman gave a bow to heaven like a hanging man to his executioner, and rolled from his saddle on to the ground.

The action is montage at breakneck speed. The anonymity of the horseman, and no less the anonymity of the violence in his wake, have overtones of various heroic and antiheroic conventions: the loner hero of the Wild West frontier or Death of Revelation 6:8, seated on his pale horse. "Hell followed with him," the biblical verse says, and indeed hell follows this horse rider, Donne, shot dead (but not dead) by Mariella, an Amerindian woman he has abused.

When Donne's name first appears, he is said to have "always possessed a cruel glory." His unspoken motto is "Gold, God, and Glory," the same as his Spanish antecedents, the first Europeans in the Americas to pursue the Amerindian legend of El Dorado and make it into a blood-drenched myth. But the name, in origin, is Anglo-Saxon. Donne is then a composite of the sixteenth- and seventeenth-century European conquistadors' demonic quest to rule the New World. Europe, the Old World, however, does not figure in Donne's quest for glory: he is the new New World, a conquistador-settler, frontier man with a plantation, the crop of which is unknown. The unknown is a seal of his cruelty.

Donne's cruelty is serious and absurd. His desire and pursuit of

Mariella and her people is a perversion of the knights in medieval romance. But his brand of absurdity is not tokenized into a chain-mail-and-steel-visor conquistador. In fact, Donne is never described, turning his invisibility into his invincibility. The chivalric crusading permits him a sincerity that is neither romantic nor sentimental.

Early in the novel he says to the I-narrator, the ghostly twin he calls Dreamer, "I'm the last landlord. I tell you I fight everything in nature, flood, drought, chicken hawk, rat, beast, and woman. I'm everything. Midwife, yes, doctor, yes, gaoler, judge, hangman, every blasted thing to the laboring people. Look man, look outside again. Primitive. Every boundary line is a myth. No-man's land, under-stand?" It is the melodrama of the plantocracy full of such maniacal flourishes. "Rule the land," he says, "while you still have a ghost of a chance. And you rule the world." With this terrible voice, Donne cries out in the rain forest for his spectral boat crew, and they arrive to fulfill his demonic quest to rule the land.

Donne's men are like the "momentous men" on Ahab's *Pequod*, adventure-seeking, ineffectual mercenaries.

As Donne is the similitude, a simulacrum, of sixteenth- and seventeenth-century conquistadors, the men, too, have their basis in history. But that history is personal, Harris's own. Mixed race and geo-graphically diverse, they are men Harris knew when he led surveying expeditions into the rain forests of Guyana in the 1940s and 1950s, all except the old man, Schomburg, who is based on Robert Her-mann Schomburgk, the nineteenth-century German-born explorer of British Guiana. The men arrive to Donne like "upright spiders," the very image of human frailty the novels will repeat. The men, living harrowing lives on the coast of Guyana, are shipwrecked even before leaving land.

They suffer more on the river, sprawled in an undifferentiated mass of the living and the dead. Indeed, the crew is dead. But the men return in a continuous cycle of death and resurrection in the name of the evil of conquest. Once again they arrive in the Amerindian village of Mariella, which the old crew, with Donne, had nearly wiped out. On sighting Donne and his resurrected crew, the surviving Amerindians flee into the rain forest. In a frozen stasis over the next three days, the crew relive, in night and day terrors, the trauma of their earlier exploits. Quickly but in slow, shadowy tableaux, they devolve into madness. The I-narrator's haunting hallucination is a vivid moment of metamorphic mastery:

> A dog rose and stood over me. A horse it was in the uncertain grey light, half-wolf, half-donkey, monstrous, disconsolate; neighing and barking in one breath, its terrible half-hooves raised over me to trample its premature rider. I grew conscious of its closeness as a shadow and as death. I made a frightful gesture to mount, and it shrank a little into half-woman, half-log greying into the dawn. Its teeth shone like a misty rag, and I raised my hand to cajole and stroke its ageing, soulful face.

The same psychic dissolution touches the landscape of Mariella. Though there is an unbroken drought, the leaves dripped like tears: drought, nature's cosmic sadness, will play out in all the *Quartet* novels. And in all the novels, torrential rain brings brief reprieve, flashing back the Edenic beauty of the landscape.

At some point Donne captures (or recaptures) an old Amerindian woman. He forces her to lead the crew upriver in their purgatorial journey—their second deaths in the final search for her elusive people, the "folk." Her presence causes new disturbances and awakenings in the crew. She stirs in Donne the tiniest inkling of conquistadorial regret. He says to Dreamer, "Your faith and intuition may be better than mine. I am beginning to lose all my imagination save that some-times I feel I'm involved in the most frightful material slavery. I hate myself some-times, hate myself for being the most violent taskmaster

I drive myself with no hope of redemption whatsoever and I lash the folk." He is only continuing his earlier monomaniacal sermon to Dreamer. Still, the pity-seeking tone displays something beyond Donne's "exasperated vanity of ignorance," to use Joseph Conrad's phrase. Notice his innocuous and nefarious terms "faith and intuition," two watchwords that the rest of the novel, and the *Quartet* as a whole, will break and renew.

Out of the mixed-race crew, the black member Carroll is the first to die. His Orphic whistle will resurrect Donne's men at the end of the novel. They arrive at a waterfall, its motionless water like a spectacular bridal train. Virginal and paradisiacal, its stone escarpment appears untarnished, yet it is not. Rough ladder steps have been cut into it. Donne begins to ascend this ladder, but it is an abysmal descent into himself. Physically, mentally, and spiritually exhausted, he presses his head to the escarpment. Inside the waterfall he sees a room, simple yet magnificent, and in it he sees a young carpenter. The carpenter has a rectangular face "cut from the cedar of Lebanon." It is the face of Christ, or so we are to imagine. Donne beholds it and beholds his end.

But Donne's end, when he falls, is in fact the penultimate catharsis of the *Palace*. The final exodus comes later in the form of the walking tree transformed into the Palace of the Peacock. In its many-windowed edifice, finally free from the accursed blood myth of El Dorado, Donne and his crew are reborn. We are to hold this massive palace in our minds as a palatial building that in the classical or ancient sense can represent government. Carroll's whistle, like Orpheus's lyre, fills the corridors with golden light. We have sailed into an artifice of eternity. No wonder Harris calls the final few pages of this miracle work "the Paradiso phase of the novel." And in miniature, it is not far off from Dante's timeless, blessed healing light.

In *The Far Journey of Oudin*, Harris departs the Guyana of the conquistadors. The rest of the *Quartet* is set in the 1950s, the decade before Guyana gained its independence from Britain, in 1966.

The departure is psychic before it is historical. As in *Palace*, the same intensity of imperial horror prevails. But with the greater specificity of a contemporary moment, the greater specificity of Guyana's new sociopolitical realities rises to the surface. The novel broods on post–World War II disaffections directly affecting a poor East Indian village on the Demerara–Mahaica frontier of Guyana's east coast.

At a meeting in a rum shop between the soon-to-be-bankrupt estate owner Mohammed, grieving the death of his brothers, and the old Faustian moneylender Ram, Mohammed, himself Faustian, notices "people are saying the atom bomb trials had affected and altered the climate and weather in every continent, reducing a large psychic pool and crowd into a crumbling reflective stream." Their exchange, which comes near the end of the novel, brilliantly compresses the tinderbox politics of Guyana, set to explode in the coming decades and turn Guyana, a nation of just over three hundred thousand prior to independence, into a major flash point of twentieth-century geopolitical rumblings.

"The world is a powder keg, man. Why the newspapers say communists penetrating this country from Russia and everybody is to be called 'comrade.'" His eyes glinted with satisfaction when he saw Mohammed had begun to show interest and to warm up. "What you mean." "I mean you family is not the only one dying out, Mohammed. You is not the only man frighten of being lonely and disinherit in the future. The other day," Ram continued, "look what happen. We talking international story of 'comrades' so let we talk." He saw Mohammed was leaning towards him. "Korea—a country just like this I would say"—he waved his hand generously—"split in half, man. What a mix-up family story. God know who is killing who. You is not the only one in this new family trouble. And what happening to you is private, plain AND ordinary compared to that."

Ram's speech, as monomaniacal as Donne's, captures the double conflict of *Oudin*: inheritance and intimate caste war.

Despite the insistent realism of the passage above, the plot of the novel is an evanescent blur. The novel's Tolkienesque title helps: it states a quest adventure and names its peripatetic hero, Oudin. In a society made depraved by the narrow conspiracies and superstitions of village life, Oudin lives in a middle earth of his own brokenness. He is a total isolate, the story's one absolute loner. The abject loneliness is enclosed in his name: closer to Norse myth, another Tolkienesque aspect, it doesn't appear to have a connection to an East Indian (whether Hindu or Muslim) identity. The makeshift caste system imported from India absorbs him into the category of the subhuman as it does other characters, primarily women. Oudin eventually becomes enslaved to the Brahmin-like Ram, though Ram's ancestors are likely Kurmi, a low cultivator caste from the Gangetic plain of India. Ram, then in a grotesque rehearsal of the British nineteenth-century system of indenturing East Indians to the colonies, indentures Oudin to Mohammed.

The narrative at various points wishes to make Oudin something other than a double slave: an earth deity. The most startling instance of this is when Beti, the illiterate teenager recently orphaned to Mohammed's household, sees Oudin in the mud amid a cluster of "courida," the swamp trees of Guyana:

> Staring at the apparition of Oudin that seemed to accompany her all the way, like the sun dark on her shoulder, in the hallucinated trees. Oudin's extremities—hands and feet—had turned to mud. He had crawled and crept far. He had risen to his feet to follow her, but he carried with him rings around his ankles, and islands off the foreshore, and it was with difficulty he still uprooted and extricated himself.

This is her second sighting of Oudin, who has arrived at Mohammed's estate to herd Mohammed's stray cattle. But Oudin has two ulterior purposes: to put his master's brand on Mohammed's cattle and, more far-reaching, to abduct Beti for Ram. The abduction is Ram's last desperate move to marry and not become, in his rum-shop words to Mohammed, "disinherit in the future."

Oudin abducts Beti for himself, thus "horning" Ram's future. The abduction puts Oudin's true far journey into motion, his thirteen years of freedom with Beti, beginning through the rain forest and eventually settling in their hut on the bank of a river, with Ram next door, demoted from his master to his landlord. For Oudin to secure those thirteen years of freedom with Beti—the universally unlucky number is charged—Oudin strikes a bargain with Ram, the Faustian devil.

The bargain, by a signed contract, is that in the event of Oudin's death all his children by Beti belong to Ram. Oudin dies, and his death, which opens the novel, reinstates Ram's future. It is a death that is both a self-betrayal and a betrayal, because it leaves Beti more dispossessed once the contract gets into Ram's hand. Knowing this intuitively (she is unable to read, and Oudin signs the contract in secret), Beti does the most ordinary and radical thing in the novel: she pries the contract from the fingers of her dead husband and eats it.

The rest of *Oudin* deals with the drama of Mohammed and his two full blood brothers, Kaiser and Hassan, and his cousin Rajah (Beti's father), bonded together in a "brotherhood of conspiracy." Their greed is boundless. It leads them to murder their unnamed half brother, who has an unspecified disability and is set to inherit their father's estate. Their greed is hereditary in part; their father, a second-generation indentured estate owner, acquired his land through hard work and saving but also "robbed and killed in the process," according to Rajah, who vehemently hates his uncle. Wife beaters, contentious and shallow, the conspiratorial brothers all die gruesome deaths in a pattern mirroring that of Donne's men in *Palace*.

Ever tragic, the moments the brothers are together are also the funniest in the novel. These moments of comic relief fit the Rabelaisian-like folk form of Guyana, called Balgobin. One splendid episode regards an early morning conversation between the brothers about their father in the hospital on his deathbed:

> "Is true-to-God story, Kaiser. False alarm after false alarm been ruling, but the doctor mek no bones yesterday. When ah leffing the hospital he gie we daddy two day at the most . . ."
>
> "He lose consciousness yet?" Kaiser asked.
>
> "The old man keeping conscious to the end. But he losing all pain. He lying there like a king. He beard white-white like snow Ah never see Ah tell you. And his face still black-black with the sun."

The half-blind old man placed his will made out to his illegitimate son under his pillow. But Hassan has replaced it with a blank sheet of paper, breaking his father's glasses in the process. Hassan, who is something of a mock sadhu (which is part of the humor), revels in telling this story, but Kaiser, who is naively more concerned with his father's broken glasses, responds with the winning punch line: "And what 'bout the spectacle."

The comedy recedes with the conspiratorial brothers' deaths—Hassan from a stroke, Kaiser in a rum-shop fire, with Mohammed present, and Rajah, years earlier, from a lightning strike. Mohammed is the last to go. Grieving his brothers, he begins to lose his conspiratorial command, withering deeper and deeper into alcoholism. Finally, he is goaded by Ram, after Oudin's abduction of Beti, to pursue Oudin in the rain forest. It is his own death he pursues.

Right before he dies, Mohammed encounters a bull. Fleeing from Mohammed's drunken terror, Beti and Oudin had also earlier encountered the same bull. They did so by a massive "tacouba" tree in which they first made love. Back on the ground, Ariadne-like, Beti charms the bull with a touch. Perhaps the bull is a stray from Mohammed's own herd, branded with Ram's mark by Oudin. What is truer and stranger is that the bull is Mohammed himself, a stunning revelation that comes to Mohammed after his death, when it is too late to matter.

While on the run in the rain forest, Beti and Oudin in *The Far Journey of Oudin* encounter a bizarre woodsman who is described as "a kind of inferior Christian fabulist." The term perfectly encapsulates the inner workings of *The Whole Armour*, the third novel of *The Guyana Quartet*.

Set in the late 1950s on and around the great Pomeroon River on Guyana's Atlantic coast, the novel features central characters with names that come from the New Testament, except one, Abram. The Old Testament–type patriarch, at the beginning of the novel, is contemplating suicide, presumably for consorting with the prostitute Magda. Magda, a woman past her prime but the desired grande dame of the frontier, is the overprotective mother of the protagonist Cristo. On the run for an alleged murder, Cristo hides out in Abram's rain-forest hut deep in the interior of Jigsaw Bay. There is Sharon, Cristo's virginal lover (paradox abounds), whom Cristo symbolically marries toward the end of the novel. Sharon's father is Peet, a drunk and a physically as well as spiritually deformed man.

All the characters bear spiritual deformity shown as physical marks, but Peet's wooden leg, which he drags around in his drunken stupor, is the major sacramental scar of the Pomeroon's spiritual brokenness. And there is Mattias, Sharon's rich fiancé, her second, the first allegedly killed by Cristo in a brawl: Sharon's love triangle amounts to a bloody, chivalric romance as Mattias, too, will be "accidentally" stabbed to death by Peet at a wake, though really he is killed by the spectral wake crowd, pressing down on him like a Greek chorus.

The wake, staged by Magda for her fugitive son Cristo, is the spectacular centerpiece of the novel. It is like a sort of Circe island fête, delightful as it is horrible. Fête, the Antillean folklore ritual of masking, is central to the novel. It is most prominent in the novel's most poignant character, an elusive tiger roaming the rain forest. The tiger's presence, which remains invisible, comes from out of the mist of myth and history. It is the novel's frightful symmetry, tying all the others together.

As the characters function within Christian allegory, so does the narrative. But each episode spills outside this context. The narrative counterpoints high-speed adventure, spliced moments of jungle police-boat chases and late-night rain-forest assignations, mostly around Cristo, with dazzling flashbacks and dream sequences of broken lives in the wider settlements of the Pomeroon, where the tiger lurks in search of human flesh. Peet's early manhood experience is harrowed by the ageless tiger. Scarred by pre- and post-Columbian violence, the landscape is a "tragical spirit of place."

With the legacy of such a history, Cristo, paradoxically, represents Guyana's new fabulation of justice versus injustice in this world. He does so not strictly because of his alleged crime but because of the hopelessness of the people of his generation—Mattias, Sharon, and her first unnamed, murdered fiancé. They are all educated outside the Pomeroon, in Guyana's capital, Georgetown, and farther afield, Mattias at Cambridge in the U.K. and Sharon at a Roman Catholic boarding school in Trinidad. Belonging nowhere else, they find themselves back in the Pomeroon, cornered and psychically marooned by the bush and its backwardness.

It is Cristo's petulance, unhinged about his innocence, which brands his generation as lost colonials, insecure in ways their parents and the shuttered, illiterate villagers of Pomeroon cannot understand. This petulance leads Cristo to play at being an outlaw rebel of the Don Juan ilk. Peet, in a pastoral sense a generation earlier, had played at the role and failed with dire consequence: now at Magda's age, broken and in love with her, he still clings to "an outlaw's natural dignity." It makes Peet foolish.

Cristo's own play at outlaw brings dire results. Hiding in Abram's hut for months and making the old man an accessory to murder, Cristo causes Abram to suffer a sudden heart attack. Abram drops dead at Cristo's feet in a most prismatic fall:

> He reached out to tell Cristo he believed all was well and his expression wrinkled like an advocate, galvanized into frightful action, in the presence of a shocking devilish judge. It was his last image of himself he saw in the mirroring liquid eye of the accused boy, aghast and still weeping in a paroxysm of murderous rage, as he fell. He put his hand upon his chest, tottering in his chair and falling face forward upon the ground, twisting his head, wanting to say something ghostly and utterly reassuring but the confirmation of innocence froze on his lips in the self-reflection of ancient horror and reluctant fibre and dread of the unknown.

Abandoned by Cristo, two days later the elusive tiger mauls Abram's body, giving him his second death. Abram will have his resurrection as well in one of the most graphic episodes of the novel, if not the most graphic of the entire *Quartet*.

Cristo runs back to his mother's house in the village. Magda gives him a resounding dressing-down, but ever the overly compassionate mother, she promises again to help Cristo escape the clutches of the law. As such, they return to Abram's hut and find his decomposing body covered with carrion crows. Hatching a plan in her head, Magda tells Cristo to strip Abram's body of its clothing. Cristo refuses, but Magda, now in sadistic humor, forces him at gunpoint to tie a kerchief over his face—a parody of the outlaw figure—and strip, marching him to Abram's corpse. The picture grows more gruesome: the carrion crows fly off, leaving a last one vomiting a piece of Abram's flesh and rag. With great revulsion Cristo strips Abram and puts on

Abram's fouled rags, while the same last carrion crow watches the whole spectacle. That accomplished and Cristo's clothing burned, Magda turns Cristo loose into the tiger-lurking rain forest. Before departing to complete his bizarre initiation, Cristo witnesses a small sign of hope: that last carrion crow flapping to the sun is transfigured into an eagle. Cristo himself vomits like a gouged eagle as if from a grotesque morning sickness.

That small sign of hope manifests itself in the form of Cristo and Sharon's unborn child, conceived while on their forty-day run from the police in the rain forest. Over the course of the journey, Cristo undergoes multiple transformations, including dream visions of fleeing Amerindian runaway slaves and finally killing the invincible tiger. He wears the tiger's pelt as a prize, like Jason's Golden Fleece or a Roman soldier's *aquilifer*, over Abram's fouled rags. This form of warrior camouflaging shows manifold imperial corrosion. But simpler and profounder, it belongs to the splendor of Caribbean carnival, the very indestructible armor of tradition Cristo's child will be born into.

Russell Fenwick, the government surveyor of *The Secret Ladder*, calls his dinghy the *Palace of the Peacock*. He does so not as a tribute to Donne of *Palace*, though a Donne-like figure on horseback haunts his dreams. The naming arises from Fenwick's fascination with "the city of gold set somewhere in the heart of Brazil and Guyana." But giving his dinghy that name is a belated—and the only—confirmation in *The Guyana Quartet* of Donne's quest for El Dorado, a point that makes *The Secret Ladder*, the last of the tetralogy, an ouroboros of *Palace of the Peacock*.

But Fenwick is not Donne, and the men of his surveying crew are not the men on Donne's cargo. Still, there are important convergences: the same number of men of the same racial and geographic mixtures over the same seven days of creation period discover their own lostness on the river and in the rain forest of Guyana. Closing the *Quartet* thus, Harris keeps us marooned in Guyana's continual post-Edenic struggle with the evil of conquest.

Ladder takes place during a long spell of drought on the Canje River, "the blackest river one could imagine," on account of its almost uncultivable swamp soil. A second factor is its inhabitants, direct descendants of enslaved Africans from the seventeenth century who had escaped to the Canje banks and created free settlements. They see Fenwick's presence on the Canje as a threat to that ancestral freedom. Their leader, Poseidon, a third-generation-born African (said to be a hundred years old), galvanizes his followers to sabotage Fenwick's surveying work by breaking and setting fire to gauges set on the river.

During their first encounter, Fenwick cannot understand Poseidon's language. On their second meeting, during which Fenwick is installing a new river gauge, Poseidon does not speak, but his stance, like Fenwick's, is starkly clear. Poseidon suddenly appears just as Fenwick turns to his colleague, a young black man named Bryant, who imagines or desires Poseidon to be his grandfather. The moment of revelation, its baffling dichotomy, is done with extraordinary documentary and visionary precision. Fenwick says to Bryant,

> "I wonder whether it'll be safe to leave this gauge here until tomorrow?" he thought, his eyes glued to the inverting telescope of his level as he checked his reading on the bench mark. The staff suddenly pitched and vanished, and Fenwick's astonished sight beheld instead the accusing image of Poseidon, eyes inverted, brow pointing down. Fenwick shot up, and the old man straightened his bent back (upon which the sky revolved). He lifted a load of firewood from his shoulders and deposited it on the ground not far from Fenwick's feet.

These two ways of seeing, Fenwick's "inverting telescope" and Poseidon's "eyes inverted," are at the heart of *Secret*'s conflict. Their different vantage apprehends the same complex of an imperial politics: the Canje River. Its water can stave off drought, which the rising East Indian rice barons, set to be Guyana's ruling political class, need for their rice estates to survive. But to build the proper reservoirs would be unaffordable, and as Fenwick alone intuits, the droughts would worsen.

This intuition is part of the reason Fenwick grows increasingly sympathetic toward Poseidon and his followers, so much so that Fenwick tells his frustrated men that Poseidon's sabotages are more "a witness of protest, the spirit of protest" than real violence. It is the gross understatement of a liberal romantic, a sentiment Fenwick expands on in a long letter to his mother, a woman obsessed with murder mysteries, back in Georgetown.

The only woman directly present in the narrative is Catalena. She is the Portuguese wife of one of Fenwick's men, Perez, whose name evokes the conquistador Hernán Pérez. Extremely abusive, Perez beats Catalena and stakes her out in card gambling "for man to have a short-sleeping-time with in lieu of cash," says Jordan, Fenwick's possessive camp cook, memorably and cruelly. This might be why Perez had her brought to the Canje; the men gamble hard, but he claims she has been thrown out by her family. Fenwick fires Perez not long after Catalena arrives on the mail boat *Andromeda*, to stay at Poseidon's house in the rain forest.

Catalena's arrival is the catalyst for the novel's two great climactic moments: Poseidon's death and the jungle-justice near execution of Bryant and Catalena by Poseidon's rattled followers. Bryant and Catalena are spared. They become lovers, and becoming lovers, they become fugitives in the rain forest. Fenwick's spirit-level intuition seizes on the deeper mystery of their flight. For him, he believes Catalena and Bryant "had put their foot and escaped upon another rung in the secret ladder. The land was the mystery in which he would never chart where they had vanished."

The sad beauty of that sentiment hovers like a thundercloud over *The Guyana Quartet*, a work that flees into its own stubborn territory in assembling the deranging shocks of conquest, holding to the mystery of Guyana, and providing a stay against confusion for any reader who falls under its spell.

THE CONCEPT OF DREAD:
A LISTENING TO LEE "SCRATCH"
PERRY IN ZURICH, WITH
LORENZO BERNET

(Opening recording: Lee "Scratch" Perry speaking in the Black Ark Studio circa mid-1970s)

LORENZO BERNET: Good evening, everyone. I want to welcome you all tonight. I'm trying to make a small introduction and a longer one afterward, and in the meantime we're going to slowly approach, or never really, the subject we just heard speaking.

So, I'd like to introduce first Ishion Hutchinson. And maybe I should say a few words, a bit like yesterday, about how this project got together, how we're sitting here talking about Lee Perry, and how Ishion made the trip to Switzerland. So I have a bit of a personal connection with the subject of Lee Perry. I was in school, I was in early primary school, and I had this friend from my neighborhood and I'd spend a lot of time at their home, and it later turned out that the figure who was always around in the house painting stones, wearing a crown with CDs, that turned out to be Lee "Scratch" Perry.

And of course, for me personally, I had a very, let's say skeptic relationship as a child with this man, and the full dimension of it is only, is even now slowly and slowly getting aware of. And of course, I was always drawn to maybe music that was slightly influenced after him, but I never made the connection. Also in my late teens I didn't make the connection, what type of dance music might be influenced by him, et cetera. Let's say I maintained a really, like, a skeptical relationship to him, and him as a subject sort of reemerged for me when it became clear to me that yeah, part of his musical production slowly merged also into a visual production, and of course for me, as a visual artist, that was sort of an entry point into this project. For me, I remember a discussion I had with a friend some years ago, I was musing about how this guy, how I remember him dressed up, walking around with shiny mirrors. It always reminded me of a living Orthodox icon painting, and that was sort of my entry point in the project, and also my personal interests toward sort of iconography, et cetera.

And then I asked him, about one and a half years ago I asked him to organize a Christmas exhibition. That was sort of my idea I had with Lee Perry, and he was kind of into it, it seemed to make sense for him to make an exhibition about the idea of Christmas. And then throughout my research, of course I noticed that this figure—and it might sound naive—this figure is actually attached to a grand narrative, and to so many overlapping discourses. And as I was sort of talking about my little Christmas exhibition, it became bigger and bigger in the sense that more people became involved, so I find myself in the middle of being thrown into an assignment of kind of grappling with the visual legacy of Lee "Scratch" Perry. It was probably also through that, only really late, that I came across the work and the poetic work of Ishion Hutchinson. It's this moment when you read a lot of sort of nerdy music theory about a person, but then you hear one poem which is a page long, and it sort of distills exactly what I was sort of grappling and looking for. So I'm really happy that Ishion Hutchinson is doing this presentation tonight, or we're trying to sort of work on something.

Yesterday we had the opportunity to be in Schaffhausen, to make a poetry reading of Ishion's work, fully immersed in Perry's exhibition, which is sadly closing today. This kind of led to this idea of another talk which will probably more form around the musical part, the musical legacy. So I'd like to welcome Ishion Hutchinson, and maybe most of you would have some personal memory or visual memory of the figure of Lee Perry, but probably it's good to show some pictures of the exhibition, and then we would move onto the visual part. So I'll show some pictures first, before anything else.

(Shows pictures to the audience.)

So instead of showing only installation pictures, I figured it's also good to throw some screenshots I had on my desktop, because sometimes it's probably more in the favor of understanding his visual output. I'm not showing the final exhibition pictures; I'm rather showing also some stuff he did in the nineties and some pictures of his studio. It gives a better idea of how this man deals with the visual. This is the pdf. Here we have some installation views of the exhibition.

(Shows pictures to the audience.)

So maybe, as we're seeing this exhibition right now, and to remember the talk from yesterday, it was really quite intense for me, in the sense that there was a sort of also channeling happening, I felt. Ishion also elaborated on a sort of foundation of a sort of collective memory, and also a psychoanalytical, deep foundation of the music of dub, of this visuality, and of the people of Jamaica in a broader sense. For me, yeah, maybe in a later step I would like to talk again about the idea of collective memory or a wider unconscious, maybe that will come back later in the talk, because that was sort of my entry point, as I mentioned icon painting. What I also noticed coming across your work, and also being able to talk in the past few days, that we're sort of three years apart, and we're both kind of grappling with a figure like Perry, which would also mean, in a way, it's a sort of grappling with a generation that was before, and in our way or in what I can say, in a way, grappling with attributes or with a psychedelic generation. I think there might be some overlap, but also in today's talk there will be, as you will notice, a lot of strands that will sort of not come back in a way, or echo out.

To wrap this up a little, we talked about channeling and we talked about dub, and I remember at some point you said that dub, in a way, it's a sort of a constant self-revisioning device. Maybe you could elaborate on that; that's maybe an interesting starting point.

ISHION HUTCHINSON: Okay. Good evening, everybody. Can you hear me? Yes. You guys are sitting on the lights.

(Audience laughs.)

You look very strange, spotlighted. I'm very pleased to be here, and grateful, really, for Lorenzo, and the people I have met so far who have put together this show. And it's fascinating in many ways. I'll answer your question, but I wanted to just express my deep gratitude to see this kind of attention being given to Lee's work. Of course, the auditory making is well celebrated and will not now disappear from people's attention, but his visual imagination has always been part of his auditory imagination, so to see that this kind of visual is getting some emphasis is more than a delight and I think overdue. So you hear it now, Lorenzo is doing pioneering work, this is probably his stamp in immortality and his legacy, so that's really terrific.

The thing that I want to say in regard to your question about what

I said about dub being a self-revising device. Well, as you know, the form of dub essentially is assemblage. It's a collage of sounds put together based on the personality of the producer, based on what internal voices or the intuitive ways in which the producer creates a soundscape in response to pressures from within that the music places on the producer's psyche. So the basic principle of dub is that several elements are being fused simultaneously. That's the kind of technical property of the music itself. These different pieces each tell a different story, right, but the dub resists a kind of narrative that is fluid and straightforward. It's atemporal, really. So temporality is put under excessive pressure in the dub construction. I will emphasize pressure, a term which can feel somewhat abstract, but it is a key technical part of reggae, the life of that music, and in particular dub itself. What is immensely unique and makes this concept of dub and its self-revising pressure powerful and peculiar is when you place it in the context of the experiential, right, meaning where this form of music is emerging from. It comes from a place, an island in the Caribbean Sea with the history of enslavement. Go further back, and it is the history of the almost complete erasure of aboriginal people you encounter. So, within those two cases you have the history of atrocity, and those are two deep psychic wounds that the landscape of Jamaica, a small place, still deals with. And I believe those psychic resonances, those two pressure points, coming from those wounds carry over in every aspect of daily life, the daily ordinary life of a Jamaican. And within the creative process, in dub music, those resonances are intensified and given sonic shapes. So, in an ordinary day, just like here in Zurich, you wake up and you tell someone "hello," or "fuck off," it depends on your personality, I'm not sure what's the general way people deal with cordiality here. But in Jamaica, it's either "hello" or "fuck off." You guys are supposed to relax and feel free to laugh, it's all right.

(Audience laughs.)

I'm desperately trying to be funny. But imagine that one could wake up and say "hello," knowing that, for instance, in some places in Jamaica if you step outside, you're confronted with a landscape with sugarcane growing on it, and sugarcane is the crop plant that the slaves were brought over from Africa for, or rather human beings were brought over as slaves, and forced to work in those plantations. So that plant is still there; it hasn't gone anywhere. And so you say "hello"; then you walk out and you see sugarcane. There's nothing extraordinary about that, but if one takes a little bit of time to think about those two presences, the self and the landscape, it is an immense psychic leap one has to make on a day-to-day basis to reconcile oneself to such ongoing visible reminders of ancestral trauma. One's whole interaction with life is fraught with this trauma; sure, it might not exist on the conscious level every moment, but subconsciously, subtly, it is always present. So, the music then is very self-conscious about this, and is aware of it in its formation, and so the sounds of the music combine these ordinary, lovely gestures that people have and the brutality that has brought people to this point. That duality exists, coexists, and is always shifting and reconfiguring itself depending on whatever interaction. So, the way in which the social and the sociological perhaps, let's say cultural, and the will to survive, the effort it takes to carry on life knowing that one is faced with . . . Come through, grab a seat. Sit in the front. Why are you late?

(Audience laughs.)
(Inaudible audience response.)

ISHION HUTCHINSON: That's not accepted, but I appreciate you for coming. (*Laughs.*) Get them a drink . . .

So essentially the revision, the self-revising, is connected to survival. It's connected to that historical background of having lived through slavery and up until whatever point of time one finds oneself in. So this is very key. The idea that, through atrocity, through pain, or in spite of atrocities and pain, the self can live with dignity and can create and claim agency. And the music is of course the most powerful exemplar of this survival, this will to live and to live fully as a human being.

So I think that perhaps is sufficient as a response to self-revision, and we can expand on examples based on Lee "Scratch" Perry, who is himself the epitome of self-revision, self-revising, constantly reinventing himself, and coinciding with the history of Jamaican popular music. I mean, the architect of reggae, when it's entering into its mature phase in the early seventies, and then being one of the key founders of dub at the turn into the midseventies, right into—and not to discount any earlier popular forms of Jamaican popular music that Lee worked in, like ska and rocksteady—and before those, folk music traditions like mento and tambu or shay-shay—but forward into dancehall and all the other kinds of popular music that have developed across the globe that he has had some influence in either directly or indirectly. It is fascinating to think that the architect of this massive movement from that small place in the middle of the Caribbean Sea is now living in the Swiss Alps. I mean, is there anything more self-revising and self-inventive than that? I'm trying to think of a reversal. Who's a great Swiss composer? Name one. None?

LORENZO BERNET: Émile Jaques-Dalcroze.

ISHION HUTCHINSON: That guy, is it a guy?

LORENZO BERNET: I think so.

ISHION HUTCHINSON: Take someone else, from anywhere in Europe. Is there an example of a great European artist? I mean, writers, there are many great European writers who have left Europe to live in small places and have written. But to have affected the whole future of music, this is a rare case. It's something I think about a lot, and I feel that I live under that shadow. And it's a benign shadow, it's not a shadow of terror, or like, oh God, this is so—how does one—I don't have the anxiety that, I've met a few young European artists, and they tend to have this kind of anxiety that is really baffling to me, like, oh, Picasso did it, how am I going to do it. (*Laughs.*) You're very unlucky in that regard.

So, this also touches on the fact that everything in the Caribbean—and now I am going to use a term I really dislike—is an expression of "postmodernity." All of it, everything that comes out of the Caribbean is creolized. Once it enters into the sea, and finds its way to an island anywhere, it is changed. It has to live in a new dispensation. This of course includes the people. So, my ancestors who were abducted from Africa became new. They had only the memory of a place of their origin to go off of. As we know, memory is imperfect, memory is incomplete, which is why you could have a music like this that will always be fresh, because it's intuitively corresponding with that other place across the ocean, that it has to travel there through these psychic channels within blood memory, within breath, within certain ethos that can't be explained, but can never be fully grasped or be fully manifested because one is now living in a completely different state. And so dub returns the self to that other dimension, that there is a kind of urging or longing within people to know themselves, to figure out the story of who I am besides the narrow narrative of "you were placed on a ship and then taken across." That couldn't be it, you know? So that's what makes dub so revolutionary, because it has given a catholic, radical approach to identity. It has reawakened dormant selfhood or selfhood that had been enslaved. And the whip and the Bible—those two controlling devices, one for the body, one for the spirit—are hard to remove; it's very difficult to remove what those things did. And so the music comes across as the great exorcise, if you will; I would go further and say that dub is a way to redeem the self that has been shaped in the crucible of enslavement and colonization. That process of redemption is ongoing, ever revising. And in fact, the music itself, the excitement of it, particularly in the late sixties, had to do not necessarily with perfecting the form. Between, say, '62 and '81, Jamaica went through four musical genres. They just came out of nowhere. Not out of nowhere, certainly came out of that restless redemptive or emancipatory spirit which was there from the first moment an enslaved person set foot on a plantation. The inventing of a great sound, then setting that aside to create another, well, that is more than proof of imaginative bravery, a will to push to the furthest extreme of questioning and pushing against the supposed narrowness of whatever one should accept as "island" music. So the music then is that amazing psychic map layered into the social reality of a people. That's why the self-revising energy is so implicit in the musical composition, because without it it would just be hollow, and it's important that the music is definitely corresponding to real lives. If it were simply a perfect sonata, then it would be nice, but it would not be so fully engaged in what every musician knows, that the listener or the dancer comes for, which is comfort.

LORENZO BERNET: That's a great place for me to pick up. I forgot to mention that we're going to play some tunes from time to time and talk about it, a bit like in the reputable music academy. (*Laughs.*)

So maybe, I would play a first tune, it's from 1977 from the Black Ark Studio, it's not very well known, it's done together with a band called Zap Pow, the tune is called "River." I cannot say much about the production et cetera—I'm not a music journalist—but what I notice about Perry or read about Perry is that he was maybe one of the first engineers that gave another secondary role to the singers, but he made them—for the singers in this song who were as equal as the bass drum, that as all in one hierarchy, which is pretty much now our common dealing with music. So he was the first who actually saw the studio as the instrument. So I'm going to play this track called "River" by Zap Pow.

("River" by Zap Pow plays.)

ISHION HUTCHINSON: This is my first time hearing that one. But then again, it's always like the first I'm hearing a Lee Scratch, even if you're so familiar with it, it always feels new. And that's how he went about making them, because sometimes they're ten alternate versions and either one of those might be really excellent. And I think that willingness to let go of a finished product is a sort of defining attitude. What struck me about the "River" track is it has a feel of the current Afro-futuristic sound to it. Did you say "River" is from '77?

LORENZO BERNET: Yeah.

ISHION HUTCHINSON: Yeah, so it's this thing where you have certain people that outpace whatever is hip or of the moment, and certainly Scratch is ahead of the curve. So now, maybe thinking of Afro-futurism as we now know it is a way to look at this piece, how this music is synthesized seemed to be a little bit closer to something like even Earth, Wind & Fire, but that's also what is fantastic about Scratch being someone who is appropriating as a way to have conversation. One of my very favorite pieces by Scratch is called "Bird in Hand," and it's a mesmerizing dub piece and he's singing on it. And I've known this for so long, this piece, and I just want to listen to it constantly. And for years I thought I would try to figure out what he's actually saying, the lyrics, and then I gave up and thought, well, he's just doing his Scratch thing, he's not really saying anything sensible. Then I was kicking it with a friend who speaks Hindi, and I was like, "Do you want to hear this?" And it was a moment that could have gone really badly because I wasn't playing it for her because she's a

Hindi-speaking person; it just happened that Scratch was actually singing in Hindi. So I wasn't trying to impress her like, look, I'm listening to music with Hindi. And so she told me what's being said. How the hell did Scratch get Hindi lyrics to sing over in this haunting piece of music, I don't know, he probably won't tell us, and certainly an explanation would even be—there's no point in having that explained anyways. But to me what is so marvelous and connects to the idea of black survival, is just the sense of ingenuity. This restlessness, this way of moving through space that one's body's sort of hyper-watched and so on, so the black body has to find a way to move in space to protect its intimacy, right. That's why—I mean, everybody does this, but we're talking in a particular context because of that hypervisuality, that hypervisibility of surveillance that is imposed on the black body, so the black walk is a kind of protection from that gaze. But the way in which that body is so magnetic or can be so magnetic is what is so constantly fascinating, and in the case of Scratch, however he picked up those Hindi lyrics, it could be something—maybe it was a com- mercial jingle he heard while traveling somewhere and just recorded it and then took it to the studio, whatever—

LORENZO BERNET: I think I know the story.

ISHION HUTCHINSON: You know the story? Don't tell me. (*Laughs.*) But I'd love to hear it, though.

(*Audience laughs.*)

ISHION HUTCHINSON: That's what I mean is so terrific. You know, here's the thing, too, because the track that I will play—I'll say this before playing it, and it's connected to this whole idea of black ingenu- ity. I'm thinking of ingenuity in a phrase from Bertolt Brecht, where he says something about, "So much of art comes from the ingenuity of the oppressed," right. It's a very, very socialist idea, or Marxist. There's a way in which this ingenuity is a way to resist mercantile capitalism, to resist being co-opted. So regular Jamaicans, but Rastas more emphatically, created these ways of being self-reliant, right. So that's why Rastas could be so very dangerous and the government could even be more upset with this band of people who decide that "we won't really take part or take any—we won't really engage in this construct of government, we'll have our own thing going on." But it doesn't mean at all some sort of weird utopic idea of isolation, like let me go and build my own paradise and forget everybody else. No, in the case of poor people in Jamaica who developed self-reliance, they are still connected or still in tune with things from the outside. So some of the most popular things in Jamaica are things like karate films, Western films, spaghetti Westerns. So those things have just entered into the culture and have been appropriated and changed, and a lot of Scratch's music is in fact engaging these pop notions from the outside that take on bigger, more complicated expression, right. So the track that I'll play is kind of a kung fu dub responding to a Bruce Lee film. It's called "Enter the Dragon," which is of course one of Bruce Lee's first films, and very popular in Jamaica. So yeah, it's just the way that he has taken this film and made it Jamaican, made it reggae, made it dub.

("Enter the Dragon" by Lee "Scratch" Perry plays.)

ISHION HUTCHINSON: Let me immediately follow with "Bird in Hand," that cut in which Lee is appropriating Hindi lyrics.

("Bird in Hand" by Lee "Scratch" Perry plays.)

LORENZO BERNET: I have similar, let's say, psychedelic associations with this track. A story that I heard is that the singer Sam Carty came into his studio and he had seen a Bollywood movie, and it's actually from—I'm sorry to demystify this for you. So he'd seen this Bolly-wood movie and it was a really popular Bollywood movie at the time, and I think he had the melody in his head. Also with the friend he was traveling with, a friend who was Hindi at the time, and I don't know, it was one of those afternoons with Perry. Also—do you know the year? It was one of those afternoons like, "Yeah, what do you got?" Perry asking, and he just had this melody. I don't know how the title came, which the title is the most—the beautiful sort of visual associa-tion toward this sound.

ISHION HUTCHINSON: Well, the title is a Jamaican proverb.

LORENZO BERNET: Okay.

ISHION HUTCHINSON: Yeah, you know it? "'A bird in the hand is worth more than two in the bush'—so be satisfied with what you have." (*Laughs.*)

LORENZO BERNET: In past weeks I heard this other tune, it's not related to reggae, not directly, it really reminded me of it, maybe I could play it right away. I think I have to thank Sveta for it; she posted it online somewhere. It's by I think Japanese composers from sort of—I think it's 2010, around, Asa-Chang and Junray, the track is called "Hana," which could mean "flower" in Japanese, I believe. And also please feel free to mingle, because I see this also—also feel free to bring input, because it's probably—the subject—it's meant to loosen up in a way.

(*"Hana" by Asa-Chang and Junray plays.*)

ISHION HUTCHINSON: That was beautiful. Very nice. It's interest-ing, the sound, like I heard three types of drums there. You have the *funde* with the sharp slap, and what sounded like the tabla, the Indian tabla drum, right. That sound like *duhmp*, that *duhmp* sound. You hear it in raga. And then it sounded like there was a talking drum.

LORENZO BERNET: Maybe somebody could elaborate. Maybe it's a vocal technique that you would link the drum to, an automatic playing hand, I don't know. But it would be a Perry idea.

ISHION HUTCHINSON: Right, right. I guess it just, this is the thing, the memory of or the impression of other forms of music coming through in a piece. That's what I was saying about appropriation as a form of conversation, as conversing. So the appropriation isn't to— you know how in some Western contexts, appropriation just means to steal, to take what is not yours. That is a violation, an imbalance of power. On the other hand, in music you have the appropriation where things are in a disparate relation but not discursive, but not so one element dominates the other. This strange but beautiful harmony is molded into the whole fabric of the piece. And what's interesting, too, is it becomes very difficult to trace where what is from. And then, in terms of the Caribbean and why perhaps Lee is the way he is, is that there is a confluence or a flux of all these various traditions and cultures that are meeting in this one very small space. For instance, the Indians, Southeast Asians, came in the early twentieth century as indentured laborers. And their influence on Jamaican popular music is immense. This is another percussive culture, meeting with an African-derived percussive culture. In terms of visibility and, say, acknowledgment, it's not always the case where the Indian influence is so evident, or evidently acknowledged and emphasized, but you listen very carefully and it's such a major part of Jamaican music. And you could name various other cultures that are there, but as usual things have been so creolized, and the appropriation has become so transformed that there is no longer any such thing as "original." That's why the music is so futuristic, right, because it belongs to a past, and it has a history, but within the composition, within the friction of the New World, and especially with dub or really any form of reggae, any form of Jamaican popular music or music from, say, the Caribbean space, is only an approximation of what that music was in its prior realization. And it cannot ever return to that pure state, it's now so mongrelized, and has become something utterly new and unexpected and so abrupt. And so much of this is the emphasis on possibility, on the possibility of a better life, a better situation. It's dreaming something more than where one finds oneself at this moment, right now.

LORENZO BERNET: What you said earlier, as a side note, made me also realize, okay, I'm completely missing the musical vocabulary to kind of—my approach would be really coming from the visual. But the Indian influence also made me think of the Rastafari movement and the attributes it definitely has from Indian culture, words, symbolisms, et cetera, that's where it's most apparent in Jamaican culture, in the phenomenon of the Rastafari, they have this Indian— yeah, it made me also think about this other component that I'm thrilled to talk about in a way that maybe is also coming over the entry point of the icon painting, which is the spiritual, religious, theological side of this music, which is a very visual part of the whole thing.

ISHION HUTCHINSON: Yeah, you're absolutely right that this spiritual iconographic element is deeply there. But, you know, it doesn't trivialize it to say, though, that the music was made to make people dance, you know. It had to be fun. The competition was so extreme in the early decades of the invention of Jamaican popular music. So the first real big Jamaican popular music was ska; that came in the early sixties. Jamaica got independent in '62, and there was this euphoria of happiness, we're now free from Britain finally, let's just have a lot of rum and dance. So the music is fast, it's joyful, ska itself is the name of a dance, reggae is the name of a dance. Dancehall where you go to listen, dance hall is a place where you go to dance. So all of it is about movement and gesture and the body being free. But yeah, you get really into a state, a trancelike state when you're moving a certain way, which is not unrelated to many other cultures where the body doing certain things repeatedly then lifts up into the spiritual realm. Think of dervishes in Sufi tradition. One of the closest associations for reggae and Rasta is of course the Ethiopian Coptic rituals, where the priests would all gather in the church and sing and chant in a very rhythmic, constant, very closely bound movement. So the religious is sort of just twined with the bodily, and there's at times nowhere to distinguish them. But where in Rasta there's no church, that church had to become the body, had to be the physical self. Let me play a clip which exemplifies what I'm saying. It was filmed in 1969 in what's called the "Dungle," the Jamaican word for "dump"; the Dungle was a dump site in Kingston Rastas were forced to live on. The clip is a recording, one of the first recordings, of a Rasta gathering led by a charismatic Rasta elder named Mortimer Planno.

(Recording of Mortimer Planno plays.)

ISHION HUTCHINSON: Yeah, the Rastas are mad, Mortimer Planno says. That's basically it. In the background of that clip, you heard drumming, right, and it's a form of drumming called Nyabinghi, which predates reggae, but reggae is—its baseline structure, its rhythmic pattern, is derived from it. So Nyabinghi talks about the drum as the heart, right. It might sound like a spectacular cliché, but when you put it in the philosophical context, it's really mindblowing. So the sense that the drum, that the heart, the softest organ in the body, is the fountain of the greatest strength of the body, because there's no life without it. And it has to move to a pulse, which is two beats, right. One giving birth to the other. So that's where that *dum-dum, dum-dum* comes from in reggae music. And everything else is just an accompaniment. All the other parts of the instrument just decorate that, which probably connects to this notion you kind of mentioned there of Scratch's Orthodox-looking presentation, which is just highly baroque, stylized, and filigreed. What the music that evolved from Nyabinghi into reggae is really trying to do, then, is to get the body in movement, in constant celebration of its existence that was previously denied it during slavery, colonialism, and in different ways in the post-independent era.

And just one other thing, though, about that clip we just saw. The man that was speaking, his name is Mortimer Planno, and he was essentially a mentor to Bob Marley. So even before Lee Scratch became Marley's mentor, you had that dude, who was responsible, a very key figure in making Nyabinghi drumming and Rasta musical form part of the Jamaican sort of musical standard. So he brought it from the hills, from the rural sort of out-layers of Jamaica, where most Rastas lived at the point in the 1940s and 1950s, so Mortimer Planno brought it into Kingston, the Nyabinghi, and had these basically celebrations, and he was always making and inviting other non-Rastas to come to these gatherings. And so, the second thing is, of course, he said, "Rastas are accused of being madmen," and he's saying yes, the accusation is absolutely correct. Because who could live sanely and pretend to be mentally well-off in a society that is corrupt and bankrupt morally, ethically, and otherwise? So being mad is actually being sane in that context, which is what, in a way, an outlet Rasta granted to the people of Jamaica. This useful madness, this necessary way of being called mad because one is refusing to be just a cog in the colonial machinery, is a form of resistance.

Okay, so what I think we should do actually is just let music play and people mingle, because there is—oh no, maybe we should open it up, let's open it up to questions. If there are any, we could talk a little bit, and we can just play music and hang out a bit longer, if you're so willing. Any questions or thoughts that you want to share? There's a microphone for that.

LORENZO BERNET: There will be a microphone, yeah. Otherwise I would have one last anecdote that I also withheld from you in a way that made me think of this talk and be reflective, in a way, about a constellation and also the two different landscapes, again, and saying it coming from my very visual memory. I remember it was in the time I went to school with Noel, Perry's son, that we, strangely some afternoons we went to Cevi together with Noel—Cevi is a big tradition here in Switzerland, a sort of Boy Scouts or YMCA thing where you have like a football club, so that's where you might spend your Saturday afternoons building things in a forest. I remember one particular Saturday afternoon that I was with Noel and we had to build these campy music instruments out of, like, plumbing tubes and then put some cloth around it, and then it was about storming the walls of Jericho. And, you know, just thinking about it, it's how sort of the iconography of roots reggae sort of, kind of came into play. I find it a very—it's strange that I was with Perry's son reenacting or echoing this sort of dubplate, what was happening on dubplates, in a sense.

ISHION HUTCHINSON: That's amazing. Yeah, I think I played similar games growing up. Storming the walls of Jericho. You did tell me that Noel once said to you, "My dad is a king."

LORENZO BERNET: Yeah, that's also something. When a friend of yours in school says, "My dad is a king." And he's like, "Yeah, in Jamaica." For me, of course, it was a fictional place. For me, it was like from the book of Enoch. But he's like, "Oh no, yeah, we go around in boats to make a ceremony." I never believed it. Like I said before, I'm slowly becoming aware of the kingliness. (*Laughs.*)

ISHION HUTCHINSON: True. You know, I think you should play that clip of the Blue Ark. So, some of you might know that Lee Scratch destroyed the Black Ark Studio in Kingston in 1980. He burned it down, and no one can get a straight answer out of him of why he did this. But it's the myth, the story that is still told. So even people who don't know anything about the Black Ark do know that it was burned down, that there was a great studio that one madman decided to burn down. And not long after that he moved to London, then to Switzerland. So earlier, when I was talking to Lorenzo and sharing this clip with him that he's about to play, I thought it was made in the Black Ark, right? But this is in Switzerland. He had so completely replicated, remade, reinvented the Black Ark in Switzerland, that I— I have seen many photographs and footages of the Black Ark—was completely shocked that it was not it, but a place in Switzerland. And you'll see our dear friend, young Noel in the clip, at one point.

(Recording plays.)

ISHION HUTCHINSON: Yeah, so actually, we have a dub experiment. Can you indulge us? Yes?

AUDIENCE: Yes.

ISHION HUTCHINSON: Yeah, okay . . .

(Bach recording plays.)
(Ras Michael song plays over it.)

ISHION HUTCHINSON: Okay, so that was Ras Michael and Johann Sebastian Bach. Anyways, so we're going to sort of wrap up. We'll sort of play music and mingle. Any questions? Any thoughts? I have questions, but I'll leave them for later.

AUDIENCE MEMBER: Apparently, with the burning down of the studio in Jamaica, he subsequently burned down his own reconstruction of it.

ISHION HUTCHINSON: Yes, that's true.

LORENZO BERNET: You mean in 2015 in Einsiedeln?

ISHION HUTCHINSON: The Blue Ark.

AUDIENCE MEMBER: Was that intentional?

LORENZO BERNET: Was that intentional? Yeah, I mean, I think, and this is a good question, and also asking Lee Perry, like, "Hey, did you burn it intentionally the second time?" And the answer is not so nebulous like the one he burned down in the 1980s. So I think, what I feel out of it, as a reaction in answering this question, I think he didn't do it intentionally. His wife is super mad at him still. It was a candle that he'd left. Yeah, so that's that. But of course, you could say it was an accident.

AUDIENCE MEMBER: There's an obsession with fire, somehow? Like it shows you . . .

LORENZO BERNET: Yeah, candles are forbidden now in Einsiedeln. But I was recently there where he made a fire with a whole bundle if incense and with a lot of other stuff, and then closed doors. Sometimes we would film these moments, but then it's like . . . out of hand.

ISHION HUTCHINSON: Nice one. (*Laughs.*)

(*Audience laughs.*)

ISHION HUTCHINSON: Any other questions? Okay, in that case we'll play some music, and hopefully you'll stick around a little bit, and feel free to dance, I hear it's not forbidden in Switzerland.

(Audience laughs.)

ISHION HUTCHINSON: Thank you for coming out, and I want to again express my gratitude to Lorenzo and to the people that I've met here, truly very, very grateful for the activities and for the honest attention being given, and the care. So you're really being custodians to a legacy that is astonishing, so with all due respect, give thanks.

LORENZO BERNET: Thank you for coming to visit, and yeah, this intense engagement in this subject is really, as you might know, it's opening worlds. How about one poem tonight? Maybe that's a— maybe it's too conceptual not to do a poem, so on behalf of the audience maybe you could read one poem, how about that?

ISHION HUTCHINSON: There was not a huge assent of yay, a poem!

AUDIENCE: Yay!

ISHION HUTCHINSON: No, too late. (*Laughs.*) Okay.

(Audience laughs.)

LORENZO BERNET: Thanks, man.

ISHION HUTCHINSON: If you ask a poet to read a poem, they're usually like, wow.

Yeah, so I guess a lot of you were in House of Love yesterday. I'll read again the poem that I read there, and it's a poem appropriating the voice of Lee "Scratch" Perry. And what it tries to do is imagine, rather than the destruction of the Black Ark, it imagines the building of it, why the Ark came about in the first place. We all are very familiar with how it got destroyed. Actually, saying that, I'm always wary that I am wrong, that the Ark wasn't destroyed, that it was just transformed. Out of its ashes, great things have come.

LORENZO BERNET: It was offshored.

ISHION HUTCHINSON: Offshored, it was offshored. The Swiss do know about offshoring things. (*Laughs.*) So anyway, the building of the Ark is as enigmatic as its destruction, so this is a very sort of partial imagining of the reason for the building of it, and in a sense, as I said, it is a little bit in the voice of Scratch.

THE ARK BY "SCRATCH"

The genie says build a studio. I build
a studio from ash. I make it out of peril and slum
things. I alone when blood and bullet and all
Christ-fucking-'Merican-dollar politicians talk
the pressure down to nothing, when the equator's
confused and coke bubbles on tinfoil to cemented wreath.
I build it, a Congo drum, so hollowed through the future
pyramids up long before CDs spin away roots-men knocking
down by the seaside,
like captives wheeling by the Kebar River. The genie says build
a studio, but don't take any fowl in it, just electric.
So I make it, my echo chamber with shock rooms of rainbow
King Arthur's sword keep in, and one for the Maccabees
alone, for covenant is bond between man and worm.
Next room is Stone Age, after that, Iron, and one I
named Freeze, for too much ice downtown in the brains

of all them crossing Duke Street, holy like parsons.
And in the circuit breaker, the red switch is for death
and the black switch is for death, and the master switch
is black and red, so if U.S., Russia, China, Israel talk
missiles talk, I talk that switch I call Melchizedek.
I build a closet for the waterfalls. One for the rivers.
Another for oceans. Next for secrets. The genie says build
a studio. I build it without gopher wood. Now, consider
the nest of bees in the cranium of the Gong, consider
the nest of wasps in the heart of the Bush Doctor,
consider the nest of locusts in the gut of the Black Heart Man,
I put them there, and the others that vibrate at the Feast of the
    Passover
when the collie weed
is passed over the roast fish and corn bread. I Upsetter, I
    Django
on the black wax, the Super Ape, E.T., I cleared the wave.
Again, consider the burning bush in the ears of Kalonji
and the burning sword in the mouth of the Fireman and the
    burning pillar
in the eyes
of the Gargamel, I put them there, to outlast earth as I navigate
    on one
of Saturn's rings, I mitered solid shadow setting fire to snow in
    my ark.
I credit not the genie but the coral rock: I am stone.
I am perfect. Myself is a vanishing conch shell speeding round
a discotheque at the embassy of angels, skeletons ramble to check
    out
my creation dub and sex is dub, stripped to the bone, and dub
    is the heart
breaking the torso to spring, olive beaked, to be eaten up by
    sunlight.

(Applause.)

ISHION HUTCHINSON: Thank you.

("Words of My Mouth" by Lee "Scratch" Perry plays.)

LUCAS

WHEN I WAS TWELVE, AND IN MY FINAL YEAR OF PRIMARY
school, a boy I'll call Lucas and I became an unlikely pair of morn-
ing birds. My mother engineered the union. It began on the second
morning of the first term, in September 1995. I had got ready for
school in the usual ways, washing in a plastic basin in the backyard,
eating a breakfast of plantain and eggs, and drinking a cup of insipid
"gross-stake" tea—the leaves of which came from a fence tree in the
yard—then dressing in my khaki uniform, still crisp after the previ-
ous day's wear, though it now bore a distinct funk that I prayed only
I could smell. My mother and I walked downhill toward the school,
which was about half an hour away by foot.

That day, there was one break in the morning routine. After we
had gone down the hill and passed the first enormous sugarcane
field, which stretched right up to the edge of the asphalt road dusted
with old ash from burned harvests—the place was called Jane Ash
Corner—we stopped in front of a high corrugated-iron fence, col-
umned by *maka* trees. By stopping, we had violated the natural order
of things as I knew them. Adding to that disturbance, my mother
called out a woman's name, then said, "We here outside." A voice

boomed back, "Him soon ready." I waited for the earth to open up and swallow us.

The compound of disheveled wooden barrack houses behind the fence where we had stopped was referred to, in a coded but barefaced phrase, as "the coolie them place." This term was used for any number of yards, scattered across the vast, largely black ex-slave region of St. Thomas Parish, where people of East Indian descent lived. To my child's mind, these yards seemed always hidden, like this one, behind thornlike trees and corrugated-iron fences or cinder-block walls. They appeared fortified, places apart that, in our small, impoverished districts, stood out for reasons I didn't entirely understand. The term "the coolie them place" acknowledged this separateness. Perhaps it had come about because blacks and Indians met in the wake of the 1838 slave emancipation. (The Indian families in St. Thomas, like most Indians in Jamaica, had first come as indentured laborers, beginning in 1845.) Perhaps the encounter between the two groups at that time had created rivalries, for status and for work, that were never overcome. Perhaps we were both overprotective of our remnant cultures, and defensiveness became a way to cope. I didn't know. All I knew was that we mostly lived at odds, an unbridgeable distance between us.

The term "the coolie them place" also served as a warning, a caution to avoid such places. Avoid them, if you were a kid, and be spared a whipping. Not from the people who lived in those yards, but from one of your parents or another relative, once it was discovered that you had gone into such a yard. Even standing in front of one, as my mother and I were now doing, was usually enough to guarantee, for a child, a whipping. For an adult, the risk was that you could be ostracized or "go off your head" or suffer "body-come-downness"—in other words, be severely stricken by spirits in the body or the mind. Because the East Indian population in Jamaica was much smaller than its black counterpart, these yards were few. But there were enough of them to make a deep mark on the psychogeography of slavery's aftermath, an aftermath in which superstition and social discrimination touched every aspect of ordinary life. The phrase bore this shattered history into our shattered present.

To me, though, the phrase had been just a phrase, something purely rhetorical, a warning I'd heard and obeyed so as not to provoke a whipping from my mother, until a year before, when she had a nervous breakdown. Catatonic for days, she would suddenly erupt in fury, breaking objects and seeming to want to break me. I was eleven, and I had to tie her down. It hurt. Two black obeah men—spiritualists—got the credit for curing her. They confirmed the family's suspicion that her illness had come from "the coolie them place" next door to us. She had been possessed, they said, by a "coolie duppy," or a spirit. She barely survived. When she did, the obeah men gave her a strict order: "Leave this sick house." That was how we had come to live in the house on the hill above Jane Ash Corner. No wonder, standing now outside the gate of one of these yards, I was confused. I was scared.

The two parts of the gate in the fence were held together by a piece of blue fishing net. I fixed my eyes on that bolt of blue, unable to look up at my mother's face. I didn't know if she was speaking, perhaps explaining to me why we were there. All I could hear was my blood thrumming in my ears. Then, when the fishing net started to move, slithering like a snake, I almost fainted. Panicked, I stepped back; the blue disappeared, and the gates fell open. There stood a boy, in uniform, slim, about my height. I didn't notice, until she spoke, that his mother was standing beside him.

She was a very large woman. Her thin black satin wrap, sack-like and knotted on one shoulder, creased under her armpits. She used her body—I thought—to block a good portion of the gateway. She turned and pulled the two sides of the gate back toward her, speaking in a flurry as she tied them with the blue net. I picked out of what she was saying that she was chastising the boy, who kept his head lowered.

Then she boxed the back of his head and said a word I would hence-forth hear repeated every morning for a year: "What a boy fi *titivate*!" What a boy for primping!

Two other things struck me: the mother and son didn't look like each other; nor, despite the yard they came from, did they look Indian. Their noses and lips were like mine and my mother's. His skin was coppery, and his hair was black, like mine, but with matching copper highlights. His mother was near white with a pink undertone, what Jamaicans dismissively called red. I had never seen that color in our district. Where was she from?

"See Lucas here," his mother said, as if presenting an item for ap-praisal. He gave the merest lift of his head, then dropped it. He stepped over to the asphalt side of the road, where my mother and I stood. My mother did not appraise him at all, this boy now standing shoulder to shoulder with me. She only said, with an unchallenged finality, "All right, go 'head to school."

So we did, taking the bend around Jane Ash Corner that led out to the town's square. From there, we would climb a hill and cross a field to school. Neither of us spoke. I glanced over at him; his head was now raised, and his eyes dead straight ahead. I registered more: he had a light coppery fuzz of baby hair on his cheek, and tiny brown spots were sprayed across the side of his face that I could see. I didn't know then that these were called freckles. I thought of an overripe banana, and I wondered if he had a nickname, some variation on the word "speckled." Maybe he was just called Banana.

But I kept returning to the fact that he didn't look Indian, not like the Indians I'd occasionally seen entering or leaving the yard next door to where my mother and I used to live. Perhaps he didn't belong to the yard that he and his mother had emerged from; maybe the two of them just happened to have been there that morning. Could be he was . . . well, maybe he was Indian after all. India was a big, big country, I'd heard. Maybe there were Indian people who looked like him, and I just hadn't seen any yet. My thoughts were racing every which way.

"Mind your eye them drop out." He said it quietly, his head still pointed directly in front of him. I hadn't realized that my glance had turned into a stare. I wondered whether to apologize, but found myself hissing through my teeth as I said, "Is my eye them, come jook them out."

He turned full face to me—more freckles and a pebble-size, scabbed-over gash on his forehead—and I saw his eyes for the first time. They were amber colored, gold. He assessed my challenge, then decided I was too petty to be taken seriously and turned his face back to the road.

But I felt as though the stinging stare of his eyes remained on me. I had never seen eyes like those before. They had not only blinded my own eyes, per my suggestion, but had done away with my tongue as well. As soon as we got through the school gate, he went his way without ceremony. Just as I had never seen him on the school grounds in my previous four years at the school, I didn't see him a single time that day.

And for the rest of that year, I never saw him around school— neither on the playground during break times, nor at the concrete water troughs, which were always crowded, nor at any of the shade spots where lunch was eaten and scandals were stirred. Nor did I see him in the evening when school was out and little gangs were formed to raid mango groves or go off to find sweetshops somewhere behind God's back or simply to play-fight in the field before rushing home. Lucas was nowhere to be seen. I saw him only in the mornings, when I arrived at his gate, without my mother, who accompanied me just that first time.

In the evening of that first day, when I got home from school, I asked my mother a barrage of questions. I sought desperately to know two things: Who were those people, and why was I to go with Lucas to school? My mother's answers were less than extraordinary. Those people, she told me, were people from down the hill; the mother she knew from "back in the days." Yesterday, she'd run into her and found out that she had lived in Jane Ash Corner for "donkey years now" and had a "wash-belly" boy my age who attended the same school as me.

Out of this last tidbit, somehow, the arrangement was made for Lucas and me to walk to school together in the morning. After all, we were both in sixth grade, our last year of primary school, and "it would be nice." The mothers had also talked about us walking home together in the evenings, but after school Lucas went with his father and older brothers "far, far clear over Holland Bay," where his father had a farm and set fish pots to catch "tom tom"—river mullets. Lucas's mother sold the farm produce, along with the fish, at big markets like the one in Morant Bay, a principal town about fourteen miles outside the district. This farm-going in the evenings explained why I never saw Lucas when school was out. It did not explain why I never saw a peep of him during school hours. That, and so much else, was left unanswered.

I hadn't formulated the right question. I don't remember if it was the next evening, or the evening after that, or over the weekend— after I'd tolerated Lucas's silence on the walk to school for the whole first week, his head obstinately tilted forward and eyes averted—that I finally figured out what to ask my mother.

"How them different from who sick you?"

She considered this a while. Her words came out slowly: "Well, they is me friend, you know. From small days, me friend and her man flexing. Their people—them couldn't change that and them did have to accept them. That is how love strong. Look see, they live years on top of years with them pickney them in the same yard. I didn't even know that, since me did move away. Is plenty generations over there in that yard, you know."

From this, I guessed that Lucas's father was Indian, which would have made Lucas "coolie royal," a designation reserved for someone of Indian and black heritage. The matter should've ended there. But, within the blurred and shifting boundaries of my surroundings, I was still confused. Lucas didn't seem to fit into the "coolie royal" category. According to my understanding at the time, to be "coolie royal," Lucas would have had to have mahogany skin and silken, loosely curly black hair. Many of the students with Indian blood at our school fell into that category. Thinking about this now, from my writing desk in upstate New York in 2022, I realize that "coolie royal" was another of those cynical colonial concepts—like "high-brown," which Lucas, though his skin was literally brown, was not. How much energy is wasted on defining visible distinctions within the fluid spectrum of Creole identities?

I began to wonder. If Lucas was not Indian, or "coolie royal," like some of our schoolmates, or "red," like his mother, how was he to be classified? It wasn't classification in and of itself that I was curious about but something for which I wasn't sure language existed. Curiosity was hard to kill, and Lucas didn't make it easy.

The following Monday morning, I arrived at his gate and announced myself. His mother shouted his name from in the yard, followed by her variation of "What a boy fi *titivate*!" He exited—quickly drawing and tying the gates shut—with his head hung low. I smiled and gave him a friendly greeting. He walked past me, saying nothing. Taken aback, I stood awhile, long enough that I had to trot to catch up with him. As he had on the mornings of the previous week, he held his head forward, eyes averted, in a world of his own. Still, I played it cool and said, "Wha'gwaan?" I rushed to add, "You going Holland Bay this evening?"

He stopped abruptly, turned to me with a screw face, and spat out, "You a watchman?"

"Watch you? No, is me mother say . . ."

"Your mumma a watchman, too?" He drew closer to me; his

innumerable freckles seemed to speak. "Stop follow, follow me, you hear? Me not Jesus, me don't want no followers." I actually found his last statement funny, but he had also provoked my ire.

"Eh, eh, look here, Christ"—I couldn't resist—"you are nobody for anybody to watch, worse to go follow, so settle your nerves." Still a hair's breadth away from me, his face glowered. At any moment, I expected him to strike me. But, just as he had done the first morning, when he had decided I was too petty to be taken seriously, he turned his face back to the road and started walking. Sure enough, I followed him.

I returned the next morning. The routine began afresh: my call, his mother's response, his exit through the gates, the silent walk to school. The same routine the morning after that. Every morning, when I woke, the first image in my head was the face of that surly boy with whom, locked in a spiky quiet, I walked to school. This was my life now. I hated it.

Thursday morning came. Just as we had rounded the bend of Jane Ash Corner, I said to him, "We not have to walk together to school at all, you know. There is plenty way to get there. You take one, me take one." I said it, half looking at the ground and half looking at the side of his implacable face. The humiliation made me furious.

A beat or two passed before he said, "No, it all right." Then, with what could be best described as a hen's cackle, he laughed and said, "Me know you love to follow me!" Laughing still, he continued, "Just don't ask me a bag of questions, like you is the district constable."

"You see me with big rum belly like constable?" I said, chuckling.

"That soon come, man. Two twos and your waist will have no line." We were beside ourselves with laughter. Over the next few weeks, this evolved into a private language between us. So that we were, for a good half hour of every morning, on our walks to school, oddly birds of a feather.

There were other little groups of students walking to school, some with parents or other grown-ups. They would stare at us—at him, really—but they never interacted with us. Lucas was unfazed. He kept his focus on me, if we were talking, or else in front of him or on the roadside bushes, his head held high. This made him seem aloof, a posture so different from the dejected, low-hanging-face boy who exited his gate every morning, the posture he maintained for the first few minutes of our walk.

In rare moments, somebody from one of these little groups, as if sent on reconnaissance, would draw near to us. He—it was always a boy—would scuttle back to his group after getting a version of the stinging stare that Lucas had given me on our first morning. One day, someone threw a taunt, an arsenal of taunts, actually, at Lucas. Like my guesses at his nickname, these taunts were food based:

"Yow, yellow-heart roast breadfruit boy!"

"Hey, bruised jackfruit, hear me a call to you?"

"Oy there, turned cornmeal face!"

Lucas made no response, and I noted no change in his demeanor. It wasn't simply that the boy doing the taunting was ignored. He didn't exist.

People in general began to fade away in the mornings when I walked with Lucas. We existed out of reach of the ever-prying village eyes, surveilling from the doorways and yards of fenced and fenceless shanties, out of reach of the imbecilic chatter and judgment that kept the old, cold comfort of plantation suspicion alive. From the time that Lucas came out of his gate, and until we were through the gates of the school half an hour later, I seemed unable to recognize anybody but him.

One morning, there was a surprise. Out of the blue, as we were nearing the town's square, Lucas asked, "Is true say principal cut off your locks when you did come a we school?"

The question was so unexpected it took me a moment to realize that it was related to me. When I did, I wondered how Lucas could've possibly known about that incident. Well, he could've heard about it any number of ways since what had happened wasn't exactly private. The way he asked, however, suggested that he hadn't really heard about it, or had heard about it in a fragmented manner. The question spoke to his detachment; it risked exposing something that was less about me and more about him.

"True" was the answer to his question. Years ago, when my mother enrolled me in the school, I believe I was the only student there with dreadlocks. At my previous school, situated in my father's parish, Portland, where I was born, there were many other boys and girls with dreads. During the morning devotion of the first day at my new school, the principal noticed me—my hair was wrapped in a khaki turban—and summoned me to her office. She was in a state. She couldn't understand how I'd got registered at her school in the first place with that "abomination" on my head.

Bewildered as she was, she casually unwound my turban. And, just as casually, picking up the biggest pair of scissors I had ever seen, she snipped twice at my head. Several strands of dreads, lifeless like dried vines, fell to the floor. The sight of my own hair numbed me. She then told me to pick the dreads up, dismissing me home with this clear instruction for my mother: "Tell your mother, 'Finish the job,' or don't come back." I was giving Lucas a rough version of what took place.

"So what your mumma do when you go home?" he asked me.

I'd never spoken with anyone about it before, other than with my mother, who raged whenever the incident was brought up. When it had happened, and for months after, I'd thought about nothing else. Then, with time, it began to feel like a fairy tale. In my mind, it became something that had happened to someone else.

"What me mother do?" I repeated, staring back into his intense gaze. "Oh. Jesus, me don't even done talk before me mother wheel out of the yard and right over to school and into principal's office without even a 'Howdy do, miss.' Then me mother start to slap slap up principal, slap her so hard you don't know if principal black or if principal blue!"

Standing outside the office, my dreads still in my hand, I didn't see my mother slapping the principal, but I heard when the principal began to scream bloody murder. A crowd gathered in no time. Next thing, before I could make sense of what was happening, I saw my mother being taken out of the principal's office by two paunch-bellied district constables. Cursing and kicking, she was hauled into the back of a police jeep. When the jeep drove off, some people from the crowd running behind it, I moved from sobbing to wailing, believing my mother was being taken away for good. But she was home soon enough.

"Them take your mumma for that?"

"Yes."

"Kiss me rass," he said. He added, "You know it have people in India, too, like Rasta dread people, who don't deal with cutting their hair." This was utterly new to me. Who were these Indian people like Rastas? Did any of those people, relatives of his, live in his yard? But we had arrived at the school gate, and Lucas, without ceremony as usual, took his leave of me.

Later in the day, thinking about the morning, I felt a strange sense of guilt. I realized that, had our conversation continued, I would not have been able to draw on any past stories about him. I had heard nothing, and how would I? Whom would I have asked if they had heard anything about a boy living in an Indian yard in Jane Ash Corner? I could ask only the boy himself.

It was out of this mood—this strange guilt—that some days later I asked him about the shiny scar on his forehead. He traced two fingers on it and said, "This? You don't think me born with it?" I was half-ready to believe him. But he gave his cackle laugh and said, "This from long, long time, man." His finger was still on the gash, smoothing it out, like. He wasn't going to say more, and I wasn't sure what other question to ask. Instead, I said, "Lemme see it."

The last thing I expected was for him to push his head under my eyes, tilting down his forehead. Up close, I could see infinitesimal freckles, finer than the ones on his cheeks and nose bridge, covering his forehead and disappearing into his hairline. Only where the gash was—shiny like two conjoined thumbnails—there were no freckles. The gash had a slight depression. I pressed my finger on it, and he flinched; it felt glass smooth. I pressed again; this time he didn't flinch. I was wondering if freckles could ever grow back there. He pulled away, glancing up with his eyes opened wide. Their unnatural gold tint had a coronet pattern, softer in glow around the iris. "See?" he said. Had I, and what? "Yes," I said.

For the first couple of minutes of our walk, Lucas was always silent. It took me a while to realize that his silence was not due to shyness or to some reservation that he had about me. It was because a deep sadness accompanied him. Usually, when we were some distance from his yard, his mood would alter, and he'd abruptly break the silence. This became our pattern of talking, which I accepted, much as it irritated me to have to wait for him to say the first words.

On one of the last mornings of the first term, as soon as he came through the gate, I could see that an extra sullenness weighed him down. He literally looked smaller, his head bowed, and his shoulders rolled into a curve. Even when we were some distance away from his place, there was no customary silence breaking. I said something about school. He said nothing but continued his hunched walk, examining the cracked macadam under his feet. I tried again, and again silence. I let him alone, looking around to distract myself. I had been doing this for some time when I heard sniffles. I turned and saw his shoulders jerking and his palms over his face.

We had just crossed into a brushy track of tall trees, which led out to the last stretch toward school. No one else was on the track. He pulled over to one side and sat on the ground, hanging his head. He let out a single loud squeal, which quickly became an almost noiseless whimper. His body convulsed in spasms. With one hand on his shoulder, I used the other to try to lift his head. I asked, "Wha'mphen, wha'mphen?" His head was unyielding, but he didn't push my hands away. I began to pat his shoulder and said, "Everything all right."

He grew calm after a short while. Then he raised his head, his face a flushed reddish color burning with freckles. "Me all right," he said, adding meekly, "is nothing." He didn't get up, so I sat next to him—worried as hell that the morning school bell would ring and we would be locked out of school or face a despicable punishment from the principal for being late. His breathing was calmer, his normal color creeping back into his face. I sensed that he wanted to talk.

"Is what wrong?" I asked.

He hesitated a moment, then said, "Them burn me again." I shook my head. He sighed and touched the gash on his forehead. "You see this? Is them burn me. For nothing them burn me. If me sit, is problem. If me stand up, is problem. If me rest a little rest, is pure licks. Them wake me anytime a night—*go wash the plate, go this, go that*—that's why me tired so a morning. Before cock crow, broom clap me in me head—*go sweep the veranda, boy!*—why veranda to sweep and sun not even light yet? Me catch little sleep back 'cause me tired."

"So them burn you? Who?"

He looked at me puzzled; then his expression darkened. "You don't know the half. Is not no one somebody—is the all of them in the yard." I wanted to ask Lucas if "them" included his parents. But I didn't know how to ask the question. I said, "Me sorry. Everything will be all right."

Looking into my eyes, Lucas said, "Me can only do a little book way a night with kerosene lamp turn low when them sleeping. All me can see is me shadow on the book page." He spoke as if that image of himself were before him now, an image of immeasurable sadness.

It broke him. He began to sob again. He said, "I bet you, one night when them sleeping I going to take that lamp and burn down the place. You watch."

I patted his shoulder, unsure what else to do. Then I wondered where on his body he got burned this time. I couldn't bring myself to ask. "Me sorry," I said again. He nodded. The track was still empty. I couldn't tell what time it was, but I had a feeling the school bell had rung a while ago.

"Bell must be ring already. We should go."

He stared in the direction of school, blocked by trees and bushes. "Yes, bell must a ring by now. You go in first, and then me come after."

I went off, to be at the mercy of the principal. I didn't look back for Lucas. Whether he entered those gates or not that morning, I never found out.

The term ended. Christmas came, the kite season, then the New Year. Whenever I happened to encounter other sixth graders, they chanted, "Free paper burn!" Meaning, the holidays will be over and soon school will reopen. (The expression came from slavery days; "free paper" was an enslaved person's pass when leaving the plantation.)

I knew the chant well. But now it was more loaded: after this term, primary school was over for good. If you were lucky in the Common Entrance Exams, you might move on to a high school. Most kids I knew who were older than me didn't have that luck; many didn't want that luck. For some, going to high school was just delaying the inevitable. Following the chants of "Free paper burn," that inevitable was summed up in a gnomic, brutal question: "Chop or pick?"

Chop was to become a cane cutter for a place like the Golden Grove Sugar Factory. Pick was to become a banana harvester for Eastern Banana Estates.

"Chop, of course," one boy might answer.

"Pick, a must that," another answered.

There might be a play quarrel about which was better—"Pick

'cause you use machete like sword!"; "Chop 'cause billhook cut and draw same time!"—but whatever was said was said without rancor. Life was leading one way or the other—why be bitter?

Manual labor made up the income basis of every second person living in St. Thomas. My mother, when young, escaped that fate by moving to my father's parish, Portland. There, constrictions existed, but less so, or in less debasing ways, than in St. Thomas. My mother drummed into me daily that neither chop nor pick would be my destiny. "By hook or crook," she would say, "you going to high school." That was that.

As far as I can guess, Lucas's mother, like my mother, had escaped the fate of chop or pick, thanks to her position at the big market in Morant Bay, selling river mullets and the produce from her husband's farm. Was it Lucas's destiny to be a farmer like his father and brothers? I thought of how I never, ever saw him at school, not even once, after we parted at the school gates in the morning. Yet he set out every morning, just as I did. I thought of the months of walking together, the diligence in doing so, and something greater than diligence that we both were in search of.

It was the first school morning of January 1996. Lucas's mother had just shouted, "What a boy fi *titivate*!" Shortly after, Lucas pulled the piece of blue fishing net and emerged from the gate. Except for a buzz cut, he was the same sullen boy I had seen two or so weeks earlier. It was the longest I had gone without seeing him since my mother had formed the strange alliance of our morning walk last September. We strolled off quietly.

"You go beach over so?" he asked as soon as we were some distance from his house. The question surprised me. I knew what he was asking—whether I had gone to a beach in Portland. But how he had known that I spent some of the school break in Portland puzzled me. I was certain I had never mentioned Portland to him in any context. Where was he getting his information from? Perhaps from my mother through his mother, but I doubted that was the case.

"Yeah, man, plenty, plenty time. Bryan's Bay, Frenchman's Cove, and thing." I thought what to ask him. Should I ask where he had spent his school break? That would've sounded trite. If I knew a little more of his background, the way he knew something of mine, apparently, I could've formed a question. I thought of asking about the farm in Holland Bay, but before I came up with anything, he said, "You can swim good? All the black fishermen me know round Holland Bay side can't swim. Bestest fishermen them, and most of them can only splash water!" He was laughing hard. I laughed with him.

"So, wait, you a good swimmer?" I asked.

"Tops, man. Champion in the water!" I don't believe I had ever heard his voice raised so high before. He made a gliding motion with his hand—fishlike—to display his conviction.

I hissed through my teeth and said, "You all talk. Splash in river water is not swimming."

"But you see me dying trial this morning," he said, opening his mouth with mock astonishment. He added, "You must not hear what top-class fishermen call me when we take boat go places like Mackerel Bank or Pedro Bank—what you know 'bout Pedro Bank?—and clear near Cuba side"—he waved a hand in one direction—"when engine cut and me dive off boat at sea; you must not hear what them call me."

He spoke with such excitement. Everything he said was utterly new to me. I was seeing a new person, new with an added layer, a secret skein of something special, a nickname, he was about to reveal to me.

I tried to quell my enthusiasm when I asked, "What so them call you?"

"Goldfish."

Not "Speckled," not "Banana," but "Goldfish" was his shibboleth.

"Goldfish," I said.

"Yes, that's me name on water," he said. I knew right then I was never going to be calling him that. It was a name reserved for—given by—a sect who knew what they were talking about and who knew him in that light of excitement out at sea.

Probably his sharing was a leftover of the holiday fervor, for he never again shared anything of the sort about himself with me. I nudged, making tall claims about my swimming abilities (which were nil); he laughed them off, saying nothing. He never again spoke about his family, either, or about being burned. Nor did he speak again of his dream of burning down the house one night while his tormentors were asleep. I didn't nudge or try to get him to talk about it, but I thought a lot about the prism of Lucas. On one side was the champion-swimmer boy with the nickname that flashed with bright radiance. The other side was dark, the tormented boy, longing to enact a revenge of fire. The dark side was also radiant, I thought, but without shine. His many other sides were blank to me, and these two, opposing forces of water and fire, were mere outlines.

One morning, some time after the beginning of March, I asked, "You declare school already?" Long I had been waiting to ask him that question.

It was the question of the moment. For the students who were not going to "chop" or "pick," "declaring" a high school was the real sacrament marking the end of childhood. You declared by ranking a few of the half dozen or so schools in and around St. Thomas, from highest to lowest in preference. The only choice I made outside St. Thomas was Happy Grove High, a school built on a cliff on the Portland side of the border. Because I was from Portland, Happy Grove was my top choice. I felt I had a special claim on it, as if going there would be my homecoming. Later in the month, you sat for the Common Entrance Exams, the results of which would then determine the high school you were placed in. So much for ranking preference. The results were released in June. The waiting period was abominable. When I was in lower grades, I had seen sixth graders waiting, stricken by jangled nerves. One morning in June, during the devotion gathering, the Common Entrance Exams results were read out loud by the principal, the results having been printed in the Jamaica *Gleaner* that morning.

The large-format paper, with columns of names of students who had made it, gave the morning a frightening gravity. In the evening, a copy of the *Gleaner* was passed from yard to yard. To see printed in black and white the name of some known person, or even an unknown person who lived somewhere close by, was like witnessing magic.

We were at the school gates when I asked Lucas the question, "You declare school already?"

Fear had made me wait until that moment to ask. The bell started ringing, which meant that he didn't need to answer. But there was still a sliver of time. He could, if he wanted, blurt out an answer before heading off. There would be time tomorrow, anyway, and the next day and weeks ahead after that in which I could ask him the same question. But I knew that this moment was the only one. If he didn't answer now, I would never ask again. The term would be over by the beginning of July, and I would never see him again. I felt that in my bones. Still, I was hoping—the last bell had struck—that his answer would alter what I felt. As usual, we parted.

DREAMS OF STONE: LALIBELA

■

AS THE VAN FROM THE SMALL AIRPORT CLIMBED THE ROUGH-terraced mountain and the sky came close again, the driver asked what had brought me to Lalibela.

I didn't know what to tell him. I wasn't a pilgrim, nor was I strictly a tourist, like the tens of thousands of people who come each year to see the rock-hewn churches in the North Wollo zone of Ethiopia's Amhara region. I wasn't sure what I was. Saying "To see paradise, my childhood homeland, but not really, because . . ." was too complicated, would have sounded dumb, so I said something reasonable and kept quiet for the rest of the drive.

But paradise was why I had come. The idea of paradise, something whole yet imperfect that I've understood all my life only in terms of loss. With nothing but this idea, the memory of an idea—this sense of Eden gone—I had departed Addis Ababa in search of a fiction spoken of in my childhood in Jamaica, in search of that fiction and its double, history.

I was raised in a Rastafarian family in the countryside, hours away by winding road from Kingston, a place that even in the 1980s folks still simply called town. Throughout my boyhood in Portland and

St. Thomas Parishes, on the cane and banana farms that entrapped imaginations on the eastern coast, Ethiopia existed as the future fulfillment of our tragic slave past.

To the rest of the world, Rastas may seem to be black hippies: long-haired vegans practicing free love, always stoned. In reality, Rasta is a complex religion in which the late Ethiopian emperor Haile Selassie is not a god but God. Desperate were the conditions in the aftermath of enslavement in Jamaica, and neither the Western Christian churches nor the remembered West African religions seemed quite to fit the facts on the ground. We wanted a black god, but we also wanted him to be Christian.

"Jamaica is literally hell for the black man, just as Ethiopia is literally heaven," was a common expression I heard as a boy. "Ethiopia awaits his creators," the Rastafarian elders said also, almost to themselves. The word "Lalibela" was like the threshold of heaven when it was pronounced.

If I took the elders' sayings for prophecy, I never envisioned actual travel. No one I knew as a child had ever been to Ethiopia. There was a guy who'd gone to England, and his nickname was thus Ivor British. Later, in high school, and more fervently in the upper grades, I was taught that our forebears originated not in Ethiopia but in West Africa. This struck a cardinal blow to the idea of terrestrial paradise invoked daily: our ancestral claim was absurd; an entire life philosophy had been compromised.

The knowledge did not diminish, though, the private awe of what I had heard as a boy. The rosary of Ethiopian place-names chanted—Axum, Gondar, Shashamane—fixed itself in me as a truth deeper than fact, and that eternally beautiful word, Lalibela, settled and grew into something unreal in my mind, a distant planet, vague as snow to me who had never seen snow. I had, from early on, a scriptural, milk-and-honey impression of the place: a potent but indefinite sense of geographic mass. There the link between people and place was unbroken—a fact that at once divided me from and brought me closer to its enigmatic center. Then I arrived, and instantly the wonder took on real divine proportion.

As I sit at home now in upstate New York, thinking back five years to 2015, when I visited Lalibela, this is how memory has assembled that place for me: chalk-white cattle; herders in brightly colored wraps or plain white like the cow horns; children on the roadside, often carrying plastic or clay buckets; thatch houses with dung roofs and cinder-block houses mostly unfinished in the valley below.

You cannot see the churches as you approach the peaks of the Ethiopian Highlands, as you can the towering steeples of European or South American capitals. The grand cathedrals of Lalibela are hidden—built into the ground. One first comes upon them from above, and they appear as if each had been constructed, placed on a freight elevator, and lowered several stories down a stone-lined shaft. As whimsical as this might seem, it is less awe inspiring than the truth. The churches—eleven in total, some with wide, elaborate plazas—were hand carved out of stone, working downward into the rock. Every lintel, every doorway, every porch and step.

With the knowledge of what lay beneath, each thing I passed, some ordinary and familiar, seemed to levitate: every single person belonged to the churches hidden in the mountains, where eucalyptus leaves glinted their mirror signals. The closeness of the rock-hewn wonders seared suddenly like the phantasmal tug of reality in a dream.

After a forty-minute drive from the airport, I got to my hotel, Sora Lodge, where I wasted no time before hurrying back out with my guide, Theo—hurrying like someone in pursuit of something to reclaim or something that would reclaim him. Theo was of average height, late middle-aged, stubble-chinned, with kind almond eyes. He had waited more than three hours for my delayed plane from Addis Ababa. He was not certain I would see all eleven churches. "A good fortune nonetheless," he said cheerfully, for this late—it was just after three in the afternoon; I was supposed to have been there at noon—I would likely be the only visitor. "What you see you will see alone."

The sky was no longer a clear blue but crimson. Theo said it might rain. He turned out to be right, on both counts. Bolting his car the two miles through what seemed to be the town square, overtaking *bajaj*—the ragged blue-and-white rickshaw taxis that paraded in congeries and vied in harmless competition for passengers—he spoke ceaselessly, pointing out things as they flew by the window.

At a tiny, bare crossroads we came to a stop. Though not visible, the churches began to our right, up and then down, into the mountain. At the top, we hopped out and descended a pale-red slope, which gradually hardened into a sable corniche. Layers of tufa along the rock walls grew distinct and wider as we went farther. After about ten minutes, Theo paused and placed his palms flat against a jutting boulder. He was silent a while. I thought he was about to pray. Then he spoke, one hand weighing on my shoulder, his eyes fixed on mine. He told me plainly that I was about to see great buildings carved out of stone. He spoke not simply to praise the churches. His eyes held mine. I realized, or felt, he was initiating me into the lifeblood of the place. It moved me greatly, a boy from across the ocean. He was welcoming me back.

In Addis Ababa, people had seen at a glance that I was Jamaican. Travel often reduces a person to his starkest identity, and in that city it was my Rasta appearance, my dreads that inflected each of my social interactions. A man in the Wabe Shebelle Hotel bar, finishing his coffee, told me that if it were not for the Rastafarians in Jamaica, the name Ethiopia would have been long gone from the world's popular memory. "Like another Liberia," he said. I didn't get his meaning, but before I could ask, he added, "It's because Rastafarian young people know history, the struggle after the Derg." I got his drift. The Derg was the brutal military regime that overthrew Haile Selassie in 1974. The country plunged into civil war and famine, the effects of which are still felt almost half a century later.

This was typical of my encounters with Ethiopians. We acknowl-
edged what connected us: colonial struggle, political corruption,
poverty. We relished one another's native music. There was dancing
and "spice war" jokes at dinner. I recognized the amused contempt
Ethiopians have for Ethiopians returning from abroad. Jamaicans say
"foreigna"; Ethiopians say "diaspora."

Moving through the enticing chaos of Addis Ababa reminded me
of Kingston, where I had lived for three years as a university student.
Chaos in both cities stimulated, oddly, a certain kind of grace. It was a
happiness that was tender in Addis Ababa (*addis*, new, *ababa*, flower);
the mundane coexisted with the sacral: busy workaday people would
stop in traffic to make the sign of the cross when passing a cathedral,
a sight I had never seen in Kingston.

Yet, as in any city, there was something estranging. The close-
packed buildings rose endlessly, new constructions, constricting the
view of the Entoto Hills flanking the city. The buildings' proliferation
matched the city's constant accumulation of people and moments.
Some of my impressions evaporated in the haste of the place before
they could quite take shape, never to repeat, which perhaps said more
about my provincial internal clock. Indeed, the real spring of the es-
trangement was myself—for lacking Amharic, for my poor way with
time when I feel it slipping fast.

In Lalibela, far away from that urban speed and within reach of
the soul of Ethiopia—its churches—Theo's words anchored within me
all those fleeting moments. Anchored them permanently.

We resumed walking, turning down a coarse, narrow lane that
narrowed further into a kind of tunnel. Not far off, barley patches.
Women passed carrying great bundles of firewood on their heads.
Some children swinging water buckets in crisscross—to lighten the
load—followed along. Theo related the story of the sixteenth-century
Portuguese priest and traveler Father Francisco Álvares, the first Eu-
ropean to describe the magnificence of the churches, in his widely

translated book, *Narrative of the Portuguese Embassy to Abyssinia During the Years 1520–1527.*

His account of Lalibela's churches is pedestrian, rudimentary, and largely impersonal, but at a certain point an exhausted Álvares reveals what seems to be, to my ear, in that century of vast Portuguese colonization, a germ of European prejudice and its simultaneously rabid and mechanical dismissal of Africa's achievement:

> I weary of writing more about these buildings, because it seems to me that I shall not be believed if I write more, and because regarding what I have already written they may blame me for untruth, therefore I swear by God, in Whose power I am, that all I have written is the truth (to which nothing has been added), and there is much more than what I have written.

Father Álvares worries that "they"—his European audience—must naturally doubt him, a man of God, when he says that there exists a Christian place of such staggering feats of beauty outside known Christendom.

The phenomenon was too great to admit, this singular case in which beauty of form supersedes beauty of geometric reality. What is this immense beauty? The archaeologist Niall Finneran calls it a "nested, concentric perception of space." Nested space that is enough for us to formulate, as Bachelard put it, "dreams of the stone from which the principles of life are said to come." But then, in a turn that compounds and spins his denial into the absolute untruth at the heart of Eurocentrism, Álvares writes,

> They told me that all the work on these churches was done in twenty-four years, and that this is written, and that they were made by Gibetas, that is, white men, for they well know that they do not know how to do any well-executed work.

I surrendered myself to the ancient story, alert to the fresh air in the passage. Not a single *gibeta* on our path. When I asked Theo if the Italians did any "work" on the churches during their military occupation of the country in the 1930s, he told me that he had heard they'd inflicted, in the name of so-called preservation, a minor scourge of tar and red paint on some of the buildings, but that was in the 1950s. (According to a World Monuments Fund, or WMF, publication of 2017, the work was commissioned by the Ethiopian empress Zewditu, who hired a Greek architect.)

I don't remember seeing the tar, but what remained of the sinister red paint seemed a laceration left by Italy's imperial quest for Ethiopia, reaching back to the first war between the two nations, in 1895–96. (The Italians were defeated.) Other twentieth-century construction work on the cathedrals was carried out by the WMF, which erected protective awnings over five of Lalibela's churches.

I glimpsed the pale-rose summit of the largest cathedral, Biete Medhane Alem (House of the Redeemer of the World). Something echoed from my boyhood, a verse chanted at Nyabinghi—the fire ceremony of Rasta resistance: "And they shall be afraid and ashamed of Ethiopia their expectation, and of Egypt their glory." Fear and shame, and their eviler aspects, terror and humiliation, have been— sometimes with the aid of missionaries no less benign than Father Álvares—the lasting legacy of foreign encounters. The night had to pass for me to see clearer evidence of this in Lalibela. But for now, the glory was not in Egypt—which also waged war against Ethiopia, from 1874 to 1876—but in Lalibela, where I was about to walk into the living rock.

As we neared Biete Medhane Alem, a service was under way; the sounds of Ge'ez, the ancient Ethiopic liturgical language, resonated through the mighty stone pillars that greeted me before the structure itself—an auditory monument, the presence of numinous poetry, an intimation of the enormous space before me, undulating and wide. Time slowed, as it does in the opening phrase of Philip Glass's *Koyaanisqatsi*, and soon within the frame of my vision, as I turned a corner, I saw the praying people. Robed splendidly, mostly in white shawls, the supplicants shuttled through the rock passages, brushing the reddish stone with their palms, kissing it; some were huddled close into tall crevices, attenuated like cocoons, or fresco marks, which then would suddenly peel off and bore deeper into the secret caverns of this mystical edifice.

Angels, it was said, worked at night, perfecting what man did by day. I accepted the theory with the same measure of cool with which Theo recounted it, leading me up to the adobe-colored arched entrance. When I touched the rock, I felt below my palms the winged labor of opening the mountain into an abode for the spirit. I felt this not because of any religious conviction but through the poetic act, what Wallace Stevens called "an illumination of a surface, the movement of a self in the rock." My imagination bloomed sacred, but in

the form neither of the Coptic belief displayed around me nor of the Rastafarian faith I knew as a child, though the latter had prepared me to listen for myself in the rock.

The megalithic hum emanating from the facade of the cathedral was like the drone from a massive beehive: according to legend, "Lalibela"—the place so named for the monarch who established the web of churches, inspired by a Holy Land pilgrimage to create a New Jerusalem more than three centuries before Álvares's mission— means "the bees recognize his sovereignty." The recognition I felt was of this place as a singular, harmonious event. The worker angels like the worker bees, the devout working as they worshipped: all in accord, immutable as their belief in God and mine in the God caught in poetry.

Inside the sanctum of Biete Medhane Alem, the elaborate and the simple together fluently expressed the Orthodox theology: wherever there was intricacy, it was spare. Several small, cross-shaped windows, cut along niches, allowed shafts of early-evening sunlight to break the dark along the aisles and corridors. Crouched beneath some of these lights, loomed in filament, a few of the faithful read tiny, red-inked vellum Bibles.

Deeper in the interior of the cathedral, worshippers moved in procession to Ge'ez chants. A line of priests in gold-trimmed vestments, holding silver crosses, thronged by young acolytes, streamed through the congregation with holy water. All seemed permitted to move freely; the one law was that none but the holiest men could go into the sanctuary while it held the *tabot*, a replica of the Ark of the Covenant (similar sanctuaries, divided off by heavy drapes, existed in all the churches). The crowd followed the priests in a gravitational surge, stopping short of the entrance to the Holy of the Holies: there the chanting reached the pitch of keening; then the living hands of the ark returned, touching the inclined faces.

There were thick red carpets on the rock floor, through which the inexorable chill of stone, and the slight trill of voices, thrummed. My feet—I, like most others, wore only socks—moved in procession with the crowd. We were surrounded by icons of Christ (one in a large gilt frame surprisingly resembled a print of Warner Sallman's *Head of Christ*); some were mounted and others propped up on the floor. The procession often splintered as worshippers stopped to touch and kiss the portraits, an ancient ritual, unending as the church itself.

Years ago when I visited the Scrovegni Chapel in Padua, Italy, to see Giotto's famous fresco series, the barriers protecting the work felt like a deterrent not even the most pious could have surmounted. The rails, the imposed time limit, both reminders of the modern world, reduced the immediate experience of being in Giotto's time and with his work. Illusion, or any sacred wonder, was impossible; the church was just an expensive shell. But in Biete Medhane Alem, the accessibility of the art and artifacts allowed for a kind of human trust, which heightened the esoteric enchantment of Lalibela. In this simplicity was a magnificence.

Back outside, rain. Theo and I took shelter in an alcove of the Biete Golgotha Mikael, about a hundred yards from Biete Medhane Alem. We crouched and watched the rainwater, lavender pink over the reddish stone, run off into the drains, from where it would flow down to the pastures below. Centuries have not dissuaded the aqueducts from their purpose: protecting the site from floods. The rain was washing off the oil from hands and lips that touched and kissed the rock. It sounded like incessant voices striking against the stone. Nature purified. Nature made perfect. I felt blessed, a child in the rain, in this place, where, early in the thirteenth century, the Bee-King-Priest, Lalibela, humbled the stone.

I saw what they say is his tomb at the fulcrum of Biete Golgotha Mikael. Saints sculpted in lifelike reliefs on the walls chorused around him. From where Lalibela rests, he propels, and has for more than eight centuries, the life of this mountain slope that bears his name. Theo adjusted his immaculate white muslin over his head. I did the same with my indigo-blue Mali scarf, and followed as he led the way, through fine drizzle, toward the masterpiece, Biete Giyorgis, the Church of St. George.

Mountains were never my element, though I grew up under the shadow of the Blue Mountains in northeastern Jamaica. It was the sea for me, laid out like a billowing turquoise gown below Stony Hill, on which stood my grandmother's home in Port Antonio. Once famous for its tourism, Port Antonio is now splendidly antiquated, but the sea around it is divinity. For hours I would watch it rolling, from a flat rock at the side of my grandmother's yellow house.

Pirate ships—the town's European history began with pirates, before the state-sanctioned piracy of colonialism—brimmed the bay in my eyes. I was a solitary boy; Jim Hawkins was my idol. Those docked boats were really cruise liners, and the tourists they brought never stayed long, so the channel between the peninsulas below me was usually empty. I hovered above the open sea, my expanse of limitless blue, but never entered the water. Why? There is a contradiction to the serenity of the ocean: it is the crypt of the Middle Passage. I instinctively understood this pain before I heard any language about it, and every language I have heard since is insufficient. I understood the pain in a maternal way, for yearly during the hurricane season my grandmother—who more or less avoided looking at the sea—would fasten her eyes on it, morning until night, her face racked with sorrow and her lips trembling. She was nervous about her house—she had indeed seen the havoc of hurricanes—but to me she seemed to be keeping vigil for the voices of drowned slaves. The season passed, and she continued on with her old silence.

As Theo and I moved on past damp, stunted cairns along the roughly quarter-mile trek to Biete Giyorgis, the sea returned to me. There was no dissonance in this. The sea returns whenever I feel joy, in its terrible immensity. When we arrived at the high vista surrounded by juniper and olive trees where the church plunged like a waterfall down into the earth, the rain stopped. The cross set into the large square roof of the cathedral floated in the light. The inlays of engraved stone rippled. Such light! *Claritas!* After-rain light. It was a low-grade silver, transmuting into amber: the whole landscape was arrested. The waiting light, I wanted to call it. The light of ascension as I went down into Biete Giyorgis, alone, Theo settling himself in one of the arched alcoves surrounding the church.

In that rain-swept silence, I marveled at the roseate terra-cotta monument, spotted with lichens that resembled bee pollen, Lalibela's essence. The hulking structure embodied the mountain and at the same time emanated another. A silence opened within me: the astonishment at God's infinite power within the stone. Who has sculpted the sea into a place of worship? Imagine an undersea cathedral; imagine fording to the deep unknown to know the Unknown. This was the great triumph of Lalibela. The king of that name rendered, with an important shift of preposition, what Christ said to Peter: "Upon this rock I will build my church."

It was a superb grammar—the movement of a self in the rock—an experience Álvares never had. His journey as he tells it ends in a prodigious anticlimax. About Biete Giyorgis, he can only report, "The doors are very well worked outside." He then adds tersely, "I did not go inside, as it was locked." Lalibela himself also never stepped inside Biete Giyorgis. According to tradition, the masterpiece may be the king's memorial, constructed by his widow after his death. The great house uniting Lalibela with Saint George—Ethiopia's patron saint—was therefore an act of love. Faith moves mountains; love moves mountains to heaven.

The doors were wide open when I approached. No one else was in sight—or not quite no one. Five hundred years ago, I was told, a pilgrim to Lalibela from Armenia decided he would not return home.

(This decision is credible, given the power of the place.) He was still there, grayish-coral bones and all, preserved in one of the inset walls of the church, his feet pointing toward the doors.

The waiting light was there as I climbed the few steps to the doorway. I crossed the threshold into an ancient stillness. The interior was a mistier dark than in the other churches. Even so, I recognized immediately the aesthetic convention: the mixing of the simple and the elaborate finding a sublime pitch. The intensity of impression here was strongest, strangest. I felt I was standing in both the depth and the height of Noah's ark. I was afloat: the rock was standing water. Was I alone inside that preternatural dark, shadows swirling around me? In a corner of the entryway was a heavy coal-black cabinet with twines of beeswax candles and matches. I took and lit a candle—darkness made visible, as it were.

When I lifted the tapered flame, I saw the luminous ornaments of a tall central altar enclosed by brilliant red-and-blue curtains. Because I could not see where the curtains hung from above, they seemed without beginning, flowing down from space. There were paintings of Christ similar in theme to those inside Biete Medhane Alem, though of brighter tones. Then my eyes caught a painting of stunning beauty and horror such that I had not seen in the other churches. It was a portrait of Saint George slaying the dragon, and in an instant it consummated the splendor of the building.

The saint sits on his white horse, a red gold-hemmed cape glimmering over his shoulder. His left hand gently reins the horse, and in his raised right hand he holds the spear still thrust through the dragon's throat. A figure partially obscured by drapery—I could make out only a fold of his blue-violet tunic—lassos the dragon by the neck. The dragon's mouth is a V spitting out a glowing tongue. I advanced closer with the flame, a votive offering. Something came alive. A priest, lying down in a corner on the scarlet-carpeted steps, rose up; the candle flame ringed his eyes and caught the golden cross he held in his hand.

I looked to the painting, half expecting to see the horse without a rider or the mysterious tunic gone. Reflexively, I prostrated myself before the priest. He brought his cross down on my forehead with a subtle force and called my mind to another fire: the Nyabinghi nights at the shore in Jamaica.

I was a boy, chanting "Ithiopia Ithiopia Ithiopia" to thunderous drums. I was a little child, and my memories of those times are now partly fable. Certain faces in the crowd remain clear. Nighthawk's came clear to me now, his matted liana-length dreads, dusted with sand, and his voice tremendous when he bellowed, "Jah Rastafari!" I was not too young to understand that we were sufferers who had found it possible to see the future. I somehow knew Nighthawk was crying psychic deliverance.

Hours might have passed. It seemed centuries did in the pulse and flash of the flame. The priest lay back down again, motionless and mythical. I, anointed with tears that shone in the fire, continued on. But I could not bear to see any more.

Outside in the twilight the air was cool, fresh as if it were the first of morning. Theo was waiting. I asked if we could walk back to Sora Lodge and he agreed. He allowed me to be with my thoughts all along the hour's walk to the hotel. I sensed he knew the priest had consecrated the welcome he had given me by the boulder at the beginning of the journey. And for the rest of my visit, as if to honor that, Theo stayed mainly silent, like a spirit, by my side. The next morning when he came, unexpectedly, to wish me farewell over coffee on the veranda of the hotel restaurant—a driver who was a relative of his, with no English, had been arranged to drop me at the airport—he would again place his hand on my shoulder. His every word enacted a binding together, a prayer.

Returning through the half-dark village, I saw derelict homes perched near the macadam road, the people shimmering by. I felt like the diver in a poem by Robert Hayden who finds at the bottom of the sea a sunken ship full of human mementos—garments, instruments, shoes—and must now "somehow beg[i]n the / measured rise." The diver's disconsolate encounter is not mine. Yet the question of what happens to a man after surfacing from such a discovery *is* mine. In such a discovery, one has come close to what is irredeemable in the world above. The diver yearns to find those people whom he calls the "hidden ones"—the drowned, those who live in a liminal death, still in transit to some port. No funerary rites, no closure: they are the voices I believe my grandmother heard. And the horror in the word "somehow"—the most appalling word, the most precise word of the postcolonial condition—that *somehow* one must go on. The encounter in Biete Giyorgis, brief and surprising, fortified my spirit to go on.

The people in Lalibela were biblical in the night. I saw them at open doors and under the infrequent streetlamps, some gathered at roadside fires, always two or more together, their muslins like folded wings down their bodies. The sky was crammed with stars, and it was cold by the time I was at my door. By then I grasped the mystery of being here. It is the way art moves the memory, the instinctive memory, of the original fire.

Poetry, what I live in and for, brings memory into the stele of the heart, and fragments of it survive on the page. Lalibela: a momentary—eternal—return to the fire. Ethiopia: "Ithiopia Ithiopia Ithiopia," the inner call of my childhood that I chanted by the sea until hoarse, until dawn became amber ash, from which glowed the answer to Samson's riddle, "Out of the strong came forth sweetness."

The morning in Lalibela: the mountains and terraced hills revealed themselves muted malachite and brown. Abyssinian thrushes twittered in the eaves. Cow and goat noises came from the nearby yards. Cooking smoke went up from hearth fires that warmed the chill air. The breeze was fragrant with coffee beans, and from deep in the valley I heard the call of a farmer. A response from farther off came shortly and closed the distance between the two. Their voices died away, and the landscape reposed, as it always did.

There is often a slight melancholy to departure, if not outright melodrama. But what I felt that morning was the deepest, most sincere human pathos of all: nostalgia. Ethiopians call the condition *tizita*—defined as "the memory of loss and longing" by my friend the scholar Dagmawi Woubshet, who had given me refuge in his home in Addis Ababa. The memory of loss was what brought me to Lalibela. Some travels confirm the existence of a place. Some travels operate the other way around: a place, *somehow*, confirms your existence; arriving there crowns a survival to which no words can do sufficient justice.

Tizita is also a ballad in the Amharic songbook. Evenings in Addis Ababa, after roaming the city, Dag would play me versions of famous, and infamous, *tizitas*, the singer's voice loaded with pain in each. Without any intention to, as I listened I heard the open wound of transatlantic slavery, the broken link my elders tried to make whole. I say "heard," but I mean I *felt* the unfathomable "ominous silence" W. E. B. Du Bois detects in the slaves' sorrow songs. The closest Jamaican mode to *tizita* is dub music. Dub, in crude musical terms, is reggae stripped down to drum and bass and given broad range inside an echo chamber. Dub's reticence—of both lyrics and instrumentation—is broken by wails and what can sound like the quarry boom of waves on cliffs. Every aspect of this sound shatters slavery's strokes of amnesia. The music imagines, acts out, an inverse passage of slave ships on the cruel, beautiful sea. In it you hear the grotesque sounds in the hulls falling quietly away into ominous silence. A silence that is the sound of the sea at night by Grandmother's house.

At dusk in Addis Ababa I had carried *tizita* in my ears and dub in my heart out to Dag's garden. As I stood by the avocado trees, barely making out the faint illumination of the bougainvillea, the flamboyant hibiscus spilling over the concrete fence, worlds blurred: the continent had become my island.

Nostalgia haunted me on the road to the Lalibela airport. We drove cautiously past beautiful schoolchildren. They moved in a swirling crowd of excitement, fearless in the middle of the road. This was another image concomitant with home.

I had been simple like them, giddy with joy to see friends in the morning, to joke and to touch the hems of our khaki-and-blue school uniforms. The day of the first snow was a far fantasy. There was only today, and all I wanted was the sun, friends, and the gold of mangoes. I wanted to avoid the green, menacing cane always within view. The children on the road stared directly into my eyes, then away. There was a man departing, and nothing else.

Despite Lalibela's enormous geographic area, it has a sparse population—only seventeen thousand, comparable to my small hometown of Port Antonio. Tourism, because of the churches, is flourishing; tens of thousands of visitors come yearly. This has caused a minuscule uptick in population, bringing immigrants from the poor neighboring towns. In a close row at the roundabout of a main square, devoid of tourists, were the ramshackle stalls, each selling the same crafts: carved wooden crosses, embroidered shawls, and coffee cups with traditional effigies painted on them. Farther down the road, by two or three lookout points, under the scant shade of trees, children out of school uniform displayed the same crafts. The gift shop at the airport did the same, at a slightly higher cost.

In Port Antonio, tourism remains a major income generator. In Lalibela there is no hawking: only once did a teenage boy bearing a cluster of wooden crosses come up to the van window; he offered them shyly to me and then, after a brief moment, went back to his friends sitting on the stone gutter. The situation would have been different in Port Antonio: *all* the boys would have been at the window, for one. The nature of tourism in both places is very different, too. The sacred is a limited commodity. In Port Antonio, with the beaches and party scene, a vendor has more to offer.

To live at the economic mercy of tourism is to be in a barely benevolent prison. And this prison is home. We drove by the new townships, squatters' corners, standing out raw and exposed in the morning light, a kind of premonition of a harder future, one wherein poverty will breed violence. The traditional round huts of Ethiopia are disappearing, Theo had told me over coffee in the morning. Progress is a leveling evil. Hotels and pensions, in varying stages of development, are rising next to the nascent slums. The young are fearless, but I fear for them. I worry, could it ever be enough, what they are given at school? How will they escape the struggle that will inevitably come? The cane fields in Jamaica eventually swallowed most of my friends. How I was spared that fate is a marvel I still find difficult to comprehend. It does not matter. There was so much delight among the children in Lalibela, parting and closing back together when the van passed through their midst.

The bright receptionist of my hotel, a boy born below the nearby bluff of Asheton Maryam, hoped one day to run his own villa there. He told me a website would help. If this happens, if he operates a villa in his own town, the people will benefit directly. He saw a possible future. I asked him about going to school in Addis Ababa or America, but that was not his real interest. His dream, an act of great courage, was to remain at home, to journey nowhere else. His name was Ambachew—roughly, "protector."

I left him sitting behind the reception desk, reading to improve his English. Whenever he wished, he could get up and turn around to see the slate-colored crouching lion of his mountain home, beyond which I disappeared. His words were the last I heard before reaching the airport.

THE NOBLE FISH: DAKAR

■

IT WAS ON THE NIGHT BEFORE EID, THE MUSLIM CELEBRA-tion that breaks Ramadan's monthlong fast, that I arrived in Senegal in 2019.

The travel there had gone smoothly, apart from a layover in Amsterdam that an unexplained mechanical failure had turned into hours of delay. During the wait, the loud, crowded lounge thinned to the ghostly quiet of only a few passengers waiting for the flight to Dakar and the one other outbound plane. On the flight across the Atlantic from New York City, I had finished rereading Saidiya Hartman's *Lose Your Mother: A Journey Along the Atlantic Slave Route*. In the hush of the Amsterdam lounge, I flitted between the two other books I had packed: my high school copy of Ousmane Sembène's 1960 novel, *God's Bits of Wood*, and a crisp 2017 edition of *Phantom Africa* by Michel Leiris.

The latter, new to me, was the first English-language translation of Leiris's 1934 travel diary of the famous—that is, infamous—Mission Dakar-Djibouti, an ethnographic collecting expedition across sub-Saharan Africa. But the characters of Sembène's novel—Ramatoulaye, N'Deye Touti, Bakayoko, striking miners—were as familiar to me as my own family members. That I couldn't decide which book to stick with for the final flight (and I felt resolute on choosing one) was like being struck by some kind of latent superstition: whatever I chose could color my journey. At some point I took a picture of the covers of both on the gray lounge sofa and texted it to a friend, along with this message: "Stuck between a rock and a hard place!" He texted back no words but a photograph of Sembène standing in a blue suit, Dakar's cityscape behind him, his body leaning forward, his ever-present pipe stabbing the air. Blazoned in a white caption was the phrase: "I myself am the sun!" Putting Leiris away in my backpack, I chose the rock.

Nine hours later, half-starved and somewhat lightheaded, I was in Sembène's beloved Dakar, the city I've visited countless times in his books and films.

On the recommendation of a friend, I had booked a room at the Casa Mara Guest House in the Amitié district. The front desk was closed when I arrived from the airport, and the Casa Mara's watchman had to be roused to let me in. In halting but clear English, he apologized as he checked me in at a table by the side of the pool, in a courtyard lined with arabesque tiling. The short date palm tree in the middle of it, strung with lightbulbs, reminded me of a *riad* in Marrakech where I stayed years ago. The aquamarine light of the chlorinated water shimmered on the watchman's military-style uniform. The light also caught his dark, handsome face, which was round, with a kind expression. He said his name was Souleymane.

When I mentioned my hunger, he apologized again, for the hotel kitchen's being closed. I told him that was all right, I'd go on a walk to find food. The likelihood that any restaurants would be open at three in the morning seemed slim to nil, and Souleymane appeared doubtful. But he gave me directions out of the neighborhood and his cell phone number, pointing over the hotel's head-high fence to a tall concrete wall beyond it. He said I should follow that wall.

My optimism floundered as soon as I got to it. Not one but several dusty lanes adjoined the wall, each heavily marked with footsteps. The dust rose two or three inches off the ground with each step and was higher still where it was banked against the bottom of the wall. The wall itself, my measure of hope, curved out of sight. Did Souleymane say I should go north? *Nord, oui?* And I must follow the second lane on the right; no, the third lane by the wall, yes? Or the fourth. I remembered that he'd said only one lane by the wall. No, two. The many-forking paths stood empty in all directions. I could hear only occasional distant traffic and the bark of dogs. Well, if Amitié is the French for "friendship," then I should be fine, I told myself. I picked a lane and started walking.

The apartments in the Amitié district appeared either newly built or newly refurbished. Most were set behind high iron-trellis gates, bursting with bougainvillea. Concrete walls were fortified with the shards of broken bottle tops. In the moonlight and under the bright streetlamps, I noticed many brand-name SUVs and sedans, some parked in commercial lots but most on the sidewalks. Some teetered on the edge of open drains.

In half an hour of walking, I saw no one on the street. The clean night air was cool as if it were about to rain. Then suddenly a scent filled the air with nothing else but itself. It stopped me in my tracks with a jolt. My mind reeled: Where was it coming from? I started down one dusty lane; then I crossed right over to another. I turned back up that one and crossed left into another before switching to the right again. I walked down it for a moment before crossing to the lane on the left, as dusty as the others. After a few paces, I started to doubt myself. The scent pulled me back to the previous lane, which I decided was indeed the lane of promise.

When I was a boy, Africa meant many confounding and elusive things to me. I was often told that we black Jamaicans were from Africa—

"back to Africa" was a frequent reggae mantra on the local airwaves—but no one could say exactly *where* in Africa we were from; no one could confirm that, say, I was descended from the Ashanti tribe, or that the language of my ancestors was Yoruba. As I learned the names of African countries, I imagined belonging to each, never settling for one over another.

When my paternal grandmother was alive, she was my closest blood tie to these several, severed ancestral Africas, though she herself had never been beyond the Caribbean, and she espoused no Afrocentrism in my presence. Yet she called her *yabba* pot her "African pot." *Yabba*, a common Jamaican word for earthenware, derives from the language of the enslaved Ashanti peoples of Ghana. That my grandmother called it her African pot set it above question or ridicule: this water jar, broken at the rim and unusable, was indestructibly African. It was her ennoblement of this rather plain receptacle that added to my wonder and desire to encounter *that* Africa—the one across the ocean—in its solid, imperishable form.

But as Teju Cole has written, "You can't go to 'Africa,' fam." You go to a country in Africa, to one or another of the current fifty-four nation-states, and hope against hope to learn something about yourself. In a way, that's what Hartman's *Lose Your Mother* is about: going to Ghana and coming close to the personal toll of transatlantic slavery. While there, she wrote that she had "entered a dark zone of private grief." Being on the continent, in situ as it were, is a distinct encounter with a kind of ground zero of oneself. My trip to Senegal was, therefore, a necessity of self-knowledge. But self-knowledge not just for me. When I travel in Africa, I do so with the full awareness that I'm the first and only member of my family, dead or alive, to have done so. I travel with them, with my grandmother in my mind.

Yet there's another awareness that I travel with, a melancholy sense of belatedness. For someone descended from enslaved African people, it is always too late, centuries too late, to return; the fatal rupture of colonialism did its work on both sides of the Atlantic. Hangovers of that rupture persisted in Jamaica after independence: poverty, mainly, but a host of other sociopolitical obstacles that prevented me, a boy from a deeply rural part of Jamaica, from getting a passport in the 1990s. Family members had no clue how to navigate the bureaucracy, nor did the rural schools I attended. It was only after I moved from the countryside to Kingston in 2003 that I got my first passport. I used it for the first time three years later, when I was granted a student visa to study in the United States. With my student stipend I traveled around the Caribbean and went to Italy on a tight budget. But a trip to Ghana or Ethiopia was out of my reach until I left university and found real employment.

Before I could see it for myself, the only Africa I knew was Dakar and Thiès in Senegal, and Bamako in Mali, the principal settings of *God's Bits of Wood*. As a teenager reading Sembène, I had no reference for cityscapes, or for the 1940s, but there was much in the humanity of the Senegalese and Malian characters that I recognized. That solidarity gave me an Africa to "return" to, a template for my own heritage. Yet reading a novel written in French, whose characters spoke that colonial language along with their own native tongues of Wolof and Bambara, didn't clear up my confusion; they seemed somehow to lack the authenticity of my grandmother's pot, before I understood that a single, unbroken Africa had never existed.

The scent of grilling overpowered me, though what was cooking I couldn't tell. But by the time I reached its source, I felt I was back home in Jamaica, in one of the harsher parts of Kingston. Then I was transported to the flanks of the Old City in Jaipur, India. Wherever I was, I was worlds away from Amitié.

Down the last of many lanes, I came to a little shack standing alone at a three-way intersection. I could barely make it out in the dim lamplight, which also illuminated an open sewer, heaped with garbage. I wasn't at all sure whether the rickety structure, a lean-to of rusty rippled zinc built right into the median of a roundabout, was a cookshop or just a mirage produced by my hunger. Above it, improbably, was a large neon sign, part of its bulb either turned off or blown, casting blotchy shadows on the ground.

In front of the cookshop was a concrete pit about two feet high and two feet wide. I could see the faint glow of coals. Now, so close to the smell that maddened me, I felt calm. I recognized this instantaneous calm: it's knowing that a home-cooked meal is waiting for you, careless of the hour of your return. The longer the time away and the farther from home, the deeper the calm. Anticipation replaces the traveler's anxiety: you are the prodigal son, and whatever you're about to eat, big or small, will be a feast.

But then I noticed that the man next to the pit, wearing a smudged white apron over his dark, long-sleeved polo shirt, was washing up utensils on a scarred, linoleum-covered table. My heart sank.

"Asalama aleykum," I said.

"Malaykum salaam. Na nga def," he said.

"Manger du poisson?" I asked.

He smiled and looked down at the dying coals. He then said something at length in Wolof, Senegal's second official language. I followed his facial expression with a pained stare, certain he meant that I was out of luck.

"Seulement le français?" he asked.

"Un peu, pardon," I said, and in English, "I'm Jamaican."

"Jamaïquain!"

He put his arm over my shoulder and led me across the street and into a bar I hadn't noticed. The inside was dim; although a blue bulb burned above the liquor bottles behind the counter, the main source of light in the empty bar was a dull streetlamp standing outside the entrance. The man banged on the counter and called out. A woman entered from a side door, one hand rubbing the back of her neck. She was tall, at least a head taller than me or her partner, and dressed in a crinkly gold frock that matched her head wrap. A fold of the head wrap was undone and covered a side of her face. She said something sharp to him. He cut her off, waved toward me, and said something punctuated at many intervals with "Jamaïquain."

The lady in the gold frock regarded me. I almost said, as if to put myself above suspicion, "Yes, I'm *Jamaïquain.*" She tucked the fold into the plumed crown of her head wrap and lifted the bar flap to come around to us.

"Jamaïquain," she said. I couldn't read her tone. She grasped my palms in hers, and her eyes, very dark and lined thickly with black mascara, fixed mine. She began to speak in Wolof. In between each little break in her words, I said, "Yes" and "Oui." Her expression was serious but then grew lighter, even playful, as she spoke. Then, to my surprise, she said in English, "Welcome, welcome to here."

"Thank you. I'm glad to be here."

"Mohmmadu says you eat *lakk jën? Jën, poisson?*"

"Yes, *poisson s'il te plait!*"

"*Oui. Jën* for Wolof."

"Yes, *jën.*"

Still holding my hands, she turned to Mohmmadu. She said something rapidly to him, and then led me to an upturned white plastic bucket at the entrance of the bar and indicated I should sit.

"Mohmmadu make for you *jën. Thiof bu ñu làkk,*" she said.

She then lifted an index finger in warning. I knew she was being playful, but it was in a serious tone that she said, in English, "One *thiof* for you," and then other words in Wolof. I tried to understand her meaning, following her eyes and her finger as she spoke. I believe she was saying that she was making an exception for me by letting me have the last fish of the house, long after closing time. The gravitas of her generosity sated a deeper hunger in me.

I nodded and thanked her.

"*Jërëjëf.* Welcome for Wolof. *Jërëjëf,* you say," she said.

"Jërëjëf," I repeated. I didn't dwell on it, but I felt a strange charm in saying the word. "Waaw, jërëjëf," she said back. She welcomed me, I welcomed her. She left, the gold of her dress glittering briefly in the blue of the bar. Mohmmadu brought the dish to me, covered with a pink oval fly protector. The fly protector, at night when there were no flies about, made me smile. It was part of the presentation, an effort at hospitality I was familiar with from home. Food, especially food that's served to a guest or stranger, is almost always presented under one of these plastic bushels, ubiquitous in Jamaican homes, particularly in the countryside. It's a small gesture of care when a meal is covered, a gesture that never goes unnoticed.

As I took the cover off the plate, a gray cat slunk in from the shadows of a fence near the bar. It purred and sat on its haunches with an expectant stare. I could hear Mohmmadu and the woman (I never got her name) talking very low somewhere inside the bar. Besides their voices and the occasional purr of the cat, all else was hush and still.

Sitting on the upturned plastic bucket, I ate the best fish of my life.

The large *thiof,* a white grouper, was grilled crisp and covered with finely chopped chunks of tomato, red onions, peppers, and a green sauce. The *thiof,* I learned later, is referred to in Senegal as the noble fish. It's something of an expensive delicacy, eaten mostly on special occasions. But in the moment, I was simply overwhelmed with my luck at having such a generous-size fish in my lap. The smell—the scent of mingled spices, char, and hot oil that I'd followed through the night—made me a little dizzy.

Just before I began to eat, to my surprise, I found myself starting to whisper grace—something I'd hardly done since childhood. It wasn't the grace prayer I learned at my missionary primary school, thanking a supreme being for my daily bread, but words of no order that poured in an unbroken stream from my mouth. I realized that I was crying.

The unchanging water of the Caribbean Sea—that's the home I know. Yet when you've lived your life surrounded by it, you develop an abiding trust in what Derek Walcott calls the "subtle and submarine" changes of history. History's cold march reduces Jamaica to certain milestones: 1834, emancipation; 1962, independence. These dates, celebrated as national holidays on a grand scale, miss the unrecorded offstage changes that truly make history. History happens when one hand slips out of another in a cane field, never to be reunited. Nothing is preserved of such intimacy, of loss that nonetheless echoes across time. Where there is no instrument to measure such changes, it takes faith—the same abiding trust—to sight up that they have occurred and keep occurring. To "sight up" is a Rasta coinage that means to see, with a double vision, the "there" that's there, the hand that is lost to sight. It's the worldview I was raised with.

In a way, if I were to claim a single ideal itinerary for travel to Senegal, it would be by sea. Before this trip, I had never seen the sea from the coast of West Africa, save for a glimpse once on a brief trip to Lagos a year prior. Other than my sense of familiarity with Senegal from Sembène's work and other literature and films I had consumed, I didn't know any of the country's languages, much less its customs. But I knew that the sea around its coast constituted a leg of the Middle Passage. I knew millions survived the horror of that journey. I knew millions were thrown overboard the slave ships.

Out of the calamity of history, in my late thirties, I found myself with this fish on my lap. The *thiof* was from that sea. The fish was dead, I knew. It had been changed by seasoning and cooking. But beneath its spices, there was the immemorial tang of the Atlantic.

What tenacity had brought me here? I had arrived at nothing

short of a missing link, present since my childhood but out of reach. Far more than the privilege of my adult work, it was my childhood that brought me to Senegal. My childhood has been my first and last impetus of travel, to experience what lived on its edges: that as-yet-imaginary Africa.

Sentimental or romantic as it may be, there's a faith I'm unwilling to concede that in eating a fish from the same terrible sea my ancestors endured or perished in, I was in spirit with them. By being here, I thought, I'm there. I accept the dire fallacy inherent in such thinking, atavistic and fatalistic without any weight on the scale of justice. A plate of fish won't assuage history's pain. But I sight up a fact that's beyond the cold statistics of death and survival. Where no traces exist to point me to my African origin, this fish was a homecoming, and, in that sense, a joy.

The cat circled my feet and purred louder. It had to wait, for I took my time filleting one side, flipping to the other side, and filleting that, and only after I'd eaten the flesh and licked clean each bone did I place them on the ground in front of the cat. Then, at last, the fish head. I sucked out its eyes and the juices between the gills. I sucked out the strips of meat in the groove of the skull, from the mouth to the back of the neck hacked off the spine. I licked all of that clean until there was nothing but a milky white skull in my fingers. Satisfied, I put that, too, in front of the cat. It immediately went to work.

Finished, I brought my plate to the counter of the bar and called out. The voices within, without my noticing, had fallen silent. There was no response after a second call. I called again, and again nothing. As I was about to call a fourth time, I decided not to. Who could know, I might be disturbing precious sleep. Setting the plate down, I took from my pocket a thick coil of bills of West African francs I had gotten in Amsterdam, put them under the plate on the counter, and stepped back onto the road.

I crossed the broken asphalt around the lean-to and stepped back into the dust of the lanes. So many lanes! And which would lead to my hotel? My own footprints were indistinguishable among the countless others in the dust. I was still alone in the silent streets. The sky was the same moon-washed dark as when I first set out an hour ago, but I could feel the dawn very close. I chose a lane at random and started to walk down it, making believe as I did that I was reprinting my earlier steps. Though aboveground, I felt all subtle and submarine.

Soon enough, I saw in the near distance the long, curving wall of Amitié. When I reached it, I noticed for the first time how much the banked dust at the base of the wall resembled wavelets, moving in near-perfect symmetry. After another twenty minutes of walking, I saw the high iron-trestle gate of the Casa Mara. I quickened my pace toward it, but as I drew closer, I heard a mewling sound behind me. I turned and saw the cat following me, the gnawed fish head in its mouth.

PRAISE SINGER:
ON AKINBODE AKINBIYI

THAT THE SEA MAKES US THINK OF ETERNITY IS COMMON-
place. Photographs of the sea arrest and at the same time transfigure
that commonplace, when successful. Such photographs are a kind of
ecstasy. They are what Henri Cartier-Bresson said photography "could

Akinbode Akinbiyi, *Bar Beach, Victoria Island, Lagos*, 1999, from the series *Sea
Never Dry*; courtesy of the artist

reach": "eternity through the moment." Cartier-Bresson made this comment in 1932 upon seeing an image of frothing waves taken in 1930 by the Hungarian photographer Martin Munkácsi at Lake Tanganyika in Liberia. Something else besides the crystalline burst of the surf shook Cartier-Bresson into his epiphany: Munkácsi's photograph depicts three black boys rushing into the ripples, their backs toward us. Naked as their bodies is their elation, which marked Cartier-Bresson and, subsequently, marked the history of photography. Such is history. Black bodies, speculated upon, revivify what time and convention have frozen. In the case of photography, the camera brings the natural life of time back into what is thought of as timeless. The meeting of black bodies with crashing waters in Munkácsi's

Akinbode Akinbiyi, *Bar Beach, Victoria Island, Lagos*, 1999, from the series *Sea Never Dry*; courtesy of the artist

photograph sees what might have remained a commonplace eternity transformed into Cartier-Bresson's suggestion of a moment's eternity, the far reach of which is the sublime.

I can see—and I can "hear"—the elation of these long-ago boys in Akinbode Akinbiyi's series *Sea Never Dry* (1982–present). No bodies rush toward the sea in Akinbiyi's photographs taken at Bar Beach in Lagos, Nigeria, yet their elation is there, embedded via different registers of photographic technique: light, shadows, angles. And it is there, too—even more vigorously—in the ways Akinbiyi captures black bodies on the move. Digressive yet determined, the artist's bodies are always in stride; stride, in fact, is the Akinbiyi visual masterstroke (he, too, is a great walker). Each step reminds us of a compass, parting and measuring the world, or worlds, for we sense in the enunciative clarity of his photographs that these bodies, striding in their routine going about, inhabit two or more realms at once. We can't say how, because Akinbiyi's images refuse direct illustration; scenes of praying and makeshift altars in the sand, though powerful, are few. This refusal magnifies a certain sense of the numinous as inseparable from the everyday. The numinous is the sea, that visible spirit of place present in all of Akinbiyi's images even when not shown, or when shown only in fade-outs.

Though the sea never fades out. It is ruminative and everywhere. It is repeated by the bodies, both in their dress—mostly surplices, white-gray like the breakers—and more significantly, the sea is repeated in the bodies' intentness on elsewhere. Even when a figure stands still, he or she appears wavelike. There is always a slight tilt, a fugitive gesture breaking straight lines. We see a hand raised or another motioning; here a head turns aslant, there another bows, acknowledging something outside our view.

One magnificent photograph, *Bar Beach, Victoria Island, Lagos* (1999), depicts a crowd along the long shoreline in a panoramic orchestration of these fugitive tilts: our eyes begin in the foreground,

Akinbode Akinbiyi, *Bar Beach, Victoria Island, Lagos*, 1999, from the series *Sea Never Dry*; courtesy of the artist

where two men stand, one in his resplendent white agbada (robe) and the other dressed more modestly in a white shirt. We then follow the ragged fluidity of bodies in the middle ground, bodies crouching, sitting, bending, and striding. We convene in the far end of the image where two high-rises can be seen, poised slightly rakishly and yet elegantly like the men at the beginning. The high-rises strike a note of indistinct translucency. They appear as clear as they are blurred, charged with an evanescence that asks us to wonder whether they are foreboding or benign. Are they hotels or apartments? Is trouble passing them by, or are they occasioning it? It is hard to say, and therein is the true tension of this photograph and others of the series: a downbeat of ambivalence, a conditional tense, that comes through because of Akinbiyi's harmonic eye.

Akinbode Akinbiyi, *Six Songs, Swirling Gracefully in the Taut Air*, installation view, February 7 to May 17, 2020, Gropius Bau, Berlin. Photograph: Muhammad Salah

Ambivalence is not neutrality. Translucency is not transparency. It is a wisdom of seeing less the eternity through the moment and more the impossible "could" inherent in creating such a moment. Akinbiyi took these photographs, starting in the 1980s, under incredible stress. The heat. The crowd. Imagine the glare, the sweat. The sea relentless with wind. We can imagine other beach noises—of vendors, from stereos and stray animals. We can imagine, too, tempers flared, some directed at a photographer like Akinbiyi with his bulky medium-format analog camera. Yes, Akinbiyi was a black body and Nigerian photographing other black bodies and Nigerians, which meant, contrary to popular belief, he could never have been surreptitious or hidden. Over the decades of photographing Bar Beach, he would have had to be as exposed and vulnerable to his subjects as they were to him. His patience must have been tested. Yet only an immense patience could see and capture in the *Sea Never Dry* series—in which, with two exceptions, we see only lone figures—the most intimate impossibility of all: quietude.

By quietude I mean what the German theologian Albrecht Schönherr said when his friend and professor the great Dietrich Bonhoeffer led seminary meetings on meditation: that "a unifying arch swung from music and play to quietude and prayer." Quietude, then, is a subtle pendulum of elation. It is an emotion of closeness not often allowed the black body. Seeing it in Akinbiyi's photographs—and here, again, I mean "hearing"—swung me back to my childhood in Port Antonio, a small coastal city in eastern Jamaica. Every weekend the beaches were a frenzy of bodies. The air thrummed with waves, music, and voices. And yet what I recall, by way of recognition in Akinbiyi's photographs, is a suspended stillness in the midst of all that joy making.

Such quietude was not melancholy; it did not counter the weekend's joy making. Rather, it anchored something unanticipated and inexpressible to most outsiders' gaze: survival. Not just surviving the Middle Passage and all the atrocities that came after but, most profoundly, how those bodies I was raised with and by bore a collective remaking of losses. The levity of those beach gatherings—so common to the Caribbean, not just on weekends—was weighted by quietude, so each instance felt like a ceremony of remembrance. I have seen that quietude distilled in photographs of vodoun ceremonies in Haiti, which is only 447 kilometers northeast of Port Antonio, shot by Sokari Ekine, Akinbiyi's Nigerian-born contemporary and a self-described modern nomad. Her photographs accurately document vodoun rituals, their intensity of drumming, singing, dancing, and possession. As such, hers are powerfully dramatic images, but what brings us closest into the invisible spirit of place and its survival is the intimacy Ekine quietly cultivates of black bodies, simultaneously at home and intent on elsewhere.

Akinbiyi seizes quietude as his unifying technique in *Sea Never Dry*. This impossibility, picked up from trawling over countless traces of human movements, becomes his indecisive decisiveness used to still their ineffable moments. With furious devotion—which is what quietude amounts to—Akinbiyi holds perpetual transience before it disappears, forever, into the soundless archive of the sand. Indeed, the supreme depiction of quietude *is* the sand, visible in its stark lucidity in all his photographs. There it is, grand and roughly hallowed by footprints or otherwise glimpsed in tiny slashes between bodies on a crowded beach day. We read the sand. Imprinted on it is the flotsam of modern life—slippers, plastic bottles, and tin cans—echoing, without irony, the makeshift altar of plastic jugs, white candles, and calabash gourds laid in front of a woman prostrated toward the sea. These juxtapositions—alterity objects and a religious devotee's relics

Akinbode Akinbiyi, *Six Songs, Swirling Gracefully in the Taut Air*, installation view, February 7 to May 17, 2020, Gropius Bau, Berlin. Photograph: Muhammad Salah

casually installed—communicate not so much the difference between the sacred and the profane as the fine line between past and fate. That between the one and the other exists a speck—a single, multitudinous grain of sand—building into a granular database of changing-but-ever-present human experiences. All of this Akinbiyi, with his camera, makes into immutable memory.

Beyond that, Akinbiyi's genius is for photographing, with a loving radiance, the conditional. He shows us the "what could" of things seen. These pictures reveal to us journeys of myriad hope and futility to come. Bodies will be gone, too, like the joy of rushing toward the sea, but, as in Akinbiyi's photographic immersion, they'll leave behind more than a single footprint melting into the wet sand. A single footprint is a kind of Crusoe-like mythmaking, a solitude nearing isolationism over which Akinbiyi triumphs. He works his way into the crowd so he can deepen the substance and spirit of a place and its people and, in so doing, arrives at artistic glory. Akinbiyi's images "sing / tongue-tied without name or audience," as the great Nigerian poet Christopher Okigbo once wrote, "making harmony among the branches." Akinbiyi lifts his camera in praise of the sand, the sea, and above all the solitary selves that people his vision.

SPLASH CROWNS:
ON DONALD RODNEY

THE SHIPS NEVER CEASE COMING. THEY COME THROUGH oblivion, the Atlantic's death clinic, to his Homerton Hospital bed. He sees them, in stark revulsion, contemporaneous with the pain that will become his own death. They haunt him to bear the brutal burden of witness.

When he sees the ships this time, he draws in his sketchbook two drips of blood suspended in the air. Where they fall, a concentric abyss rings out. In the middle echoes a coronet, the splash crown. There the ships plunge, soundlessly disappearing—condensed, but not gone, into a circular delirium that is no less the terror, as Borges once put it, "that someone else was dreaming him." The someone else, in this instance, is the artist himself, Donald Rodney (1961–1998).

Prior to, or after, one of his numerous surgeries, Rodney writes,

I was in hospital again and during the injection of Maximum dose pethidine to kill the pain I drifted off to a landscape Night-mare. I flo[a]ted above everything [on] a sea of glass on which

sailed a boat filled with slaves but somehow we were connected
by blood and bone and flesh and storms raged.

Rodney's art enacts a powerful form of inner witnessing of the
original crime of transatlantic slavery. The splash crown, drawn with
sensuous and volatile lines over many pages, alters slightly, circles what
his ancestors endured. Through it he grasps a finite view of their in-
finite pain.

Much of Rodney's brief life was spent in hospitals. A hospital,
for him, was a veritable slave ship, looming from the past to the pres-
ent, intensifying his physical and psychological torment each time
he underwent surgery. He died in one in 1998, at age thirty-six.
The cause of death was sickle-cell anemia, what he called his "BLK

splash

BLOOD DISEASE." Why, at this particular moment of agony—an operation—the vision of the slave ship, that particular oceanic pain, blurs? Inexorably, blood.

Rodney's nightmare is a mirror. The phantasmagoria of history is there as an active presence, bound to the future by blood. In his words, "somehow we were connected by blood," the "somehow" has a sincere, healing tone. This sincerity, however, is not due to nostalgia or any other narcissistic impulse; the force of the recognition of his connection is an infraction of both time and consciousness. Yet "somehow"—somehow—redeems the tragic fate of the descendants of slaves, those who are doomed to live as victims and posthumous witnesses to slavery's prevailing injustices. The blood recognition converts doom to defiance. It conducts the wrestling with history out-

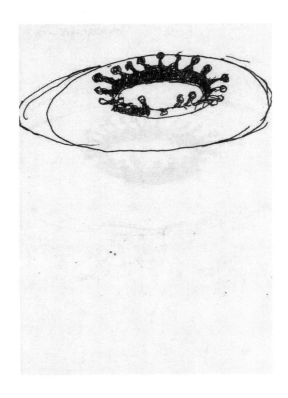

side the metaphysical prison of history and within oneself, where the struggle is most radical and most transformative. Such autonomy, the autonomy of one's body, is a politics that refuses vengeance or atavistic revenge. It is a politics that rejects purification and embraces, while it also confronts, being contaminated and the right to vigilant, explicit protest. It aims to amplify what approves life and is life's sole authority: one's blood, which cannot be refuted, neither by death nor by any other oblivion.

The result is an art of strange grace. And Rodney's splash crown series creates, in situ, a special, fluid vernacular of resistance. Resistance begins with blood.

All his work meditates on that authority of blood. Each functions as a personal documentary that questions the imperial pathol-

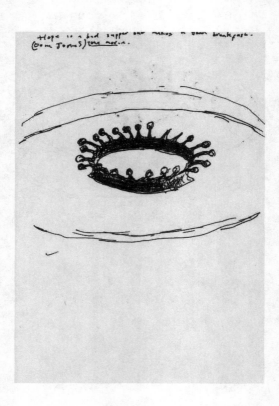

ogy, inherited—like the doctrine of original sin itself—at birth, even before he was born. The documentary moves within the scope of fable, however, and does not depend on an aesthetic of pathology. It strikes an imaginative resonance, transfiguring the appalling postcolonial body politic as he experienced it in his lifetime in England. Those were the Margaret Thatcher and the Enoch Powell years. The Thames, not the Tiber, was foaming with much blood.

But England was, and is always, royal England. There "no bloodless myth will hold," in the voice of one of its poets, though the sovereign crown represents—through inaction and silence—slavery as a fallacy of mythology. Rodney's splash crown, in turn, signifies and reminds us that slavery is monarchical, far from mythological. Atrocity flows directly from the divine head. In plain ink, his splash

crown revolts against his sovereign's violence of abstraction. By rendering visible the dark innocence pervading the crown—at times with texts, like this one—the violence becomes at once surreal and concrete:

> *this is a splash*
> *a splash of blood*
> *beauty and the beast sleeping beauty pricked her*
> *finger on a needle the blood falls to the floor*
> *and splashes as a crown for a princess*

The fable's gravitational cadence emphasizes imperial menace. Bloodlust. Other texts by Rodney convey savage mockery and indignation: "a crown of thorns"; "a nigger splash." Their effect—and

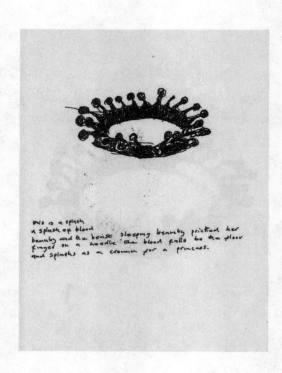

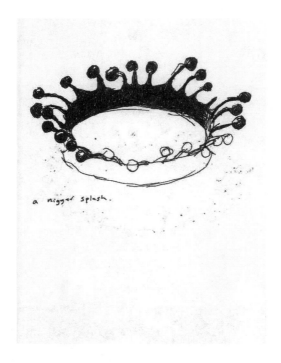

a nigger splash.

the splash crown's total visual effect—further cracks the mirror of colonial disillusionment to insist on healing. Healing: that is the lasting dignity of Rodney's splash crown, created from his hospital bed and venerating the real provenance of blood—that which survives the aftermath of surgery and slavery, and that grows, irrepressibly, without end, across the black Atlantic.

BOTTLE TORCHES:
A FANTASIA ON NARI WARD

Detail from Nari Ward, *Savior*, 1996. Shopping cart, plastic garbage bags, cloth, bottles, metal fence, earth, wheel, mirror, chair, and clocks. 128 × 36 × 23 in. (325.1 × 91.4 × 58.4 cm). Installation view, Nari Ward: *Re-Presence*, Nerman Museum of Contemporary Art, Johnson County Community College, Overland Park, Kansas, 2010

UNTOLD (2013)

At the first sign of dusk, kerosene oil is poured into the soda bottles, right up to the rim of their slim necks. The bottles are then stuffed tightly with newspaper, with the long "tail" of each paper, twisted and curled at the tip like the small intestine of the stomach, floating halfway to the bottom of each. The short "head" of the paper, the wick, is pinched into a triangular shape and then flattened. Later, just before lighting, the wick will be re-pinched into the triangular shape. Once all the bottles are filled, they are leaned upside down in rows against one side of the house or around a big rock or on the trunk of the ackee tree or in between the ackee tree's raised roots, where they resemble strange bulbous growths. As the kerosene secretly soaks into the newspaper, the men wait for darkness.

It is during this time of waiting, the dusk darkening fast, that these red, green, blue, and orange Coca-Cola and 7UP and Pepsi and Fanta bottles begin to glisten dimly like the flux of a burnished river. The men, deep in conversation, making bad jokes and teasing each other, don't see this phenomenon. But one among them happens to catch a glimpse of these faint colors moving in the dark and is suddenly filled with a nameless sadness. For somehow, the looker sees enslaved ancestors in the glimmer. Centuries ago, these ancestors lived and died on this same plot of land, which—except for the house, the big rock, and the ackee tree—remains the same, full of sugarcane fields and swamps. They dreamed of escape. They set ablaze the sugarcane fields, then fled to the swamps.

Yet they would later return to the land, the land synonymous with sugarcane. For most, there was no escaping the sugarcane. It reasserted itself many times over in the unending cycle of conflagration and return. In between recurrences of this dream—the dream that was the perpetual fight for freedom, the setting ablaze of plantations, the fleeing to the swamps—the living and dying continued to live and die where the sugarcane grew.

Somehow—the word has a shiver of terror in it—as dusk becomes night, the looker sees in the bottle torches the unfinished dream of freedom. The rivulet of colors pauses momentarily, disappears in the blink of an eye. Then, with a near-divine rage, the looker grabs a bottle from the big rock.

The action is like a signal. The waiting is over. The bottles are taken up and shaken vigorously. The wicks on top are squeezed again into triangular shapes. A lit match is put to one, then another, and another, and another. After brief sputters, wavery flames dance steadily on the torches. There's laughter.

"Ready?"

"Ready."

Swiftly the flames begin to cut into the dark to the swamp.

Nari Ward, *Hunger Cradle*, 1993. Yarn, rope, and found materials. Dimensions variable. Installation view, *Nari Ward: We the People*, New Museum, New York, 2019

HUNGER CRADLE (1993)

I wonder if Nari Ward, the installation artist known for his fantastical sculptural assemblages of found objects, who was born in 1963 in Jamaica, knows the scene I've described above. Being that he was a city kid, a Kingstonian, before immigrating to Harlem at age twelve, it might not be so familiar to him. But the scene was a touchstone of every rainy season in the Jamaican countryside and a recurring part of my own childhood in St. Thomas, the easternmost parish on the coastline of Jamaica. The ritual of the bottle torch, which still happens, is a peculiar kind of fugitiveness. It makes me think of the layers of fugitiveness in Ward's work, its engagement with various forms of black selfhood.

Indeed, Ward's work takes a "fugitive approach," in the words of his beloved friend the great Nigerian curator Okwui Enwezor. Enwezor was referring here to the "abstract" or elusive conceptual frame of Ward's work rather than the historical premise of the black quest for freedom that is also central to the work; the sculptures take a fugitive approach because they address the great burden of history sidelong, honoring its essential paradoxes. Both physically and figuratively, Ward's work conjures and grounds itself in the black quest for freedom.

In its original meaning, the word "fugitive" refers to someone who commits a crime and hides from justice. The paradox, in the context of African enslavement in the United States, is that a fugitive is someone whose crime is escaping and hiding from injustice: a paradox premised on the fact that enslaved people of African descent were not full, legal human beings. The notorious three-fifths clause of the U.S. Constitution enshrined this into law in 1787, paving the way for the Fugitive Slave Act of 1850, which required citizens to return escaped blacks to enslavement. In effect, the enslaved were taken back to the injustice they tried to escape. This practice continued until the repeal of the Fugitive Slave Act fourteen years later, in 1864.

The fugitive approach of Ward's work indirectly complicates and does justice to this heritage. Ward's painstaking process of salvaging objects that have escaped our human containment and reimagining them in ways that disturb our affective capacity reflects an ethos of private and civic rebellion.

Hunger Cradle is one such disturbing installation. I saw it in the spring of 2019 at the New Museum in New York, suspended from the ceiling like a seemingly endless galaxy: a vast, roughly undulating net above the viewer's head. You enter it through a cavernous, womb-like doorway: this kind of entranceway is a trope in Ward's work, at once inviting and foreboding.

Once inside the cradle, you can barely make out the random distribution of car parts, mirrors, PVC and metal pipes, porcelain bathroom sinks, wicker birdcages, soccer balls, wooden doors, baby cradles—perhaps the installation's namesake—tools, antique chairs, the lid of a grand piano, and, even more improbable, a very large refrigerator bulging against the net. These are the material fetishes of failed utopias. Standing under the web, you feel the weight of majesty, mutilated and turned into trifle. The frail yarn, intersecting at points to form weird star patterns, signifies the tension and entropy of material progress, much of it eked out of forced and unacknowledged black labor. The netting is the last defense against total collapse: it forms a porous bulwark against the disparity between hunger and consumption, set forth by a morally bankrupt history. It forms a kind of refuge. A skein. A skein of blackness.

This skein of blackness is identical to Fred Moten's definition of blackness: "the extended movement of a specific upheaval, an ongoing irruption that anarranges every line . . . a strain that pressures the assumption of the equivalence of personhood and subjectivity." This skein of blackness is a fugitive tilt. The tensile strength of the yarn is great because it is a mix of pliable polyacrylic and sturdy wool, which figuratively fuses the black fugitive past with the fugitive present that Ward "anarranges" into a huge, breathable tarpaulin.

This opaque breathing space shields you from the colossal wreck of empire.

I use the word "shields" to stress the overriding effect of the work's protective gesture from Ozymandian decay. But for a work that is so tender, the word "shields" risks feeling militaristic; aggression is not part of the texture of this "hunger cradle." What you experience moving under the billowing mass is something far more archaic and vulnerable. A spider's web with the strength of an ark, suspended in the air.

SAVIOR (1996)

I used to not think about the sugarcane countryside of my child-hood in St. Thomas. I preferred thinking about Portland, just north of St. Thomas: the other place I grew up. Portland is a place of ex-quisite beaches; in my mind, it is always blue and turquoise, whereas St. Thomas is green. A green edged with silver, the color of the sugarcane. As a boy, I feared walking past that green, even in broad daylight. But I feared walking through the crammed housing areas of the former slave barracks standing next to the green cane even more. These rusty board-and-corrugated-metal shacks, some on stilts, seemed to be toppling down on each other, perennially drunk. But I loved repeating the names of these former barracks, so much that they became a kind of gnomic chant I recited when doing errands or chores at home:

Duckenfield, Bellrock Lane,
Jane Ash Corner, Golden Grove,
Lyssons, Peacock Hill.

Only years later did I really start to wonder how such beautiful names could contain such deep sorrow and sadness, a sadness I must have felt when I skirted along the barrack roads and glimpsed the shacks in bright sunlight, seemingly dwarfed by the everlasting green cane.

Green, green, green, green, green.

But the green also concealed an old resilience that is not visible when looking at the landscape: that of maroonage. I'm connected to it by blood, on my mother's side. "Maroon" derives from *cimarrón*, the Latin American Spanish word for "feral animal," which by the seventeenth century had become the common word for a fugitive or a runaway enslaved person. Starting in 1655, when the British seized Jamaica from the Spanish, the captured Africans trafficked to the island fled the plantations into the mountains. In this rugged terrain—another kind of green, dense but subtler than the cane—these Maroons formed free communities. Though self-reliant in the mountains, the Maroons raided plantations, retrieving livestock and agricultural tools for their communities. They brought back other enslaved Africans to live free (technically as fugitives according to colonial law) among the trees and the rivers of the hills. They set plantations on fire. This led one of the foremost maroonage historians, Carey Robinson, to give them the infamous sobriquet "Iron Thorn." In many senses, from the economic to the psychic, the Maroons were the biblical thorns in the side of the British Empire. Their eighty-odd years of fierce guerrilla warfare with the British—in which they defeated the British militia many times—seriously stymied the sugar industry on the island.

The war ended through skulduggery when the Maroons signed two peace treaties with the British by 1740. While the Maroons forced the British Empire to acknowledge Maroon sovereignty, they were made to do so in a manner that upheld chattel slavery, underscoring the impossibility of universal black freedom. The treaties state that "all hostilities shall cease on both sides for ever" as long as the Maroons return fugitive slaves to the plantations and stick to the land ("the amount of fifteen hundred acres," according to the first treaty) designated by the British. The final article of one treaty, which gave the British governor of Jamaica the eventual right to appoint leadership over the Maroons, definitively signaled their lost sovereignty to the British.

The resilience and ingenuity of Maroon culture are nowhere more spiritually present than in the *abeng*, a symbol at the center of Maroon life to this day. Carried by Maroon leaders, the *abeng* is a hollowed-out ram's horn with a small hole at the narrow tip. In shape and design, it resembles the smaller Jewish shofar. Like the shofar, it is ceremonial

Nari Ward, *Savior*, 1996. Shopping cart, plastic garbage bags, cloth, bottles, metal fence, earth, wheel, mirror, chair, and clocks. 128 × 36 × 23 in. (325.1 × 91.4 × 58.4 cm). Installation view, *Nari Ward: Re-Presence*, Nerman Museum of Contemporary Art, Johnson County Community College, Overland Park, Kansas, 2010

and sacred. And as with the shofar, its shrill sound travels for miles, ringing the alarm of terror for the sake of redemption:

> Blow ye the shofar in Zion, and sound an alarm in my holy mountain; let all the inhabitants of the earth tremble for the day of the LORD comes, for it is nigh at hand.
>
> (JOEL 2:1)

When I first saw Ward's sculpture *Savior* in the same exhibition at the New Museum, I heard the *abeng*. I heard it in the sculpture's large horn shape. Constructed from a shopping cart, wrapped with black and red plastic garbage bags and studded with bits of mirror, cloth, metal fence, clock, bottles, and dirt, *Savior* resembles a behemoth that has walked through fire: a goatlike sacrificial animal crowned with a small chair. The sculpture is like a lookout peak of a mountain in St. Thomas, a spot in which a camouflaged Maroon might wait for the ultimate redeemer. I heard the *abeng*, blown not by a great Maroon warrior like Cudjoe or an elusive leader like Nanny but by a boy. I hear the *abeng*, its outlawed dialect, and look up.

I look down, and nothing is green.

> A day of darkness and of gloominess, a day of clouds and of thick darkness, as the morning spread upon the mountains: a great people and a strong; there hath not been ever the like, neither shall be any more after it, *even* to the years of many generations.
>
> (JOEL 2:2)

TROPHY (1993)

What are you looking for?

The soda bottle torches flit through the swamp, low and slow. What are they looking for? Hushed, incessant voices rise as if from the mud.

"Got one, got one."

"Same, same."

"Plenty more this side."

The torches move in broken unison toward the voice.

What are you looking for?

It is May, crab hunting season, and the men are hunting land crabs in the swamp at Holland Bay, St. Thomas. Holland Bay—one more haunting Anglo-Saxon name!—has a long coastline thick with mangrove and windblown palm trees. Holland Bay used to be part of Holland Estate, one of the most profitable sugarcane plantations in the New World, owned by one of Jamaica's wealthiest sugar planters, Simon Taylor. Green swamp has now engulfed the estate and subsumed the plantation. Its vanishing makes the mud, in the wet season, an uncommonly fertile breeding place for crabs. The flames of the torches highlight the pale blue shells of the crabs as they try to scuttle back, in the thousands, to holes in the muddy ground. But a hand, quick and dexterous, often catches several at a time and puts them in sugar bags.

Consider the sugar bags.

Called crocus bags in Jamaica, they are burlap sacks woven mostly from Indian jute. The enslaved people, like the ones who lived and died on Holland Estate, filled millions of these bags with sugar. The bags were then shipped to markets in every crevice and corner of Europe.

What are you looking for?

When the Maroons raided the plantations, crocus bags were one of the staple items they brought back to their mountain communities. Almost every aspect of Maroon life (consider the *abeng*) was touched by these crocus bags. They were repurposed as clothing, as gunpowder satchels, as bedding, as carriers for the *abeng*, as tinder wrapped around the ends of sticks to light aflame and hurl at the plantations.

What are you looking for?

The sugarcane burned. The green burned. The boiling house burned. The curing house burned. The great house burned. The barracks burned. The spectacular banality of avarice burned. All those souvenirs of suffering, candied into molten fire.

Thinking of that burning, I remember the conflagrations I used to see as a boy, when the green canes were lit and left to burn overnight before harvesting began in the morning. I remember those flames in the dark. In my memory, they resemble the thin gelatinous glaze of Tropical Fantasy soda Ward poured on a baby stroller and left to harden with garbage bags, old clothes, plants, and other found objects, in a sculpture called, with striking irony, *Trophy*.

It is a nightmare vomit, a mutant of imperial creation. Do you see?

IRON HEAVENS (1995)

The torches, burning at the low ebb of predawn darkness, echo the stars melting like crushed ice in the sky.

I hear a conflagration, not of fire, but of wings, myriad wings unfolding like those of bats, or those of angels, whether ascending or descending it is impossible to tell, neither does it matter, for what I hear in these wings is an exultation that makes of the human, angel, and of the angel, human: such are the multitudinous wings rattling louder because charred. They clatter with joy, a joy eclipsing suffering and anything else that might corrupt the immense, apocalyptic upheaval of laughter in the swamp.

The wings are the same as the men's hands, sinking deep into the mud to catch crabs. The wings are the same as the hands that sank deep to pick the cotton and sank deep to cut the cane with the same devotion, though not with the same fury. They are filling the crocus bags with crabs. They do so with an intimacy that comes from the authentic faith in the work of the hands of humans or angels. They reach deep down into the mud. It could be that they are reaching into the sky, opening a portal.

Nari Ward, *Trophy*, 1993. Baby stroller, found objects, sugar, Tropical Fantasy soda, car battery. 65 × 55 × 31 in. (165 × 138 × 79 cm). Installation view, *Nari Ward: We the People*, New Museum, New York, 2019

BREATHING PANEL: ORIENTED LEFT AND *BREATHING PANEL: ORIENTED RIGHT* (2015)

I can't breathe I can't breathe I can't breathe I can't breathe
I can't breathe I can't breathe I can't breathe I can't breathe
I can't breathe I can't breathe I can't breathe I can't breathe
I can't breathe I can't breathe I can't breathe I can't breathe

Morning light sifts through the swamp. The otherworldly, serpentine roots of trees emerge from the ground, covered in morass and mud. The island has traveled overnight. A womb. A slave ship. An ark.

None and all. The damp mud stench has the new freshness of sea salt. How, all along in the night, the sea was hidden! The salt freshness at dawn now suddenly fills their nostrils.

The Coca-Cola and 7UP and Pepsi and Fanta bottle torches are out. The crab hunters, in a ragged single-file line, make their way home, back to the shacks of the barracks of Duckenfield, Bellrock Lane, Jane Ash Corner, Golden Grove, Lyssons, and Peacock Hill. Their crocus bags, twitching on their shoulders, are full of crabs.

Then the same looker from several hours ago, now at the back of the line, sees something unexpected: hundreds of herons rising from a cluster of swamp trees. The looker stops to watch them. The others keep walking toward the green, their voices sparse but loud. The herons fly seaward in a single soundless arc. Then, just before disappearing from sight, they seem to pause, as if on the threshold of an entrance in the sky. The looker's eyes widen in astonishment. The birds disappear through the invisible portal, and when the looker turns to the others, mouth opened to shout to them, they, too, have already disappeared in the morning expanse of Caribbean light.

THE FIRE THUS KINDLED, MAY BE KINDLED AGAIN: THE FIGURE OF FREDERICK DOUGLASS

NO DEATH IS PERFECT. BUT EVEN THIS FREDERICK DOUG-lass defied brilliantly, and his death, when it occurred on the evening of Wednesday, February 20, 1895, while in conversation with his wife, Helen Pitts, struck like a moment's perfection. The two were alone at their Cedar Hill home, in Anacostia, Washington, D.C. Earlier in the day Douglass had attended the National Council of Women's triennial session, not as a speaker, but, in fact, as a surprise guest. He sat beside Susan B. Anthony on the platform, his presence underlining the gravity of the occasion; there he was, the struggle and the triumph, the living colossus urging America to change, silent and listening. He returned to Cedar Hill, to relax and prepare for a lecture he was to deliver that same night in the city. At home, "while cheerfully recounting the incidents of the day," Helen would later reminisce in a memorial piece published in 1897, "the strong, sweet Angel of Death drew him gently within the vale, and he was with God."

I wish to institute a cult, the worshipping, if you will, of a man.

He slips easily into myth and is often reduced to mythic proportions: the survivor and the hero. The beauty in him that is beyond myth is also beyond us. It is what we grasp for and what compels us to worship him. The beauty in him that is beyond us is nonetheless with us, invincible as poetry. "The poets are with us," he often repeats, a phrase that equates to his beauty. I want to be, have to be, empathetic about his beauty: it was denied him, brutally, but he redeemed it himself. Self-redeeming beauty is a superb part of his beauty, one that centers on justice, the supreme tenet of his life. The cult's name is his name. We members of the cult, his worshippers, are called kindlers. I hope to work my way around to why we are so called, but you can already hear it lodged in my title: "The Fire Thus Kindled, May Be Kindled Again."

* * *

Douglass died talking in the most private way, speaking to his beloved. His voice ended—no, was transfigured—at the precise instance of the consummation of lyric poetry; it brimmed with happiness and gave delight to his intimate listener: her phrase "cheerfully recounting" could serve as an epitaph to his life of vigilant public advocacy. Poems about Douglass strive, on their own terms, to kindle the felt intimacy of his passing with his immense legacy. Many have attempted to reconcile this burden, of intimacy and legacy, in words and have found the height unscalable. The attempt started early and with the most formidable interpreter of Douglass's magisterial oeuvre.

On the same day Douglass died, more than four hundred miles away, in Wilberforce, Greene County, Ohio, the twenty-six-year-old W. E. B. Du Bois, receiving the news of Douglass's death (by wire I assume), opened his notebook and wrote this poem he called "The Passing of Douglass":

> *Then Douglass passed—his massive form*
> *Still quivering at unrighted Wrong;*
> *His soul aflame, and on his lips*
> *A tale and prophecy of waiting Work.*
> *Low he chanted, and his hot accents,*
> *Fell in rich melodious cadence*
> *'Fore God's altar. Then—O, Christ!*
> *Not as the sickening dying flame,*
> *That fading glows into the night,*
> *Passed our mightiest—nay, but as the watch-fire,*
> *Waving and bending in crimson glory,*
> *Suddenly flashes [into] the Mountain, and leaves*
> *A grim and horrid blackness in the world.*
> > *Selah.*

Live, warm and wondrous memory, my Douglass,
Live, all men do love thee.
Amen!
Rise weird and weary wheeling wave, waft
My Douglass on, o'er earth and sea—
Strength of the strong sweep round us.
Alleluiah!

Rest, dark and tired soul, my Douglass,
Thy God receive thee
Amen
and
Amen!

Kindlers, this is a first prayer. It feels summoned out of a dark-night-of-the-soul shock, in which the luminary's passing is still so fresh to the speaker that the first half of the poem is a double modulation of that passing while the second is an immediate imperative to resurrect the newly dead. "Passed" is itself a euphemism, and this poem, to an extent, is an intensification of euphemism. The poem concludes with a gentle coda, less an elegy and more a lullaby.

Rest, dark and tired soul, my Douglass,
Thy God receive thee
Amen
and
Amen!

Hearing it, I see the deathbed photograph of Douglass. A serene play of a smile is on his face. Indeed, he appears to be asleep, in becalmed gray-bluish light, dreaming, perhaps, of the Tuckahoe Creek of his early boyhood on Maryland's Eastern Shore, the creek he loved in spite of the bondage he endured mere yards away from its banks.

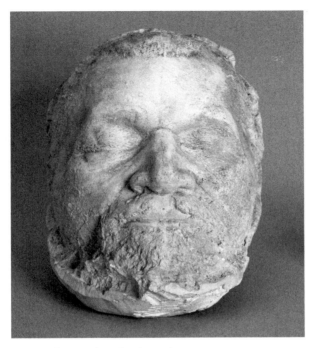

Frederick Douglass death mask

"Cheerfully recounting," Helen said, and it is this we hear in the photograph—"cheerfully recounting"—the sounds of sunlight commingling on water.

I said Du Bois's "Passing of Douglass" is an intensification of euphemism. Du Bois's poem is not without faults, but I won't dwell on them. One or two points are necessary, however, for me to elucidate my main focus when I turn to Robert Hayden's "Frederick Douglass." To do so, let me go back to the sound of the photograph.

Douglass was an astute critic of the art of photography, as well as the most photographed person of the nineteenth century. He considered photographs music for the eyes and heart. For him, also, the aesthetic value of photography was as an aesthetic-political vision, a true democratic art. In two separate lectures, "Age of Pictures" and "Pictures and Progress," delivered during the Reconstruction era, 1865–77, he made the following observations:

> It is an attribute of man's nature thus to convert the subjective consciousness into the objective form. The exercise of this divine faculty, or element of our nature, may be made a source of great happiness or of great pain . . . [T]he habit of making our subjective nature objective thus becomes evermore a matter of vast importance for good or for evil.
>
> All subjective ideas become more distinct, palpable, and strong by the habit of rendering them objective.

And this splendid combination of the aural and the visual over a philosophical map of desires culminates in something indissoluble. Douglass wrote,

> All wishes, all aspirations, all hopes, all fears, all doubts, all determinations grow stronger by action and utterance, by being rendered objective.

Du Bois's poem is an imperfectly beautiful and moving tribute to Douglass, and Douglass exists in it, but only as a subject. The failing largely is in forging the twin pillars, intimacy and legacy, into an irreducible, integrated object. Du Bois essentializes Douglass. Those three cries of "My Douglass"—

> *Live, warm and wondrous memory, my Douglass*
>
> *Rise weird and weary wheeling wave, waft*
> *My Douglass*
>
> *Rest, dark and tired soul, my Douglass*

—are raw and true but are not finally worked up into the reciprocal gesture of lyric poetry.

Let us leave Du Bois and move fifty-two years ahead to Robert Hayden's "Frederick Douglass." Here we have shifted to another century and psychic state: Hayden transfigures, surreptitiously, Du Bois and places, as it were, a complete bust of Frederick Douglass on the plinth. Here is solid, flexible resonance, a river honeyed out of a fountain whose tone resembles the great compact, conical stone tower inside the Great Enclosure at Great Zimbabwe, the noble sedimentary we hear shafting like water lights, weathered, layered, and fissured "stronger by action and utterance." Hear:

> When it is finally ours, this freedom, this liberty, this beautiful
> and terrible thing, needful to man as air,
> usable as earth; when it belongs at last to all,
> when it is truly instinct, brain matter, diastole, systole,
> reflex action; when it is finally won; when it is more
> than the gaudy mumbo jumbo of politicians:
> this man, this Douglass, this former slave, this Negro
> beaten to his knees, exiled, visioning a world
> where none is lonely, none hunted, alien,
> this man, superb in love and logic, this man
> shall be remembered. Oh, not with statues' rhetoric,
> not with legends and poems and wreaths of bronze alone,
> but with the lives grown out of his life, the lives
> fleshing his dream of the beautiful, needful thing.

Two silences surround the poem, holding words in a parenthesis, in medias res, a lyric station in which words, concentrated, radiate with awe and move "with the silence of music, rather than sound," moving in two directions at once, vertical and horizontal, curving into the final oval of eternity. The music of a river dreaming itself. Two silences, the first devotional. Devotion, Douglass tells us in the "Pictures and Progress" essay, is "the prelude to the vision and transfiguration, qualifying men and women for the sacred ministry of life." The second silence is the poem's greatest paradox: posterity. The first silence requires that the poet be an absolute devotee of techne, and in this matter, in his attentiveness to craft, Hayden has an almost infallible ear.

Let's take a brief survey of the poem. It is a sonnet: a poem of fourteen lines. The deeper qualification of this obvious stricture is Dante Gabriel Rossetti's famous line "The sonnet is a moment's monument," a convenient illumination of my credo that Hayden's sonnet is a textual monument. Rather than a sonnet, Hayden's poem is sonnet haunted; it subsumes the ghosts of traditions in order to stake new claim to the form, beyond simply—though it is a major innovation—reversing the octave and the sestet. The implications of such a movement are far more intense and crucial for the language of the poem, which sustains an asymmetrical progression from abstraction to act. But language begins in the ritual of the form; its slant and its slanting posture underline the immensity and upright figure of Douglass.

But language begins in the ritual of the first silence, that of devotion. To hear the silence, let me turn back to Du Bois.

The most poignant moment for me in Du Bois's "Passing of Douglass" is the abrupt vocative "O" of line seven—"Then—O, Christ!"—interrupting the ecstatic, elegiac musings of the preceding lines. The "O" forms the void of the mouth filled with pain: pain, for sure, and also the primal elation of the mouth shaped into a cipher through which, to repeat again Douglass on the photograph, "the prelude to the vision and transfiguration, qualifying men and women for the sacred ministry of life," may pass and is passing. This is the echo—the exclamation "O, Christ!"—vibrating behind Hayden's sonnet, not as a literary antecedent but as a much more palpable haunting: the haunting of inheritance. It matters little if Hayden knew Du Bois's handwritten manuscript; what matters is Hayden's devotion, the first silence in which he heard and imagined with devotional clarity his own Frederick Douglass. Race is not the pivot of the palpable inheritance I am speaking of, and that inheritance is not exclusive to historical pain and black joy, but belongs to the sacred ministry of life or, to riff on Coleridge, adheres to the secret ministry of form—the haunted sonnet—as a form of moral obligation. Inheritance, like influence, cannot be fathomed. "When it occurs," writes Elizabeth Rottenberg in her book *Inheriting the Future*, "an act of inheritance (the acceptance of a legacy) is an extraordinary act: on the one hand, because it elicits from the heir a response to a chosenness; on the other hand, because any true act of inheritance always implies momentous decisions and responsibilities." Hayden, the belated heir, forgoes the exposed lyric "I" and takes up his obligation in praise of Douglass, unlike Du Bois, impersonally but not self-effacingly. We hear him as we see him.

When it is finally ours, this freedom, this liberty, this beautiful
and terrible thing, needful to man as air,
usable as earth; when it belongs at last to all,
when it is truly instinct, brain matter, diastole, systole,
reflex action; when it is finally won; when it is more
than the gaudy mumbo jumbo of politicians:
this man, this Douglass, this former slave, this Negro
beaten to his knees, exiled, visioning a world
where none is lonely, none hunted, alien,
this man, superb in love and logic, this man
shall be remembered. Oh, not with statues' rhetoric,
not with legends and poems and wreaths of bronze alone,
but with the lives grown out of his life, the lives
fleshing his dream of the beautiful, needful thing.

The clarity is brisk. We hear the shuttle of a single thought, the first sentence breaking at breakneck speed over eleven lines to a period. What follows is a brief gasp—"Oh"—for breath, an intake of air in order to rev again, at an almost similar pace, though covering the shorter ground of three and a half lines, toward the final period. "Oh": a little word, a little sound. Oh. Oh. Oh. Let us consider it the demotic vocative inhalation of Du Bois's oratorical vocative "O." "Oh," so splendidly timed in Hayden, deepening the tide of the poem's first movement, is also the structural linchpin, fastening the second movement into the one fluid whole. There is a further masterstroke in that little sound: Geoffrey Hill has suggested that the demotic "Oh" in certain poems celebrates the democratic values embodied in "my brothers and sisters in arms." "Oh" turns to us; "oh" involves us in a close-up recognition: oh oh oh. "Miss May grandson? Him somewhere in England talking."

This, then, is the whole of the poem's architecture, a wheel constructed around a rhythm of "perceived periodicity," one that "acts to the extent to . . . alter in us the habitual flow of time," to cite Pius Servien. Time is river time, elusive, rivering. Yet time can be perceived, and marked, in subtle shifts of syntactical gradients— nineteen commas, three semicolons, and a colon—and also in the rich and variegated blend of assonance and consonance, constructing on either side of the two periods, a patterned freeness. We hear it in the melody of Hayden's voice, which has the rich echo of the wind passing inside the stone walls of the Great Enclosure at Great Zimbabwe.

I said earlier that Hayden's sonnet is sonnet haunted. Should I have said it is a haunted sonnet? His cadence also has the compound spirit of many poets who significantly altered the sonnet, perhaps most emphatically Hopkins and Auden (who was one of Hayden's early mentors). But where Hayden's sounds lift the enigma of poetics into a moment's monument, starting with the monumental gesture of "When," the first word of the poem, we hear not the glimmer of poets who might have influenced Hayden but instead the very voice of Douglass:

> When the dogs in your streets, when the fowls of the air, when the cattle on your hills, when the fish of the sea, and the reptiles that crawl, shall be unable to distinguish the slave from a brute, *then* I will argue with you that the slave is a man!

A spectacular example of the orator's classic parallel structure. Balanced vehemence, the anger pitched with dignity, with the cogent wash of a photograph developing the irrefutable. This sentence is from Douglass's speech "What to the Slave Is the Fourth of July?," delivered on July 5, 1852, in Corinthian Hall, Rochester. It is a master class in oratory. The twisted frame of the oratorical structure enacts the helices of political and social change culminating in America's declared independence from Britain on July 4, 1776. Douglass's interrogative "when," four times repeated before each blunt phrase, bears the propulsive speed of attack, an attack relentlessly seeking the recompense of justice. The frame of the octave of Hayden's sonnet draws from Douglass's oratory, mirroring the "when" clauses, but darkly converting Douglass's acceleration into momentum.

We sense in Hayden's "when" anaphora the widening evocation of a kind of plea:

> *When it is finally ours*
>
> *when it belongs at last to all*
>
> *when it is truly instinct*
>
> *when it is finally won; when it is more*

The evocation Hayden stirs here as if by divining water is both a recalling and a calling. Douglass calls things by their names—dogs, fowls, cattle, fish, reptiles—and in so naming confounds those who may argue the slave is a brute and needs the salvation of slavery. And Hayden? Hayden condenses substantives by way of rhythm into something nameless and elemental, something that is at once a striking and a frightening lamentation: it / it / it / it.

It is freedom and liberty, two differing things, of course, which are the "it" of Hayden's plea. But let's call the plea of the poem both material and immaterial, set off by the "when" clauses. The immaterial I have mentioned already, textually, as the ghosting of syntax between two periods. The immaterial is also inside the black body and activates in four ways: "truly instinct" as imagination; "brain matter" as intelligence; "diastole, systole" as compassion; and "reflex action" as sensitivity. These are all distinct characteristics of Douglass's beauty, and are all characteristics of the freedom and liberty that the American slave system denied, or tried to deny, to his body.

If "when" establishes in the octave an urgent plea for time, "where," at the beginning of the sestet—the conventional *volta* position of the Italian sonnet—sets up or rather locates the place for the time of freedom and liberty. Where is where? Where is where you find the body. In a world. Well, not just a world, the whole phrase, broken over the eighth into the ninth line, is "visioning a world / where." We are called to think of survival. We think of the effort to continue and become better: the present progressive melody of "visioning" demands and triggers such self-reflexivity. It is the world inside the black body that vision makes possible, "where none is lonely, none hunted, alien" and all is graspable, tangible, livable.

These poles, when and where, are far from a dialectic of time and place. They are not adjuncts of Hegelian "progress," which has been used to justify slavery. When and where are the simultaneity of the conscience and the will of a man's—Douglass's—self-redeeming, essentially private, labor within the public sphere of American plantocracy. Even so, the poem clearly creates a continuum in which "when" and "where" can be taken as a ritualistic pattern of "an implied movement from abstraction to act," to borrow from the great poet Jay Wright. Whether sonnet haunted or a haunted sonnet, Hayden's poem absorbs abstract nouns ("liberty," "freedom") within the texture of its rhythm to produce toughness and elasticity: concrete, marmoreal, and vivid. The form's ritual, not the semantic signifiers "liberty" and "freedom," gives us an order intrinsic to Douglass's life. What ritual teaches—to cite Wright again, from his essay "Desire's Design, Vision's Resonance"—is reverence and compassion, visual and auditory rigor, emotional and intellectual rigor (what we may call discipline of imagination, the freedom of rule), respect for history and memory, respect for vision and desire, and, finally, the ability to face up to the seriousness of life and the inevitability of death.

These are the conditions of "truly instinct," "brain matter," "diastole, systole," and "reflex action," performing the act I would call—and which this poem enshrines—remembrance. "Frederick Douglass" appeared in Robert Hayden's 1962 collection, *A Ballad of Remembrance*. It is the final poem of the collection. The collection houses remembrances for historic figures such as Nat Turner ("The Ballad of Nat Turner") and Harriet Tubman ("Runagate Runagate") as well as remembrances of Hayden's living contemporaries, such as Bessie Smith ("Homage to the Empress of the Blues") and Mark Van Doren ("A Ballad of Remembrance"). Astonishing from our vantage now to think that both Bessie Smith and Mark Van Doren were just under one year old when Frederick Douglass died in 1895. The title poem of the collection closes with two stanzas addressed to the distinguished older poet:

Then you arrived, meditative, ironic,
richly human; and your presence was shore where I rested
released from the hoodoo of that dance, where I spoke
with my true voice again.

And therefore this is not only a ballad of remembrance
for the down-South arcane city with death
in its jaws like gold teeth and archaic cusswords;
not only a token for the troubled generous friends
held in fists of that schizoid city like flowers,
but also, Mark Van Doren,
a poem of remembrance, a gift, a souvenir for you.

The lines register a young poet's gratitude to the older poet for helping him (Hayden) discover a voice to rise above terrible reality and to, as it were, add to the stock of available reality: the ideal interfacing with the actual.

Included in *A Ballad of Remembrance* is Hayden's masterpiece, the epical sequence "Middle Passage." "Middle Passage" deals primarily with the African experience in the transatlantic slave trade. Voices mutilated, pitched in hymns, songs, and speech; vernacular and formal, oratorical and oracular, the lyric here, broken and breaking, is as mesmerizing as concussed sea waves. I want to briefly draw attention to something Jay Wright said about "Middle Passage" that I find deeply revelatory in regard particularly to the last lines of Hayden's sonnet. Wright says the voices of "Middle Passage" take us "from chaos to what we may call an 'antithetical chaos' to a realization of latent human possibility and perfection." Again, the voices take us "from chaos to . . . a realization of latent human possibility and perfection."

Oh, not with statues' rhetoric,
not with legends and poems and wreaths of bronze alone,

but with the lives grown out of his life, the lives
fleshing his dream of the beautiful, needful thing.

America's chaos, slavery and its aftermath, shapes American life. So much of that life is violently suppressed and forced into dormant, insentient abstractions. Douglass wakes the inert perfection in us and wakes us to our capacity to change: What exactly *is* Douglass's life? "I . . . saw myself . . . as my voice in the great work of renovating the public mind, and building up a public sentiment, which should send slavery to the grave, and restore to 'liberty and the pursuit of happiness' the people with whom I had suffered." His life is a voice, and so he declares it in his final autobiography, *Life and Times of Frederick Douglass.* Hayden in effect sharpens the last four lines out of Douglass's voice into an antithetical chaos, and we hear it as a continual future manifested in the present:

Oh, not with statues' rhetoric,
not with legends and poems and wreaths of bronze alone,
but with the lives grown out of his life, the lives
fleshing his dream of the beautiful, needful thing.

The syntax coupled with the *via negativa* statements, deliberately and carefully and tenderly measured like two people really in love ("cheerfully recalling"!), insists that it is life and only life—not statues' rhetoric, not legends, not poems, not wreaths of bronze: none of these emblems of power so subjected to patriotic degradation but the living voice—that changes what is to what can be.

The living voice alone stands—as I am standing here, echoing Hayden's praise of Douglass into that second silence I called posterity. And this gathering an echo

but with the lives grown out of his life, the lives
fleshing his dream of the beautiful, needful thing

the poem ends. Hayden refuses, at its end, to be an elegist of the past. The poem ends. On the page, that is, the poem ends.

Beauty desires to replicate, not replace, beauty. Those final lines of Hayden's replicate in my ears the final lines of Milton's great sonnet 18, "On the Late Massacre in Piedmont." In horrific language, centering on the apocalyptic, Milton describes the terrible slaughter of Waldensian puritans by Catholic troops in northern Italy in 1655. The horror resounds in the wide vowel *o* dominating the end rhymes of the poem—"bones, cold, old, stones, groans, fold, roll'd, moans, sows, grow, woe"—elongating midway of line 12 into this sublime turn: "that from these may grow / A hundred-fold, who having learnt thy way / Early may fly the Babylonian woe." This utterance, one commentator has written, "reveals itself more in the poet's strength of imagination, the strength to interpret the slaughter providentially." I do not know about "providentially," which hinges too near the parasitic for comfort. But that Hayden's cadence— "the lives grown out of his life, the lives"—replicates in my ears Milton's—"that from these may grow / A hundred-fold"—embodies the secret ministry of poetics suddenly affirming the sacred ministry of life.

Let me now allow that affirmation, in what really is a lyric transgression of Douglass's voice, to rise up and name us:

> *The fire thus kindled, may be kindled again;*
> *The flames are extinguished, but the embers remain;*
> *One terrible blast may produce the ignition,*
> *Which shall wrap the whole South in wild conflagration.*
>
> *The pathway of tyrants lies over volcanoes;*
> *The very air they breathe is heavy with sorrows;*
> *Agonizing heart-throbs convulse them while sleeping,*
> *And the wind whispers Death as over them sweeping.*

Kindlers: from *kynda*: Old Icelandic: to ignite, to catch flame: influenced by Old Norse *kindill*: candle, torch—two universal images of hope strengthened against existential chaos, and in this passage Douglass perfects "some association between an internal approach to greater light and purity and the kindler of this dark lantern of our external existence." Hayden's sonnet refracts this hope. How? Because "the foundation of hope," to borrow from Geoffrey Hartman, "becomes remembrance," and since remembrance is the ritual of Hayden's homage to Douglass, the self—any of us—hearing this poem becomes it, becomes a kindler, a radical, an agitator of and for this freedom, this liberty.

The lines of Douglass are the last two quatrains, rhyming aa and bb couplets, from a twenty-nine-stanza poem titled "The Tyrants' Jubilee!," printed in the January 16, 1857, issue of *Frederick Douglass' Paper*. "The Tyrants' Jubilee!" is Douglass's longest surviving poem, spoken in the voice of a white southern slaveholder. We know this in part because of the poem's subtitle: "An Address Supposed to Have Been Delivered on the Occasion Celebrating the Suppression of the Recent Apprehended Insurrections at the South." The subtitle hints that the poem is a satire or parody. More significantly, the subtitle hints that the poem is one of ironic reversals. The year before its publication, 1856, saw many violent suppressions of slave revolts across the South, and the tyrants, the white slaveholders, were indeed jubilant. The ultimate reversal is that the planter speaker, as he feverishly denounces "the Insurrections," unwittingly praises the slaves' bravery and their indomitable spirit of survival:

We whipt them and whipt them and whipt them in vain;
We wore out our whips, and whipt them again.
Seven hundred stripes we laid on one brave;
Yet he died like a freeman and not like a slave.

His praise admits the slaves' humanity and, by so doing, posits an insurrection within the oppressor's self; the slaveholding mind, discovering, sick as it is, that it, too, is human—and human truly, and human only, with the recognition of the others' humanity. At this moment Hayden's phrase of the third line of his sonnet, "when it belongs at last to all," flows back onto us like the "terrible blast" in Douglass's "Tyrants' Jubilee!" as the total expression of antithetical chaos and radical hope.

Further, by utter serendipity the word "terrible" in both poems resounds within the same exact scansion and so the locution gains an elemental pressure like cold air on the face that is felt down to the toes, exacting the poetic credence of the phrase: "The fire thus kindled, may be kindled again":

Hayden: "and terrible thing, needful to man as air"
Douglass: "One terrible blast may produce the ignition"

And this gathering is an echo.

The city of Newcastle stands—*kynda*, *kindill*—in special reverberation to the memory and life of Douglass. It was a refuge for him during the fugitive years in England, as were other British cities, from 1845 to 1847. But it was at Newcastle upon Tyne on December 12, 1846, that Douglass's freedom was purchased for $711.66 by Ellen and Anna Richardson, two Quaker sisters, residents of Summerhill Grove. This purchase, Douglass said, "made a present of myself to myself and thus enabled me to return to the United States and resume my work for the emancipation of the slaves." We can hear in his gratitude the codicil of lyric, the essential bonding of transcendence ("myself to myself") and purpose ("resume my work for the emancipation of the slaves").

*   *   *

Frederick Douglass in his study at Cedar Hill

Let us imagine Douglass seeing his voice as if it were a photograph, perhaps one hanging above him in his home, Cedar Hill, in Anacostia, "making manifest the invisible, and giving form and body to all that the soul can hope and fear in life and death," a photograph hanging like a poem and hovering like music inside a death mask.

UNBENDING PROGRESS: ON CLAUDE MCKAY

What is it you want me to reconcile myself to? I was born here almost sixty years ago. I'm not going to live another sixty years. You always told me it takes time. It's taken my father's time, my mother's time, my uncle's time, my brothers' and my sisters' time, my nieces' and my nephews' time. How much time do you want for your progress?

—JAMES BALDWIN, FROM A 1984 INTERVIEW, INCLUDED IN THE DOCUMENTARY *JAMES BALDWIN: THE PRICE OF THE TICKET*

FOLLOWING JAMES BALDWIN'S INIMITABLE VOICE WITH MY own is as unwise as performing after James Brown, a lesson the Rolling Stones learned all too well at the infamous Teenage Awards Music International (T.A.M.I.) show in 1964. The Rolling Stones were scheduled to headline, much to James Brown's sore displeasure and constant complaint, none of which the promoters heeded, and so the schedule went on as planned. Incensed, Brown took to the stage, and like a Revivalist preacher possessed by something more than the Holy Spirit, he delivered what many believe was the most electrifying performance of his life. It lasted eighteen minutes and saw, among other things, the birth of the "cape routine." Reflecting years later about his T.A.M.I. performance, James Brown said, "I don't think I ever danced that hard in my life, and I don't think they'd ever seen a man move that fast. I danced so hard my manager cried, but I really had to. What I was up against was pop artists—I was R&B. I had to show 'em the difference, and believe me, it was hard." Add "sing" next to "move" and to the twice repeated "danced," and you get a more complete portrait of the artist's fiery apotheosis. After demolishing the stage, James Brown strutted off, passing the trembling Rolling Stones in the wings, according to legend, and dished—still according to legend—the now immortal punch line: "Nobody follows James Brown!"

I'm no Rolling Stones, yet I tremble hearing Baldwin's voice, out of both fear and admiration for the way it projects, as inseparable from a highly personal account, an act of civic witness to the appalling nature of progress on black people. The pitch of the whole passage has an unsparing *saeva indignatio*, but the ax blade of indignation falls on the word "progress," splitting it open. The sharp, blunt ring rightfully incriminates the word as a central hypocrisy of what broadly can be called the Western cultural mission. Closer to home, the pitch conveys Baldwin's gift and singular authority of working justice and grace into the register of a language that still seeks, after four centuries, to erase and obliterate him and his family from the deleterious experiment of life in America. His lyric anger "show[s] 'em the difference," to use James Brown's caveat, in how it tackles language's entrenched resistance to change. Adopting a semblance of that personal account, and doing so from the position of a listener and a Caribbean poet living in the aftermath of Baldwin's America, I want to approach the fraught word "progress" by trailing another voice, that of the Jamaican-born poet Claude McKay (1889–1948), who died when Baldwin was twenty-three years old.

Separated by two generations, both black gay men who grew up in poverty, McKay and Baldwin wrote fiction, poetry, and polemical essays. They shared a conflicting relationship with the Western tradition of Christianity, which, nonetheless, had a strong influence on the texture of apocalyptical lyricism in their writing. Both restless travelers, they spent long stretches outside the United States, where Baldwin was born in 1924 and to which McKay immigrated in 1912. Despite their exile, they both called Harlem, the city of Baldwin's birth, home. Long after they had left Harlem behind, Harlem remained home for them and was the direct or sublimated subject of their writing: Harlem appears in the title of five of McKay's seventeen books. Baldwin's and McKay's travels in Europe, and especially in North Africa, deeply impinged on their pan-Africanist sensibility, which bore intensely on their assessment of life in America. Like Baldwin, the authority of McKay's voice is its unflinching witness to the peculiar compounding of progress and racial injustice in the United States.

This witnessing takes many shapes in McKay's writing. In his poetry, it does so mainly in the verse form of the sonnet, generally categorized under two useful but reductive labels, that of the "protest" and allegorical sonnets. Rather than any rigid divide, they are better understood as mutually contentious counterparts, embodying, in form as well as in content, a volatile nature. In this sense, McKay's sonnets are embattled poems. It is the embattlement pervading in one of them that I will hover over, to hear how it activates a pitch of indignation consonant in spirit with, but deviating at the same time from, Baldwin's lyric anger of "show[ing] 'em the difference."

Let's first listen to McKay's sonnet:

Their shadow dims the sunshine of our day,
As they go lumbering across the sky,

Squawking in joy of feeling safe on high,
Beating their heavy wings of owlish gray.
They scare the singing birds of earth away
As, greed-impelled, they circle threateningly,
Watching the toilers with malignant eye,
From their exclusive haven—birds of prey.
They swoop down for the spoil in certain might,
And fasten in our bleeding flesh their claws.
They beat us to surrender weak with fright,
And tugging and tearing without let or pause,
They flap their hideous wings in grim delight,
And stuff our gory hearts into their maws.

"Birds of Prey," the name of this poem, appeared in *Harlem Shadows*, McKay's volume of 1922. Two years before, a slightly modified version was published in the British socialist newspaper *The Workers' Dreadnought*. There it was signed under McKay's pseudonym Hugh Hope. While the newspaper's name and its slogan, "For International Socialism," supply good clues, if not justification, for the brand of leftist communist sentiments lurking behind the poem's allegorical curtain, McKay's choice of pseudonym signals a deeper play of miry sarcasm concealed in the poem's indignation. The historical Hugh Hope (1782–1822) was a nineteenth-century Scottish civil servant of the British East India Company, the crown jewel of British imperialism. The name shores up the hypocrisy of progress; no less a slave-trading company than the Royal African Company, the British East India Company denied its role in both the transoceanic and the transatlantic slave trade. This fact, ingrained in the name McKay decides to sign the newspaper publication of the poem with, and the newspaper's socialist bent as well, are not conjectural but vital contextual factors in assessing the poem's central burden. They narrow and sharpen what is meant by the broad predicament "leftist communist sentiments." They do so in a manner similar to Baldwin's repetition of the accusative "you," pinpointing without labeling the agents of historical materialism that he and McKay are "up against" in their work.

The poem itself adheres strictly, and at times awkwardly, to the Petrarchan form of the sonnet. Unlike other sonnets in *Harlem Shadows* in which the artifice of the form generates genuine surprise on the level of structure—"The Harlem Dancer," "The White City," and the famous "If We Must Die," for example—the artifice of "Birds of Prey" does not, to again riff on James Brown, dance hard enough. As a result, some of the sound of its language is patently derivative. At the same time, however, the form pushes many of the lines into memorable sonic and linguistic tension. "Birds of Prey" is good proof as any in McKay's oeuvre that his creative power is not ancillary to his political urgency. That power exists as an imaginative indwelling *within* the political sentiment of his language.

Set up in the first line, the poem unfolds into a pattern of contrast between dark ("shadow") and light ("sunshine"), with attendant pronouns ("their shadow" and "sunshine of our") delineating the oppositional position of one to the other. A listener is immediately called to think of the proverbial—and McKay means it proverbially—struggle between good and evil. Such theological speculation is unsurprising. "Birds of Prey" relies heavily on book 3, lines 431–41, of Milton's *Paradise Lost* for its ornithological and religious conceit. The "their," the birds of prey, are the symbol of evil, and the "our," the prey, are the symbol of good. The position of the birds of prey is depicted as elevated, "on high," a height that is sarcastically Luciferian: an "exclusive haven." In contrast, the position of the prey belongs to a fallen realm beneath the birds of prey. Its featureless existence in the poem makes it a type of voided place, yet a place felt palpably as the drained but oddly invigorating landscape of, say, Fritz Lang's *Metropolis* or Charles Burnett's *Killer of Sheep*. There's a striking filmic quality to the movement of the poem: the panoramic sweep in the octave ("across the sky") gives way, Kubrick style, to close-up shots ("swoop down") in the sextet. The switch in perspective is a switch in perception; when it happens, a listener is brought down into the terrible orifice of hell. Hell being a recognizable corner of earth.

Though Milton the theological thinker is on McKay's mind in these cut and clear distinctions between good and evil, it is Milton the hierarchal agitator that McKay channels when he meditates on the violence enacted by the ruling class on the proletariat. Both straight-forward and amorphous, the "greed-impelled" violence can be seen as the vicious extreme of Wordsworth's condemnation of avarice in "The World Is Too Much with Us"—a sonnet standing silently be-hind McKay's sonnet—as "Getting and spending, we lay waste our powers." It is within that vein of wasting powers that the sensuous field of action in McKay's poem moves from an exercise of theological ornithology to a visceral portrait of the dismal reality of progress. The move (in turn) increasingly turns the listener's experience of the poem into one of shock and revulsion.

Highlighting that sensuous field of action, as if by echolocation, we hear in all the gestures ascribed to the birds of prey a dry and re-morseless vivification of violence. Mostly monosyllabic, the action can be pared down to an emaciated sonnet of brutality:

dims
lumbering
squawking
beating
scare
circle
watching
swoop
fasten

beat
tugging
tearing
flap
stuff

The prey put up no counteraction to these hostilities, except for the one that defines their abject state of powerlessness: "surrender." There's a small but glorious semantic and structural miracle in that word where it appears in the sonnet, struck with some of the semantic force, though not the scorn, with which Baldwin sounds "progress" in his passage.

The *volta*—"From their exclusive haven—birds of prey"—merely fulfills the rhetorical demand of what's expected in line 9 of a Petrarchan sonnet. There the imagery and action of the predators scaring away "the singing birds of earth" are emphatically em dashed, thus inaugurating the sonnet's "resolution"—or "anti-resolution" in McKay's case—to unfold in the concluding six lines of the poem. But "surrender," coming two lines after the *volta*, upsets the binary flow of the Petrarchan form that McKay follows with not much formal (or informal) innovation. The effect is more than a delayed voltaic jolt on the adamantine clad of meter and form. It is that, but also a real turn—*volta*, Italian: "turn"—of another matter. It is an unexpected surge of psychic resistance coming from the seemingly nonresistant lumpen proletariat majority in face of the hegemonic violence sponsored by the ruling class minority.

There is more. I want to eavesdrop further on the line and hear how the cadence enacts a poetic conversion of "surrender" into a pitch of resistance.

Let's hear it again, isolated, and loud:

They beat us to surrender weak with fright.

Iambic feet counterpointed with, and affected by, anapestic feet, the line is a collision of the conversational—"they beat us to surrender"—with the "poetically" heightened—"weak with fright"—tone. This mingling of registers is claustrophobic, intense, and frightening, which makes a listener feel affected by and with the violence being described. "Surrender," the lone three-syllable word in the middle of the line, is hammered from both sides by blunt monosyllabic words.

Indeed, "surrender" seems besieged by whips, rifles, pistols, batons, bricks, stones, bottles, and tear gas. A protester surviving a beating by a mob or by the police at a march could describe the terrible event by saying, "They beat us to surrender," pausing, out of breath, then adding, "weak with fright." The line's beauty is its extemporized naturalness. Even the poetizing second half of the line is inflected with a vernacular, on-the-spot shiver following the anapestic middle word, "surrender." Historical records have shown that it is not uncommon for survivors of state-sanctioned violence to express the traumatic event with language that verges on, what might be called by shorthand, "the poetic." Survivors do so in the very moment, or in the immediate aftermath of the event, and these shattered bits of language sometimes become simultaneously a record of a historical pain and the evidence of resilience against such history once the events recede further away into the deep past. Hearing, for instance, a survivor of violence say, "We were really afraid and we hid behind the piano at my aunt's house," communicates evocatively and affectively the fear felt and the action taken, but the specificity of "the piano at my aunt's house," rather than being a mere sociological detail, has a dimension of "the poetic" a listener hears in McKay's "weak with fright," which serves to amplify the existential horror just lived through. While the allegorizing language of "Birds of Prey" makes the poem "universal" and thus applicable to any civic unrest, a listener can assume it bears witness to a specific place and time pressed under a specific set of conditions.

For me, "surrender" is the note anchoring that history. Earlier I said the word is besieged by brute mob and police force and that its rhymical position in the line, contrary to the word's usual meaning, is an act of resistance. This is not willful, speculative narrative but an attempt to ground the poem in a specific moment of racial injustice, that of the 1919 Red Summer anti-black riots in Chicago. In those riots, twenty-three black people were killed by white officers and civilians either by being "burned alive, shot, hanged or beaten to death," according to one report. Hundreds more were injured, some maimed for life, and thousands were left displaced. The sentence "We were really afraid and we hid behind the piano at my aunt's house" is spoken in 2019 by a 107-year-old survivor of those riots, Juanita Mitchell. She was eight a hundred years ago when her uncle hid her and her sister behind her aunt's piano. Outside her aunt's house, white terrorists went pillaging and killing. Although she was relatively safe inside the house from the physical violence, the invasion caused lifelong suffering: "I remember how afraid my mother was, afraid my aunt was. And I'm going to never forget the tears in my mother's eyes as she cried in her sister's house." In the wake of this extraordinary violence, McKay wrote a series of sonnets (and other poems) directly protesting the brutality, including his most famous poem, "If We Must Die," considered the defining poem of witness to the violence of Red Summer. "Birds of Prey" must be heard in the same lineage. Like "If We Must Die" or the more pointedly titled "Exhortation: Summer, 1919," it is a witnessing to that murderous moment of racial violence. But pinning, as it were, "Birds of Prey" to the 1919 Red Summer riots has at least one major kink.

Nineteen nineteen is also the year the first violent wave of Red Scare hysteria spread across America. The law enforcement agencies, in reaction to radical left-wing communists setting off bombs in American cities, imposed swift, far-reaching anticommunist punishments. Blacks, already heavily discriminated against, were either assumed to be or pigeonholed as communist, and thus suffered doubly under these crackdowns by law enforcement. Though he was not an anarchist, McKay's sympathies were with the communist—he would make what he called his "magical pilgrimage" to Russia in 1922—and his sonnets and other writing of the period respond directly to that historical crisis. A listener might point to the word "scare" in line 5 of "Birds of Prey"—"they scare the singing birds of earth away"—as squarely implicating the poem in the Red Scare nexus of the bloody upheavals of 1919. Such an observation is just. But considering that the figurative origin of the word transmuted, as I believe, from the phrase "scarce of prey" in book 3, line 433, of Milton's *Paradise Lost*, the pitch dislodges the word from one explicit resonance or reference.

McKay appropriates many other phrases from that section of Milton's *Paradise Lost* that he spins into a taut, unstable web across his poem. For instance, that same phrase of Milton's, "scarce of prey," and another, "bent on his prey," from line 441 of Milton's book, are condensed to form the final em-dashed phrase of the *volta* in McKay's sonnet. All of this, plus the allegorizing of events, ensures there's no easy division in the poem between Red Summer and Red Scare. I don't mean nor am I implying that the word "scare" is used abstractly, or worse, has been eked out of Milton and as a solipsistic form of subjectivism. Caught between this private literary antecedent and the public circumstances of terror, "scare" is both a multifarious and a multivalent word. McKay's pitch of it as a gesture of witness to violence bears out how the *Oxford English Dictionary* defines it: "a sudden fright or alarm; esp. a state of general or public alarm occasioned by baseless or exaggerated rumours," with "exaggerated rumours" here meaning, of course, statecraft and vigilante violence. The word, then, is ambivalently "applicable" to one or another circumstances of 1919, and just as well to circumstances of a similar nature back in the distant past or ahead in the distant future. But considered in relation to the latter keyword, "surrender," "scare" coincides more strongly, by inference, with the existential horror of the Red Summer riots.

What is less ambivalent and a clearer signifier of violence and racialization is the use of "gray"—"beating their heavy wings of owlish gray"—the only color adjective in the poem. McKay again appropriates the word from Milton. It appears only once in book 3 of *Paradise Lost* at the literally pivotal moment when Satan, perched like a vulture on an outer orb of earth called "the Lymbo of Vanity," watches the building of "New *Babels*" by different races, which he describes as "Embryo's and Idiots, Eremits and Friers / White, Black and Grey, with all thir trumperie." The masterful conflation of race, vanity, and insignia in the building of "New Babels" is a world "where *Chineses* drive / With Sails and Wind thir canie Waggons light" becomes vulnerable to imperial exploitation. In alighting on "gray" to characterize the birds of prey, McKay's aesthetic alertness affirms, or assents to, Milton's dissenting voice in this new arena of brutal commodification of human labor. The need for a rhyme word ("day" with "gray") is a chime and corroboration of a spirit to act against such imperial exploitation. In this limbo land of progress, a megalopolis stuck between war and peace, "gray" is the ugly trumpery of its attrition and neutrality.

The martial cadence of "beating their heavy wings of owlish gray" summons the haunting echo of a battlefield. Indeed, there is a mood of postwar dissipation or torpor in other lines, shored up strongly by words like "spoil" and "surrender." "Gray" itself is another of those words, and it raises the specter of a specific clash of civilization. No African American at the turn of the twentieth century would not recall that gray is the color of the uniforms of the Confederacy: "Gray," indeed, is the shorthand for the Confederate army during the Civil War of 1861–65. In 1919, the Civil War had ended only just over fifty years earlier. In the decades after, veterans of this defeated army and their descendants flocked to American cities like Chicago, swelling the already inflated racist legions in every sector of the society. These "owlish gray" predators—"predators" meaning "plunderer" in the primary sense—seen in their ponderous flight, belong, then, to the evil omen of "America's original sin." "Negro Slavery," wrote John Adams in a letter to William Tudor Jr. on November 20, 1819, "is an evil of Colossal Magnitude," and that is the extreme evil being resisted by the word "surrender" in the poem.

If we listen again to the migratory ponderousness, so to speak, of "beating their heavy wings of owlish gray," its martial cadence brings to mind another clash of civilization whose reverberations are closer to the Red Summer terrors of 1919 than the Civil War: World War I. Many of the victims of the Red Summer violence were African American World War I veterans, recently returned from the European theaters of war. Their sacrifice abroad was a sacrifice of necessity, in large part, to secure greater quality of life at home. "We fought gladly and to the last drop of blood for America and her highest ideals," wrote W. E. B. Du Bois in a 1919 article called "Returning Soldiers" for *The Crisis*, adding, "We fought in far-off hope; for the dominant southern oligarchy entrenched in Washington, we fought in bitter resignation." These black war heroes, subjected to menial service on and off the front, came back to poverty and lynching, to a liberal democracy of hate. To Du Bois, as for many others, there is no possibility of being a "regular" citizen in the dehumanizing warlike conditions of Jim Crow America. Impassioned, Du Bois ends his article with "But by the God of Heaven, we are cowards and jackasses if now that that war is over, we do not marshal every ounce of our brain and brawn to fight a sterner, longer, more unbending battle against the forces of hell in our own land." In both a subliminal and a sublime way, Du Bois's conclusion connects back to what Olaudah Equiano, the ex-enslaved African veteran of the Seven Years' War (1756–63), writes in his 1789 book, *The Interesting Narrative of the Life of Olaudah Equiano, or Gustavus Vassa, the African*: "When you make men slaves you deprive them of half their virtue, you set them in your own conduct an example of fraud, rapine, and cruelty, and compel them to live with you in a state of war." Note here how Equiano's incriminating tone, in his style of address, the repetition of "you," seems to anticipate, by 195 years, Baldwin's own pointed use of the "you" in his interview passage. The "you" remains, in different guises, the same "evil of Colossal Magnitude" duplicated across time to satisfy the insatiable "maws" of empire. Enslavement and its afterlife are consigned to an unresolved "state of war."

I want to make a sharp turn to yet another sort of battlefield. I am doing so still in the shadows of migratory ponderousness and enslavement as an everlasting "state of war" haunting progress, a state that one word in McKay's "Birds of Prey" pitches a formidable resistance against.

Though unverified, it is long believed by many that Winston Churchill recited "If We Must Die" before the House of Commons in 1939 as a patriotic hymn to spur on British soldiers entering into battle during World War II. In full flight of Churchillian grandeur, Churchill did not acknowledge the poem's author, nor any of the poem's originating circumstances, the Red Summer racial injustice of 1919. Racial hatred was not exactly anathema to Churchill. In 1937, for example, he says this piece of an unflagging white supremacist's statement to the Palestine Royal Commission (or Peel Commission): "I do not admit for instance, that a great wrong has been done to the Red Indians of America or the black people of Australia. I do not admit that a wrong has been done to these people by the fact that a stronger race, a higher-grade race, a more worldly wise race to put it that way, has come in and taken their place." It is therefore not egregious to say that Churchill's co-opting of McKay's poem for British wartime propaganda performs an ontological silencing of McKay. Further, that ontological silencing is an imperialistic whitewashing of the black resistance allegorized by McKay's poem. McKay uses allegory with the full knowledge of the history behind the terrible predicament—Churchill's passive "great wrong"—being faced down in his poem, a predicament rooted in the transatlantic enslavement of black people by Europeans.

In addition, bearing witness to the racist murders of 1919, "If We Must Die" is conscious of eighteenth- and nineteenth-century Anglo-American tradition, both progressive and conservative, of portraying black revolutionaries as nothing but marauding rebels, rather than resistance fighters in the line of, say, Garibaldi of Italy or Mierosławski of Poland. As such, the poem is eager to assert against this dehumanizing white gaze the humanity of these black resistance fighters. Not only their humanity, but their nobility. The nobility of Telemaque, Tacky, Nat Turner, and scores of black resistance fighters whose names are lost to history. The poem is in search of acknowledgment from them and not from the "cowardly pack" of whites. Its fierce bid for recognition is addressed to "kinsmen," fellow blacks in the struggle, contemporaries a century later of those enslaved black resistance fighters. Although that struggle appears suicidal—"what though before us lies the open grave?"—the poem insists it is not only human but also noble to surrender to that faith rather than to live life scared of predatorial white (or gray) violence.

This returns me, for the last time, to the line "They beat us to surrender weak with fright" in "Birds of Prey." Specifically, to the medial word "surrender." In the onslaught of violence radiating from the verbal field of the poem, "surrender" is one of the subtle turns, a quiet undertow, belonging to the black tradition of resistance. For a black poet, such a subterranean withstanding of plunderers is at once a clear and baffling form of purposeful belonging to blackness. This makes me think of the only existing audio recording of Claude McKay reading "If We Must Die" sometime near the end of his life. In what is left of his rapid, careful rural Jamaican accent above the crackle of the vinyl, he prefaces the poem by saying, "'If We Must Die' is the poem that makes me a poet among colored Americans." If McKay's statement feels a little hinged on the limbo cliff of vanity, it is because solidarity is often, for the poet, a tenacious earnestness of spirit. To survive, and bear witness to survival, is a deep form of contradictory omen.

Perhaps omen of some sort was on my mind when, in the late autumn of 2006, I wrote these lines dealing with, among other things, an imaginary encounter with Claude McKay in Manhattan:

> *Drizzle above the high-rises.*
> *Through the street, coats swish by;*
> *black boots clomp into a coffee shop.*
> *Nina Simone pours pastel blues—*
> *I know this; a finger of memory*
> *lifts to the waitress and to forecast*
> *the rain back home. Remember island rain,*
> *Claude? Grass and asphalt blending,*
> *the road a crucible, even the dog-shit*
> *smells good, even the hot cane field?*
>
> *She takes the signal,*
> *brings us two steaming cups.*
> *You take off, Harlem or Russia. Doesn't matter.*
>
> *Now is right—my status alien—to weigh my lines.*
> *Most are antique, and have entered antiquity*
> *with my slow pace. In my coffee a hurricane is brewing.*

The passage is from "Autobiography of Snow," a longish poem included in my first poetry collection, *Far District*. The collection, to a large extent, takes the measure of living as a Caribbean poet, as an alien, in America. In terms of the modern era of English-speaking

Caribbean poets, this process, many have argued, began most prominently with McKay. Adrift in the city, I read McKay and other Caribbean poets and writers to better grasp this form of estrangement from home. Kamau Brathwaite (1930–2020) was one such figure whose work helped me to come to grips with this condition. The phrase "contradictory omen" is in fact an echo of the title of Brathwaite's 1974 monograph, *Contradictory Omens: Cultural Diversity and Integration in the Caribbean.*

Contradictory Omens is vintage Brathwaite as firebrand cultural theorist of the Caribbean. The slightly bureaucratic subtitle, accurate as it is, belies the monograph's impressionistic style. Indeed, the monograph is a compressed follow-up to Brathwaite's now classic *The Development of Creole Society in Jamaica, 1770–1820* of 1971. When I first read *Contradictory Omens* in Jamaica, in around 2003, it went over my head. But one passage was lodged in my mind for the way it illuminated what I felt intuitively around me and gave language to that feeling. The passage is fairly well known. In it, Brathwaite formulates his own version of "creolization" as a cultural process that

> may be divided into two aspects of itself: ac/culturation, which is the yoking (by force and example, deriving from power/ prestige) of one culture to another (in this case the enslaved/ African to the European); and inter/culturation, which is an unplanned, unstructured but osmotic relationship proceeding from this yoke. The creolisation which results (and it is a process not a product), becomes the tentative cultural norm of the society.

Not just the argument, but the eddying snags and rush of the prose, thrilled me. The syntax catches the unruly shape of my landscape and the psychic condition underpinning that landscape, the volatile history that began with European conquistadorial genocide, then four centuries of African enslavement, followed by Indian and

Chinese indentureship, all done in the name of progress. Yet out of this violent osmotic pressure, surviving the progress of empire—namely, the British Empire—comes everything around me, the terror and the beauty of the Caribbean. Brathwaite's revelatory parenthesis—"(and it is a process not a product)"—shields the essence of what that survival is, and means, from the degradation of progress.

Later I want to juxtapose this passage from *Contradictory Omens* with the passage from James Baldwin's 1984 interview with which I began this listening, eavesdropping on Baldwin's highly personal pitch of the word "progress" in a way fitting to the lyric resistance or re-visioning I have here been conducting through close listening to McKay's "Birds of Prey." With my lines dealing with an imaginary encounter with McKay, I have already moved into the Baldwinian highly personal direction and will go further down that road. As jaunty and reckless as the highly personal approach is, or might turn out to be, it is the best way a young poet shows his indebtedness to his inheritance, a gift of bewilderment from his background, for which he will forever be happy and uneasy.

As such, I want to recall a memory of seeing Brathwaite in Washington Square Park in New York City. He was dressed in a dark overcoat and wearing his signature knit blue tam, afloat on his head like a small bolt of immemorial Caribbean cloud. He was standing very still in front of Garibaldi's bronze statue in the slanting midafternoon light of autumn. I had never seen him before in the city. My first impulse was to run over and greet him—we had met a few times in Jamaica and had exchanged emails—but something stopped me in my tracks.

He was not just looking at Garibaldi's statue; he was contemplating it. The more I lingered and watched him, the more I thought something else was going on. He seemed to be communing with the statue. Leaves and trash swirled at his feet. People passed him by; he didn't move or moved so slightly I couldn't make out that he did. Uncertain what to do, I sat down on a bench adjacent to where he stood. Seated, I realized that though Brathwaite's face was tilted upward to the statue, his focus seemed to be on the marble pedestal, plain but for Garibaldi's name and dates of birth and death. I felt I needed to be there with Brathwaite, for him, that my "unplanned" witnessing of this moment wasn't a coincidence that could be explained away by the fact of us being in the city at the same time. Over the next two years I lived in the city, I never saw him again. I felt, inexplicably, I was seeing "a shadow of reality to come," like what Keats said of Adam's dream.

What was Brathwaite contemplating? Did he see someone or something, *non-finito*, straining out of the marble pedestal? Could it be a radical "dis/location," to use a Brathwaite-like slash, of some type? It was—and remained—unknowable. But his intense attention to the statue (or the pedestal, who knows?) made me think of isolation. The isolation of the poet from his Caribbean, at this moment, standing in the heart of the new imperial center. To give even the smallest fraction of the bewildering set of implications that come with such isolation for a Caribbean poet would be like hearing a voice speaking out of its pedestal. But it remains silent, about alienation and the pain of empires, new and old.

Whatever Brathwaite was contemplating or communing with in front of Garibaldi's statue was characterized by, as Brathwaite wrote in *Contradictory Omens*, a "creole way of seeing." And here was the obvious and mystifying thing, I was seeing this moment in a Creole way, too. I was an acolyte to it, offstage in the wings of a ceremony I didn't understand. This was something I couldn't have gotten at a poetry workshop table or in a lecture hall. I doubt if I had happened upon Brathwaite this way in Jamaica or in Barbados I would've been as mesmerized—struck, yes, but not as mesmerized. Here, I saw no exhibition of an eccentricity. I saw a great Caribbean poet and thinker, isolated and locked deep in a penumbra of his own thoughts.

I remained watching Brathwaite for however long he stood, seemingly motionless in front of Garibaldi's statue. He watched for a while, which, in retrospect, felt even longer. When he finally left, simply turning to his right and walking off under the Washington Arch, as if "evading believers"—me in this case—like the weeping man in Les Murray's poem "An Absolutely Ordinary Rainbow," I remained seated, grounded by some kind of radiance lingering in the space he departed from. Indeed, like the man in Murray's poem, Brathwaite was to me "not words, but grief, not messages, but sorrow, / hard as the earth, sheer, present as the sea."

With those quoted lines of Murray's springing in my head, I tried to chalk a parenthesis around that enigmatic sighting of Brathwaite in a sonnet sequence I wrote about a year later. Here is the third of the sequence, a votive candle held toward Brathwaite:

> *Man's hardest divorce is from the sea.*
> *He hears in the Village's meridian*
> *the sea-lice's dividing eggs, the tree-frogs' plea,*
> *losing their accents to the American*
>
> *babel, through the amnesic marble arch;*
> *past Garibaldi's half-sheathed sword,*
> *their sounds with fifes and white flags march;*
> *the leading professorial frog bellows, "Words,*
>
> *you dimwit fireflies, light up History,*
> *for we been in dark now we in New York!"*
> *All in his head, this malarial memory*
> *sickens him, he shivers like a stork;*
> *worse now the bridal sea recedes in foam.*
> *At every corner, leaf-wet whisper, "Go home."*

In my sonnet, the visible reality of that moment reassembles itself around an ironic prosopopoeia, an imaginary carnival in which the Caribbean is sounding through the city the "dis/location" a Caribbean poet endures while living outside the Caribbean.

Is the sonnet form, as signaled by its bipartite structure of octave and sestet, inherently the form of exile and home? I distrust this "little song" of Italy, invented about a century and a half before Columbus's 1492 voyage to the Caribbean. Yet surrendering to its demands is one of the ways I sense that my language grows beyond a formal hectoring pitch, to love, to an ethos of what Brathwaite calls "a process not a product" in his passage cited from *Contradictory Omens*.

With a more bracing lyric vigilance, the passage by Baldwin enacts, as Brathwaite's own, a similar attentiveness to the "yoke" of history. The burden of Baldwin's passage is the way his two questions function as an invisible parenthesis around a trauma that is tacitly, meaning superficially, "absorbed" by or into the empire's progress, a progress that has no serious interest or commitment to true reconciliation.

Let's listen again to the pitch and tone of Baldwin's voice:

What is it you want me to reconcile myself to? I was born here almost sixty years ago. I'm not going to live another sixty years. You always told me it takes time. It's taken my father's time, my mother's time, my uncle's time, my brothers' and my sisters' time, my nieces' and my nephews' time. How much time do you want for your progress?

What I marvel at here, among other things, is the way the ghost of the iambic rhythm of the final sentence—"how much time do you want for your progress?"—is reconciled with the savage indignation of the statement. It has a suddenness that overrides its rhetorical encasement, so the question is no longer a question or even the accusation underlining the question. Engrafted on the ghosting pentameter is an energy expressive of a faith analogous to what is being said. That is the marker of an isolated powerful line or word in a poem. In this regard, Baldwin's sentence lives within the recalcitrant texture of McKay's line "What though before us lies the open grave?" from "If We Must Die." Even more, without the rhetorical question, I can hear Baldwin's sentence subsumed in the vivid witnessing invoked by the cadence of McKay's line "They beat us to surrender weak with fright" from "Birds of Prey."

"How much time do *you* want for *your* progress?"

No one knows. Perhaps the question all too easily answers itself. On that, this passage from "The Price of the Ticket" will have to be, for now, the last words:

> Spare me, for Christ's *and* His Father's sake, any further examples of American white progress. When one examines the use of this word in this most particular context, it translates as meaning that those people who have opted for being white congratulate themselves on their generous ability to return to the slave that freedom which they never had any right to endanger, much less take away. For this dubious effort, and still more dubious achievement, they congratulate themselves and expect to be congratulated—: in the coin, furthermore, of black gratitude, gratitude not only that my burden is—(slowly, but it takes time) being made lighter but my joy that white people are improving.
>
> My black burden has not, however, been made lighter in the sixty years since my birth or the nearly forty years since the first essay in this collection was published and my joy, therefore, as concerns the immense strides made by white people is, to say the least, restrained.

THE BEARINGS OF THE ISLAND

A DEFENSE OF POETRY IS A CONTRADICTION IN TERMS. THE honor to speak this evening, which I accept with great humility, though inevitably unnerving, I will use to contradict myself with some vignettes, as if through a glass darkly, in the light of that beautiful, abstract theme-word, "visions." What is vision is in part the same question as what is a visionary; who is performing the visioning; to what end: this is the trajectory I wish to amplify in this talk.

The title of my talk is "The Bearings of the Island." It is snatched from the first sentence of Robert Louis Stevenson's *Treasure Island*. The phrase is resonant for me due to a certain bounty of my background that is at once simple and strange: the sea. I grew up above that inexorable axis on which everything turned in my hometown, Port Antonio, a harbor village on the northeastern coast of Jamaica. Port Antonio has had its modern fame in the swashbuckling character of the Australian-born movie star Errol Flynn, who in 1946, when he docked his yacht the *Zaca* in the bay, trumpeted like a latter-day Christopher Columbus, "Here is a place more beautiful than any woman I have ever known." His pronouncement brings Auden's powerful definition of the sea to mind: "The sea . . . is that state of barbaric vagueness and disorder out of which civilisation has emerged and into which, unless saved by the effort of gods and men, it is always liable to relapse."

In Flynn you have the tone of the marauder, the romance colonial empires derived from, and it was this flourish that launched Hollywood briefly in Port Antonio. The rich flocked there and created an outpost of tropical pleasure, where women more beautiful than Flynn ever knew, women like my grandmother—women who would have been slaves three or four generations before Flynn arrived on his *Zaca*—became the exotic backdrop to this fantasy. Suddenly they were natives, extras for the silver screen's one-dimensional vision: banyan skirts and madras, heavy women.

But that was before I was born. The Hollywood affair was brief. The era of Flynn passed like smoke, leaving Port Antonio, as I grew up in it and it is now, splendidly antiquated, most of its shores lined with skeletal coconut trees, the town leafing through days without interest or self-importance, checking its incessant calendar of rain and sun by the sea.

When the sea was not in our direct vantage, it fell like fragments of silhouettes into our lives. It appeared imperceptible from moment to moment, and was hardly ever acknowledged in conversation, unless it was to prophesy rain or the greater calamity of hurricane, when clouds would darken into cancer over the water. But to me the sea, whether dark or bright, was the town's mirror crammed with voices, phantoms whose blurry features resembled mine, staring at me with confounded eyes. I was anxious and unable to name them. And this paranoia intensified in me due to the roster of cruise ships that, on occasion when I was a boy, arrived with tourists. More often, though, were the slenderer banana boats that came every other Thursday, their glide secreting the very word "merchant" into the harbor. But they never stayed long. By Friday morning, and for the rest of the week, the bay between the twin peninsulas would tingle like a wound whenever one vanished beyond the sea's pale of topaz infinity, vanished to other worlds from which I had already started to imagine or dream I had emerged and to which I belonged and from which I was irrevocably an exile in this my world of light on my grandmother's veranda.

A sensitive child-seer into whom the sea beat the language of loss, I felt unique in this pain.

I was mistaken, of course. This inner conflict of dispossession was, and remains, a shared ancestral and historical yoke. Tragic conditions brought us to the island. No, not "conditions"—for the conditions were, and remain, the terrible consequences of, put accurately, the tragic visions of European colonial imperialism that steered the slave ships to the island. Often, I saw those ships in silent montage, a harmonious pageant of fused cruise ships and banana boats, bearing the muted tumult of uprooted tongues, wailing in their purgatorial hulls.

Sometimes my eyes contracted, too, and I would catch something else that deepened a coastal shelf of grief and love inside me: someone walking before the lynchets of waves, increasing as they receded, unfinished in thin curdles that never reached the villas in the cliffs with their rich-flowered lights and cacti growing out of the rocks; a maid in her uniform, bent into a figurehead at the lilac and rose hour of day, walking, not looking back.

When I saw her, the star-apple blood smell raged in my eyes.

The violent visions of a European ideal of progress have long culminated in a metaphysical prison, one that has to be met with purgation through the terror of beauty, through a process of radical re-visioning.

To be a visionary, I think, is to "walk[] in the light of inward heroism," a phrase the nineteen-year-old James Joyce wrote to Ibsen when Ibsen was on the threshold of death at the beginning of our last century. "Inward heroism" is the defiant condition present in the Caribbean character, like the maid (anonymous and one of many) I saw walking before the waves, a condition V. S. Naipaul dismisses when he writes his famous, brutal proposition on the Caribbean: "We lived in a society which denied itself heroes."

The phrase is tangled in the mangrove of its own genius, expressive of a thoroughly educated colonial mind that sees horror and pessimism everywhere, where in truth there is radiance. There is the radiance of self-reliance and self-actualization through and after slavery, emancipation, and the modern malaise called independence. There is radiance in the everydayness that is not the torpor of servitude. The radiance is an anguished kind of nobility. As when the sea is glowing embers at noon and all is still, except for a fisherman sitting on his beached, upturned boat, repairing his fishing net; that mundane webbing is emblematic of Penelope's spiritual resistance and whatever other mythical origins the fisherman echoes, but are hard to name or even identify because they have been obscured by colonial history. Still he enacts their presentiment in the movement of his shuttle repairing not just his net but the sea, and we have to see this fisherman as I have seen him, the way Joyce says Ibsen sees "with large insight . . . with the sight of one who may look on the sun with open eyes."

The sea revises itself and outlasts empires with that defiant, exultant yes.

Let the poet's own shuttle go through a million failures to get the exact shape of the dimple crest in his grandmother's cheek while she rests, half-asleep in her lattice veranda chair, tired from hanging laundry, her stocking cap pulled back on her forehead to show its copper waves going into the gray foam of her hair; in front of her the sea light is trembling on the zinc shanties on the hillside with the dateless light of poetry. I think this is the radiant core of poetry Novalis means when he writes, "The more personal, local, peculiar, of its own time, a poem is, the nearer it stands to the centre of poetry." Even so, given my background I am sketching here, I would go further and add that human moments magnified over historical time do not lessen the complicated involvement with history and this is the revisionary poetics that makes a subject more than an image caged in rhetoric. It turns a subject into an event.

This is why I reject any vision which states that the poet speaks for his community or tribe as an insult both to the poet and to the community or tribe. What such vision demands is an annihilation of personality, and doing so would be to perpetuate one of the first tenets of the colonial order: the extinction of the individual. The demand is arrogant and requires that the poet commit the second worst sin of all, provincialism.

I should be clear that I am not advocating nor do I care for a poetry of the merely personal, of inchoate individuality. I mean personality as presence, alert to voice and its characteristics and the visible and invisible surrounding of the local terra firma; one for whom writing is a way to be "in concert with strangers within oneself," to use Wilson Harris's striking phrase. Further, I mean the personal when the lyric self significantly approaches what John Berger describes as the "will to preserve and complete, to create an equilibrium, to hold—and in that 'holding' to hope for an ultimate assurance—that this derives from a lived or imagined experience of love." Love, the lurching, healing shuttle of poetry!

Vision in the context of any tradition, it seems to me, is borne on an authoritarian pedestal, sepulchral as Roman marble: it achieves its formal contours and is celebrated in the airy domes of museums or in the gusting thoroughfares of the literary canon: rarely is it left in the open air, to the elements—sun and sea—which will gradually alter its perfection, until it dissolves into what it aims to imitate. Where it does alter, it becomes ruins. But it emerges from the ruins, patched together by subjugating asbestos and not the fisherman's or Penelope's patient needle. Its achievement is in its solidity as a monument erected wherever conquests are made. It speaks the one language of the conquistador, power, and responds only to the awe of terror, and its special brand of terror is to turn one passive, to paralyze with its elegiac, Parnassian cloud.

Visions calcify culture into egotistical civilization. This Aimé Césaire condemns as "that projection of man onto the world; . . . that stamp of man's effigy on the universe," but Césaire also praises, at a different pitch of distinction, writing, "True civilizations are poetic shocks: the shock of the stars, of the sun, the plant, the animal, the shock of the round globe, of the rain, of the light, of numbers, the shock of life, the shock of death." The motto is one and the same under the spirit shuttle of poetry: *Le dur désir de durer*. It aims to outlast what it repairs.

All these shocks in Césaire are shocks of time. Time on an island of the Caribbean is what I would call genesis in medias res: a space within which the Old World, as it is known, picks up in the middle of the unknown New World, unaffected by metropolitan time. An island, in reality, comes closest to what Coleridge means when he speaks of poetry as "that willing suspension of disbelief for the moment, which constitutes poetic faith." Derek Walcott puts it succinctly in his luminous epigram "Poetry is an island that breaks away from the main."

And what does that breakage sound like? Take this late poem by Walcott, since I have invoked him. In it we hear how he defies its Virgilian or Augustan coolness with subtle varying of Antillean cadence, syllables set down with such caring, careful love we hear and feel a negative voice cleansed of bitterness, widening into the evocation of grace. The poem, at its core, is a prayer.

Keep vigil with it now in my voice:

No opera, no gilded columns, no wine-dark seats,
no Penelope scouring the stalls with delicate glasses,
no practised ecstasy from the tireless tenor, no sweets
and wine at no interval, no altos, no basses

and violins sobbing as one; no opera house,
no museum, no actual theatre, no civic center
—and what else? Only the huge doors of clouds
with the setting disc through which we leave and enter,
only the deafening parks with their jumping crowds,
and the thudding speakers. Only the Government
Buildings down by the wharf, and another cruise ship
big as the capital, all blue glass and cement.
No masterpieces in huge frames to worship,
on such banalities has life been spent
in brightness, and yet there are the days
when every street corner rounds itself into
a sunlit surprise, a painting or a phrase,
canoes drawn up by the market, the harbour's blue,
the barracks. So much to do still, all of it praise.

Revision is literature as resistance. Poetry, whose spirit is reciprocating and anarchic to a greater degree, ignites the re-visionary force because of its "devotion to abandoned or exiled or obliterated myth" (Césaire again). What happens in the Janus-double of revision, therefore, is a bond of redemption *with* survival in an attempt to shatter the psychic structures of the oppressive order.

There are innumerable great examples of this kind of revision in reggae, but one significant instance, for me, actualized with sharp hydraulic energy splintering the monument of the English language, is a poem called "Mabrak," by the Jamaican Rastafarian poet Bongo Jerry. The elemental tongue of patois, that sphere of demonic utterance, punctuated with quick shafts of sunlight and rain breaking off broad thunderheads in the distance, is alive in the poem, which itself is charged with the biblical heritage of prophecy alive in Rastafarian revolutionary ideology.

Two things, though, before I read Bongo's poem.

First I want, perhaps unjustly, to set it against this remark by El-
iot: "The aim of the poet is to state a vision, and no vision of life can
be complete which does not include the articulate formulation of life
which human minds make." Vision here is expressed in the bureau-
cracy of prose. It mounts the imperial idea of eloquence—"articulate
formulation"—which often denies voice and agency to the so-called
inarticulate or mute subaltern.

Second, I will not go into the confluence of traditions behind the
poem, so the reading may sound a bit like glossolalia, which is the
strange effect that the poem is after; the prophetic apocalypse in it is
serious and deliberate:

> *Lightning*
> *Is the future brightening*
> *For last year man learn*
> *How to use black eyes*
> *(wise!)*
> *Mabrak:*
> *NEWSFLASH!*
> *Babylon plans crash*
> *Thunder interrupt their programme to*
> *Announce:*
> *BLACK ELECTRIC STORM*
> *IS HERE*
> *How long you feel fair to fine*
> *(WHITE) would last?*
> *How long calm in darkness*
> *When out of black*
> *come forth LIGHT?*
> *How long dis slave caste*
> *When out of*
> *The BLACK FUTURE*

Comes
I
RIGHTS
?
Every knee
Must bow
Every tongue
confess
Every language
Express
WORDWORKS
YOU
MUST
COME
To RAS
MABRAK,
Enlightening is BLACK
Hands writing the words of
Black message
For black hearts to feel.
MABRAK is righting the wrongs and brain whitening HOW?
Not just by washing out the straitening and wearing dashiki
ting:
MOSTOFTHESTRAITENINGISINTHETONGUE so
HOW?
Save the YOUNG
From the language that MEN teach,
the doctrine pope preach
skin bleach.
HOW ELSE? MAN must use MEN language
To carry dis message:
SILENCE BABEL TONGUES; recall and

recollect BLACK SPEECH.
Cramp all double meaning
And all that hiding behind language bar,
For that crossword speaking
When expressing feeling
Is just English language contribution to increase confusion in
Babel-land tower
delusion, name changing, word rearranging
ringing rings of roses, pocket full of poses:
SAR instead of RAS
Left us in a situation
Where education
Mek plenty African afraid, ashamed, unable to choose
(And use)
BLACK POWA (strange tongue)
NOT AGAIN!
Never be the same!
Never again shame!
Ever now communicate for now I and I come to recreate:
Sight sound and meaning to measure the feeling
Of BLACK HEARTS-alone-
MABRAK: frightening
MABRAK: black lightening
The coming of light to the black world: Come show I the way
Come make it plain as day now-come once, and come for all
And everyone better come to RAS
For I come far, have far to go from here:
For the white world must come to bloodbath
And bloodbath is as far as the white world can reach; so when
    MABRAK
Start skywriting,
LET BABYLON BURN

JEZEBEL MOURN
LET WEAK HEART CHURN
BLACK HOUSE STAND FIRM: for somewhere under
    ITYOPIA rainbow,
AFRICA WAITING FOR I

The exacting rhythm concatenates a new nobility in the spirit that Tasso outlines, that "the poet's objective takes him beyond simple, or even sophisticated, mimesis—beyond imitating existing forms into copying the perfect eternal forms . . . [T]he poet can penetrate and express the secrets of creation: and by so fashioning literary analogues to God's creation, the poet identifies himself as a true visionary who both views 'the sacred Forms' and *perceives mentally* what the design of God is." Jerry's poem is essentially spoken from the clouds and the ground at once, not in verbal utterance but in something unbidden to us like rain and roots, the one replenishing the other and vice versa into an endless circular design whose end or beginning we could never reach, and so when we come to the last line of this poem, we begin again. The shuttle moves thus.

I want to bring into focus here near the end in a far too summary manner the great visionaries in the Anglophone Caribbean tradition of twentieth-century fiction, whose superb re-visionary faculties have questioned handed-down vision and empowered Caribbean narratives with strange and unpredictable cosmic reality. One name came up earlier in my remarks, the Guyanese poet and novelist Wilson Harris. Harris was a land and hydrographic surveyor of the forests of Guyana in the 1940s, and his fiction has the precision of looking through a theodolite, where at first things appear oblique but then, in the arc of a second, they appear intensely brilliant. The enigmatic tension in the texture of his language retains strong traces of the pre-Columbian peoples of the Caribbean, enmeshed with the post-Columbian in a vivid, irreducible fiction that sustains, in his own words, "an involvement with the past that is equally an involvement with the present, even as the present becomes a threshold into the future." No other fiction from the Caribbean has haunted me more. Take just the opening passage of his first novel, *Palace of the Peacock*, published in 1960, which depicts in a dense phantasmagoria a triple death:

> A horseman appeared on the road coming at breakneck stride. A shot rang out suddenly, near and yet far as if the wind had been stretched and torn and had started coiling and running in an instant. The horseman stiffened with a devil's smile, and the horse reared, grinning fiendishly and snapping at the reins. The horseman gave a bow to heaven like a hanging man to his executioner, and rolled from his saddle on to the ground.

Nothing is taken for granted. The language creates a music that fuses landscape and character and makes us witnesses of what is actual and of the multiple possibilities our imaginations will have to work out. Further, Harris has said, "One's craft has to be linked in some way with some unconscious force, some sacramental energy that has been suppressed and lost." What I have been contending is that a wholeness of vision is incomplete—insufficient, even insipid—without re-vision, and re-vision is a constant revitalizing force attending to what has been suppressed and lost. Re-vision is creating with a kind of "sacramental energy." One looks out at the sea at immeasurable loss, and sees gain too great to put into words. And yet, and yet the hand moves to try.

My life is that trial. To close, then, on a rather bold note with such a trial of my own, I will read a poem called "A Surveyor's Journal." I wrote it about ten years ago in honor of and dedicated to Wilson Harris, who is ninety-five years old this year. In it I am attempting a sacramental bow toward heaven, striving to hold the mind's elation at having grown up by the sea where my ancestors call out to me onshore.

I took my name from the aftersky
of a Mesopotamian flood,
birdless as if culture had shed its wings
into a ground vulture on the plain.
Beneath the astral plane, a war-ripped sail,
rigged to its mast a lantern and a girl
who swayed and stared
off where the waves raced backwards.
I begged her in signs. She jumped
overboard, arms sieving seaweed, eyes netting home.
Dear Ivy, you live in my veins.
Spurned flesh, I couldn't bridle
the weathervane's shift; it turned and turned
into a landfall, and I, panting panther,
sleek carnivore of the horse-powered limbs,
ran from a reign of terror.
All my despairs in green rain, on leaves
I prayed to the mantis, head wrapped
in white, reading the "Song of God"
over a bowl of beef. Afterwards,
I hemmed into my skin this hymn:
O lemming souls of the mass migration that ended in drowning
O embroidered heart and marigold wrists that brushed the
  copperbrown field
O cargoes that left the dengue jungles and ended on the yellow
  fever shores
O compass points that needled the new to the old, stitching
  meridians into one tense
O reflecting telescope that spied the endangered specimens
Clashing head-brass,
the vertical man vs. the horizontal man,
those who lost their surnames

to the sea's ledger, beached up on the strange coast,
waiting for the Star Liner
to cross that imagined Mesopotamian water,
the ship's bulwarks in sleep,
weighed down a spirit-bird,
my calm, to never flounder,
to walk holy and light on this land.

A VOICE AT THE EDGE OF THE SEA: AN INTERVIEW WITH DEREK WALCOTT

JOSEPH BRODSKY ONCE SAID THAT WHEN YOU HEAR DEREK Walcott's voice, "the world unravels." It is a voice concomitant with the sea, and by connection, history. As I listen to its garrulous rise and fall from the veranda of his home by the sea in St. Lucia, the sphinx-head bluff of Pigeon Island keeping watch in the distance, an opposite understanding of Brodsky's statement takes hold: this is the voice that knots worlds together, or more accurately, re-knots worlds into the singular experience called the Caribbean.

After six decades of making the language that has elevated his Antillean world into the permanence of poetry, Walcott, at eighty-four years old, a Nobel laureate, maintains there is "so much to do still." Such a statement is impressively humbling—a mark of the vigor of a writer whose love of his island and the poetic craft has never diminished, for whom these two things have congealed into one great echo. Though moments of silence gather during our talk—moments when he looks out to the humming sea—his voice returns with the fulgent light "that reads like Dante" of his poetry, each time with greater magnificence. There were often, too, glittering moments of irreverence and laughter, including his fondness for puns, such as those by James Joyce, one of which he recited from memory.

Walcott's poetry, from its very early beginning, possesses a chromatic fluency that accelerates the sensual pulse of the moment, converting ordinary images beyond their actual reality, into the colloquial magnitude of fable. His landscape, named, vivifies "every neglected, self-pitying inlet / muttering in brackish dialect, the ropes of mangroves / . . . / losing itself in an unfinished phrase." The "unfinished," fragmentary by nature, is a vital feature of Walcott's poetics, which resemble his life and belief that "poetry is an island that breaks away from the main."

In 1964, Robert Graves praised Walcott's *Selected Poems* for handling "English with a closer understanding of its inner magic than most (if not any) of his English-born contemporaries." The true aspect of that inner magic is its outer votive life not at the core of English, a life that is the multitudinous heritage of the Caribbean, finding sublime utterance in Walcott. Shabine, the poet-persona of the brilliant poem "The Schooner *Flight*," declares what the phantasmagoria of that self is:

> *I'm just a red nigger who love the sea,*
> *I had a sound colonial education,*
> *I have Dutch, nigger, and English in me,*
> *and either I'm nobody, or I'm a nation.*

"English," Walcott once remarked, "is nobody's special property. It is the property of the imagination," and from this private sensibility evolves an oeuvre—seventeen poetry collections, nine volumes of drama, and a book of essays—of a pelagic imagination, inexorably striving against the stream, with unparalleled strength and beauty.

Recognized for a lyric torque of elemental potency in such poems as "Love After Love," "Coral," "Star," "A Sea-Chantey," among many others, it is the lush, anticipatory cadence of his serial style, beginning with the book-length poem *Another Life* (1973), in which the full force of dramatic poetry coheres into the tremendous music that has secured his lasting reputation. That music reaches its oceanic magnanimity in the epic poem *Omeros* (1990); in it Walcott's genius for breaching the membrane between metaphor and metonymy reads, in the words of one of its stunning moments, like "doors [that] dissolve into tenderness." The collections following *Omeros*—*The Bounty*, *Tiepolo's Hound*, *The Prodigal*, and *White Egrets*—all move serially, completely in sway with the early vow made in "Islands":

> *to write*
> *Verse crisp as sand, clear as sunlight,*
> *Cold as the curled wave, ordinary*
> *As a tumbler of island water;*
> *Yet, like a diarist, thereafter*
> *I savour their salt-haunted rooms.*

To savor, yes, and to repeat and conclude with the last line of the epigraph to Brodsky—a poem I consider the verbal companion of van Gogh's *Painter on His Way to Work*—we read Walcott's poetry and we "dissolve in a fiction greater than our lives, the sea, the sun."

ISHION HUTCHINSON: Every time I arrive here in St. Lucia, I remember these lines from your early poem "Homecoming: Anse La Raye": "and never guessed you'd come / to know there are homecomings without home." How has the tension or paradox of home evolved for you?

DEREK WALCOTT: I don't think we ever have complete homecoming. There is always a little extra left that we need to occupy, or something to contradict the elation of being home.

What contradicts the elation of being home for you?

I think the reality of being in the Caribbean, the poverty, the reality of the illiteracy; it is a reality a lot of writers do not try to confront. I guess the poverty particularly.

From the standpoint of craft, what enabled you to achieve the amazing synthesis of autobiography and the reality of your island in your work—I am thinking especially of *Another Life*?

One of the big influences on the book [*Another Life*] is Pasternak's *My Sister—Life*. He is a tremendous writer.

What about, and this is going to sound academic, someone out of the twinned idea in the Romantic tradition of self and landscape, Wordsworth in particular?

That's very academic.

Let me stop.

(*Laughing*.) No, no. You can ask the question. I think we do not make [a] distinction about people's nationality. I mean, the move from Wordsworth to Pasternak is basically very simple, and there is no real distinction between Englishness and being Russian. In fact, it is a good, surprising comparison because the affection Wordsworth has for his landscape and Pasternak for his is identical.

You have said you consider yourself at the beginning of a Caribbean tradition. What do you think has happened or is happening in that tradition?

Well, what I think is quite apart from what I knew might [have] happened. What has happened is astonishing. The amount of young, good writers is quite phenomenal, I think. Don't you think?

Absolutely. Because of your work and others who were at the beginning, now we are able to see ourselves in a way which illuminates our own attempt of what is possible.
Yes. In a way it was inevitable, though. You can't have such a history and so much urgency to talk in the experience of that history. You can't muffle those voices, you know, they would be articulated, they would be uttered anyway. It is just that they are being very well uttered.

In both poetry and prose?
Not so much prose.

Why is that so?
Because you have to be, for you to write prose, really, really great to do it. You can get away with a lot [in] poetry. You have things that are for you—your history, your race, your language, all these things. You begin with pluses. I don't think you begin this way with prose, that you need them at the beginning. But they are inevitable in poetry; they are inside you, you know.

One of the great prose works of not so long ago is *Texaco* by Patrick Chamoiseau, which you have praised—
Oh yes.

For its "adjectival style" over the nominal. What exactly is the adjectival style?
You'd have to have a melody. An example in mine—in fact I did not remember that is one of the qualities of Patrick's work—in fact I don't remember that now, but if I saw it, I will know it.

You said it is the gesture of the storyteller. I get that to mean it is expansive, broad gestures, which I think of as an element of your work. It made me think about the usual thing of poetry as compressive, more so than with prose.

The people who have influenced me or whom I have imitated are writers who are compressors, like Hemingway particularly. Pasternak, too. But I think if you are influenced by great poets like that writing prose, that what you pick up from them or what you have to pick up, is what I would call simultaneity. The one instance of several things going on, and I think in any West Indian instance there is a tremendous amount going on, in race alone, you know what I mean?

I do. We have been talking about prose, and you have published essays, but never any fiction.
No.

You never wrote any?
Yeah, I wrote a very bad novel. A terrible novel. I think if you deal with theater, it takes up where the novel might anyway; you have to deal with plot, character, and the story, very fictional.

On occasions you have spoken about poems you return to—Walter de la Mare's "Farewell," for instance—not necessarily for their technical brilliance, but for the force of the benediction. Are there any of your own poems you go back to for the same reason?
That's a very good phrase, "force of the benediction," that is [a] terrific way to put it . . . I have read parts of work of mine that are irrepressible in terms of reciting them.

I have seen you recite "The Light of the World," and it brought you to tears.
Yes, yes. It is a long poem.

It is a majestic poem.

(*Laughs.*) Thank you.

You told Edward Hirsch in an interview when your *Collected Poems* (1986) came out that there are "deficiencies" there. Has *The Poetry of Derek Walcott, 1948–2013* corrected those deficiencies?

I don't remember what poems, if any. There weren't many alterations or adaptations or changes in this collection. It was done by Glyn Maxwell, so he ran the whole thing. It is his book, kind of. He did a good job, I think.

He did a phenomenal job. So there were no revisions to any of the poems?

Not really, no.

It made me wonder—since some of your earliest poems are here— about the impulse to revise early work. Auden, for example, famously revised his early work. Lowell is another. Did you have that impulse?

No, I can't say so. I'd probably rewrite. I would just write another poem, or something.

Are you writing poems now?

Yes. I am working on a book about a painter. I think the shape is going to be several poems. I think so. The painter is Peter Doig. You know him? . . . He lives in Trinidad, a Scotsman. I like him a lot.

Would you say the new poems resemble the serial blank verse of *White Egrets*?

I have not done enough yet, I don't know. I have done a few like that, but in fact I don't know quite what I am doing. I think constantly I am trying to find a natural link between prose and poetry. For me, unless a writer has that quality—I mean if a prose writer has that quality, then it makes good poetry; the prose, as it is done in Pasternak. You don't have to scan it; it divides itself rhythmically.

You have never done a book that is a mixture of prose and poetry.
    No. I don't believe in the idea actually, although I practice it. I think for a poet to set out to do a prose and poetry book is a kind of cop-out. If he has set out to do it, then it is a cop-out. If it has happened, then it is a different thing. See what I mean?

It seems to happen in some contemporary poets really well. The one that comes to mind now is Alice Oswald.
    I like her a lot. You know her? . . . You must tell her how much I admire her work. I really enjoy it.

I will. Speaking of that, I read in Bremen [Germany], and Les Murray was present. I know you admire him.
    Les is great, really terrific.

What would you regard as your greatest strength as a poet?
    I can't tell. I think there are lots of times when I have maybe caught the light in certain passages; certainly they are informed by the presence of the light a lot. The Caribbean light at sunrise and sunset.

Do you have a favorite of your collections?
    I think it would be what do I enjoy reading. I like reading "The Spoiler's Return," maybe because it is so direct.

There is a recent documentary, *Poetry Is an Island*, about your life. What do you think of it?
    I think it is very well done, it is not fussy, and it gives a lot [of]

room to my friends. It is good; the director, Ida Does, is a sensitive woman.

As you mention friends, I did want to ask you, finally, about your late friend Seamus Heaney. Is there a memory of him that endures with you?

When I sit here, I can see him at the edge of the water [Walcott points to the sea] or sitting on one of the chairs, you know. Yes, he's right there, I see him at the edge of the sea.

THE CLASSICS CAN CONSOLE?

HOMECOMING, IN THE ODYSSEAN SENSE, IS THE SOURCE OF my title. I will arrive there by circumvention. I promise. I am going to take the mythic way and traverse many siren songs getting to my source.

I will start with a sound you cannot hear.

The name for that sound, a strange word from my childhood, is *kaachi*. That word—*kaachi*—ordered life in the sugarcane districts of St. Thomas, the easternmost parish in Jamaica. When it sounded, conversations ended and bodies departed abruptly. After the rush of their disappearance, a brief silence always followed. I heard in that silence the sharp green of the sugarcane flags. I heard the heat rising off the asphalt. And, if it was late at night when the bodies left, I heard the many sighs between bush and stars. The *kaachi* had been sounding and ordering lives in St. Thomas for centuries. Perhaps at first it was an iron bell, like that one shaken at my primary school. Or it was no other instrument but an overseer's voice, calling the enslaved people to the sugarcane field. History has swallowed its origin whole.

The *kaachi* I heard growing up was neither a bell nor a voice but an electric horn that blared from Tropicana Sugar Estate's factory.

The sound traveled miles. The sound reached into the barracks of Jane Ash Corner, Duckenfield, Cheswick, Hampton Court, Dalvey—all those gently falling Anglo-Saxon district names—out of which bodies rose up at the break of dawn, at midday, at dusk, at bedtime, and at midnight and filed off down the marl-and-ash road to sweat in the satanic vats. Time was shaped by the *kaachi*'s relentless change of shift. What I heard was the sound of a tragic pastoral, the sound of a place blunted into routines of and for survival, routines intimately tied to the sugarcane crop, the original sin of suffering. Sugarcane. *Saccharum officinarum*. The sound has a terrifying pathos.

But you cannot hear the incessant shrill hiss of the *kaachi*. It is a sound I would not *want* you to hear. I want you to hear another sound, one that even as it issues—even as it is uttered—from the pain of the sugarcane, out of the despair of history, manages to bear an elemental cry that imagines itself beyond pain, beyond despair, beyond cane, and beyond history.

Here is that sound:

Half my friends are dead.
I will make you new ones, said earth.
No, give me them back, as they were, instead,
with faults and all, I cried.

Tonight I can snatch their talk
from the faint surf's drone
through the canes, but I cannot walk

on the moonlit leaves of ocean
down that white road alone,
or float with the dreaming motion

of owls leaving earth's load.
O earth, the number of friends you keep
exceeds those left to be loved.

The sea canes by the cliff flash green and silver;
they were the seraph lances of my faith,
but out of what is lost grows something stronger

that has the rational radiance of stone,
enduring moonlight, further than despair,
strong as the wind, that through dividing canes

brings those we love before us, as they were,
with faults and all, not nobler, just there.

This poem is called "Sea Canes," and it appears in Derek Walcott's 1976 volume, *Sea Grapes*. Five tercet stanzas set between a quatrain and a couplet, alternating full and half rhymes, "Sea Canes" has the skewed formality of a cultivated sugarcane plot, lost in a dense forest of classical oaks and beech trees. This cultivated structure falls away where the rhythm of the poem commingles into an Antillean melody, and you hear, with pictorial clarity, a landscape that is asymmetrical, self-creating, and involved in the speaker's lament. A reminder of the dead and the radical site of consolation. How does the poem become such a site? A fair amount of classicism drives the matter.

There's the ecologic convention; there's the apostrophe to earth, earth that is allegorized into a speaking subject; there's the elegiac final couplet with a last line ghosting dactylic pentameter and standing like a funeral epigram; and above all, there's a Grecian, and later a Roman, stoicism in light of death—both acceptance and refutation—that marks the poem's consolation. Such artifice appears naturally embedded in the poem. The poem overcomes this classical artifice in one way I find crucial, and that is in the ritual journey of the first-person singular, "I," to the first-person plural, "we"—the private to the ceremonial. This journey encompasses "the work of mourning." Framing the classics in this light would seem to give a positive answer to my title's question: "Yes, the classics can console."

The work of mourning (Freud's phrase) is a transmutation of the self into an other. If we begin, though, to consider the work of mourning within the context of the Caribbean's colonial history—and there's no escaping taking stock of that history—an irreconcilable difficulty presents itself. This history already consigns the Caribbean self into the position of the other. The immediate first question is, Does the work of mourning, illustrated in poetry forged out of classicism, constitute a hollowing of the other?

The question isn't naive. There is no doubt as to the convergence of the classics, works written throughout the period of the Greco-Roman Empire, with the colonized world of, say, the British Empire of the nineteenth and twentieth centuries. The classics of the former empire were the cherished cultural property of the latter. They were deployed as a tool in the colonized space to reinforce and validate the "civilizing mission" of British imperialism. This raises immediately a second question: What recourse of language, then, does a person with a sound colonial background, one inevitably shaped by the classics, inadvertently and directly, have when considering the work of mourning? The question put this way would seem to imply a negative answer to my title's question: "No, the classics cannot console."

Well, neither quite no nor quite yes. The situation calls for a far more diffident response. A collision. Such a word exists, though it resides for me outside the English language or any other standard European language. The word I am thinking of is *pallaksch*, a word the German poet Friedrich Hölderlin invented during his madness while translating Sophocles's *Antigone*. *Pallaksch* means yes and no. *Pallaksch, pallaksch*. Those of you who recognize the source of my essay's title might understand immediately why Hölderlin's self-othering word *pallaksch*, yes and no, such a beautiful agon of bitter ambivalence, is the just response.

Or you might be thinking something else altogether. You might be thinking the question mark is a caricature of the end-stopped original. My question mark imposes an unheard pitch of defiance against a system of power and domination in which the classics play a central role. The imposition of the question mark, moreover, is an act of doubt. The question mark is an agon of *pallaksch* rather than a reproach to the certainty of the original end-stopped statement, "The classics can console."

One of the powerful ways in which "Sea Canes" overcomes classical artifice is through the ritual journey from "I" to "we," a democratization of mourning. By crossing from the personal into a civil polity, "Sea Canes" enacts a metaphysical trespass that is poetry's natural habitat. The poem discovers there is "something there" in the landscape, a landscape as much insulted as it is romanticized. The "something there" is a "numinous consciousness," to use a term coined by the early twentieth-century German Lutheran theologian Rudolf

Otto. "Sea Canes" writes into the genius loci, recovering choric pres-
ences obscured by history. At every turn, we find the landscape in
motion: "the faint surf's drone," "the moonlit leaves of ocean," "owls
leaving earth's load," "the sea canes by the cliff flash[ing] green and
silver," and "the wind . . . through dividing canes," all of which, in
effect, brings consolation.

These simple, radiant turns of image not only retrieve vanished
ancestral presences (as if from a sunken archive) but also refuse to ide-
alize the dead, as is typical in the classical tradition of the elegy. The
final tercet encloses "the rational radiance of stone," erecting a living
memorial in which, when we return to it, we encounter a deep humil-
ity akin to what Otto calls "mysterium tremendum": its simplicity is
the terror and awe of beholding the ancestors.

That couplet again:

brings those we love before us, as they were,
with faults and all, not nobler, just there.

The dead are recognized by the epitaph "those we love," which
might appear commonplace. But those words are the choral recog-
nition and a claiming of the hard-stressed love from the historical
violence of the sugarcane. The phrase also signals a declaration of love.
An act of vigilance.

Those we love before us: how numinous it sounds!

My reading of Walcott here is an attempt to show how certain
modalities of the classics impinge upon a reader's desire for consola-
tion. I mean a reader growing out of the cane, for whom the trauma
of colonial history is ongoing and contingent on the classics. I am that
reader. Such a reader faces what Simone Weil calls "piety with regard
to the dead: to do everything for what does not exist."

*   *   *

When I was eight years old, I was sent to purchase charcoal from a man named Maas Brown, a charcoal burner who lived deep in a clearing at the edge of a former sugarcane plantation. Acres of cane grew there still. I knew nothing much about Maas Brown, a widower with no children, except that when he was a young man, he had fought in some war overseas. He was not liked. No one spoke fondly about him. But he was tolerated, being the closest charcoal burner in the district. I had gone to his yard before to purchase charcoal, but always with cousins or other company. Those walks were filled with dread. The talk was of Maas Brown's varied wickedness, the highlight of which was how he butchered little boys and fed them to his pack of mongrels, the hounds that roamed his yard. And on this occasion, alone, I was to go buy charcoal. The snarls of the dogs were in my ears even before I arrived at the ash mound outside Maas Brown's corrugated-iron gate. I couldn't hear my voice calling his name. But I heard a voice saying, "Come in, come in. The gate unlatched." I heard the dogs, whimpering, snarling, growling. Sense prevailed. I shouted to the voice behind the gate that I was afraid of the dogs. Maas Brown, who I could now tell spoke from the tree stump at his front door, the one he sat on to measure out charcoal, said I had nothing to fear. "I'm with them. Come in." I pushed the gate, went in. The pack circled me—yapping and snapping at each other, barking at a low thrum—but kept their distance. I was in shock and stood paralyzed. Then one broke from the circle, rushed toward me. I heard Maas Brown shout, "Don't run"—but I did, and the entire pack chased me as I fled, and they seemed to multiply by the hundreds, seething mongrels, heated, maddened for flesh, for blood, for bones. And they got it: I fell, and their teeth sank in. Claws ripped my skin white, then red. I was dragged around in the ash-and-dirt yard like a rag doll, fainting in and out, barely conscious of Maas Brown, his tall angular figure, black as the charcoal he sold, risen, beating off his dogs vigorously with a stick, and as he did, swinging and wailing, calling out their names: "Virgil, Homer . . ." There were other names, too—Bismarck, Churchill, Napoleon—none of which I had ever heard, all foreign, distant, hard sounding. And as he called out their names and the pack receded from me, I heard his voice in a half-chanting, consolatory tone, "Homer, Virgil," and so on, a dim glimmer until all went black.

All the names of the dead in Homer's *Iliad* appear laid out, indiscriminately, Trojans and Greeks, in eight columns of the opening pages of Alice Oswald's *Memorial*, published in 2011. Two hundred and forty names. *Memorial* is Oswald's fugitive lyric translation, an excavation, of Homer's *Iliad*. Oswald calls her digging into the *Iliad* "a kind of oral cemetery." If it is indeed an oral cemetery, it is the kind the philosopher Gillian Rose termed "a borderless cemetery in the air" after seeing the death camps in Poland. Air. Breath. That is what Oswald excavates, recovering and making an inventory of these names from the epic's bulk. They're etched on vertical columns, to stand before us, as they were, with faults and all, not nobler, just there.

PROTESILAUS
ECHEPOLUS
ELEPHENOR
SIMOISIUS
LEUKOS
DEMOCOON
DIORES
PIROUS
PHEGEUS
IDAEUS
ODIOS
PHAESTUS
SCAMANDRIUS
PHERECLES
PEDAEUS
HYPSENOR
ASTYNOOS
HYPEIRON
ABAS
POLYIDOS
XANTHUS
THOON
ECHEMMON
CHROMIUS
PANDARUS
DEICOON
ORSILOCHUS
CRETHON
PYLAEMENES
MYDON
MENESTHES
ANCHIALOS
AMPHIUS
TLEPOLEMOS
COERANUS
CHROMIUS
ALCASTOR
ALCANDER
HALIUS
PYRTANIS
NOEMON
TEUTHRAS
ORESTES
TRECHUS
OENOMAUS
HELENUS
ORESBIUS
PERIPHAS
ACAMAS
AXYLUS
CALESIUS
PEDASUS
AESEPUS
ASTYALOS

PIDUTES
ARETAON
ANTILOCHUS
ELATUS
PHYLAKOS
MELANTHIUS
ADRESTUS
MENESTHIUS
IPHINOUS
ENIOPEUS
AGELAOS
ORSILOCHUS
ORMENUS
OPHELESTES
DAETOR
CHROMIUS
LYCOPHONTES
AMOPAON
MELANIPPUS
GORGYTHION
ARCHEPTOLEMOS
DOLON
RHESUS
ISOS
ANTIPHOS
PEISANDER
HIPPOLOCHUS
IPHIDAMAS
COON
ASAEUS
AUTONOOS
OPITES
DOLOPS
OPHELTIUS
AGELAOS
AESYMNUS
ORUS
HIPPONOUS
THYMBRAIUS
MOLION
ADRESTUS
AMPHIUS
HIPPODAMOS
HYPEIROCHOS
AGASTRAPHUS
THOON
ENNOMUS
CHERSIDAMAS
SOCUS
CHAROPS
DORYCLES
PANDOCUS
LYSANDER
PYRASUS

PYLARTES
APISAON
DAMASOS
PYLON
ORMENOS
HIPPOMACHOS
ANTIPHATES
MENON
IAMENOS
ORESTES
EPICLES
IMBRIOS
AMPHIMACHOS
OTHRYON
ASIUS
ALCATHOUS
OINOMAOS
ASKALAPHOS
APHAREUS
THOON
ANTILOCHUS
DEIPUROS
PEISANDER
HARPALION
EUCHENOR
SATNIUS
PROTHOENOR
ARCHELOCHUS
PROMACHUS
ILIONEUS
STICHIUS
ARCESILAUS
MEDON
IASUS
MECISTEUS
ECHIUS
CLONIUS
DEIOCHUS
KALETOR
LYKOPHRON
KLEITOS
SCHEDIOS
LAODAMAS
OTOS
KROISMOS
DOLOPS
MELANIPPUS
PERIPHETOS
PURAICHMES
AREILYCUS
THOAS
AMPHICLUS
ATUMNIOS
MARIS

KLEOBULOS
LYKON
AKAMAS
ERYMAS
PRONOOS
THESTOR
ERYLAOS
ERYMAS
AMPHOTERUS
EPALTES
TLEPOLEMOS
ECHIOS
PURIS
IPHES
EUIPPOS
POLYMELOS
THRASYMELOS
PEDASUS
SARPEDON
EPIGEUS
BATHYCLES
LAOGONUS
PATROCLUS
EUPHORBAS
HIPPOTHOUS
SCHEDIUS
PHORCYS
LEOCRITUS
APISAON
ARETUS
PODES
KOIRANUS
IPHITUS
DEMOLEON
HIPPODAMAS
POLYDORUS
DRYOPS
DEMUCHUS
LAOGONUS
DARDANUS
TROS
MULIUS
RHIGMOS
LYCAON
THERSILOCHUS
MYDON
ASTYPYLOS
MNESIUS
THRASIUS
AINIOS
OPHELESTES
HECTOR

What else is being recovered? Irrecoverable time. The lyric moments, about the length of a name, buried within the poem's narrative are grace notes, interludes of consciousness. Oswald's columns make us think of certain architectural war memorials, for instance, the Vietnam Veterans Memorial in Washington, D.C., or the Australian War Memorial in Canberra. On a monumental scale, they appeal to our historical sense of consciousness, a form of commemoration Oswald's columns are engaging with. But I think the grace notes of lyric consciousness in Oswald's are closer to the obduracy of lightness we find in the sculpture gardens of the Scottish poet and artist Ian Hamilton Finlay.

Why is looking up at the list-nakedness of Oswald's columns so moving? Silence permeates them. They await recitation. "Homer makes us hearers," Alexander Pope says, and the names, simply by standing before us with such immediacy, awaiting recitation, are speech made

flesh. Oswald's mnemotechnic columns, then, operate as a form of recalling, each victim summoned to bear witness—to self-testify—to the dignity of the individual in the face of extreme violence. Since each victim is a soldier, inevitably subscribed to the heroic code, *arete*, that greater violence is death.

The greater violence, though, is not death itself but more what Homeric death does: it turns a subject into an object, a person into a thing. This form of objectification is where death succeeds in the total erasure of one's name from time. Weil defines this violence of erasure—"the true hero" of the *Iliad*—as force. In a moment, I want you to think of this force as a peculiar American systemic power of abuse that subjugates and is the cause of innumerable erasures, for over four centuries. For now, I want you to think of Homeric deaths the way Barbara Graziosi writes in her luminous book on Homer:

Homeric deaths have their roots in experience, it seems, rather than gruesome fancy.

Each man dies in a particular way. Each has a name, a family, and a specific life that has been cut short. There is no "unknown soldier" in Homer: every casualty is named.

The stark litany of Oswald's names fills the ear/air as prayer. Each name is a prayer, is a bid for futurity, a plea that can only be made in doubt, the most vulnerable human position imaginable, which, when the stone columns speak together across three millennia, we hear the street outside this building, wailing. Make note of this wailing.

That's our aural experience of Oswald's columns. They allow no comforting fiction—no narrative—to intervene between our position as spectators, shaping our imaginary empathy, and the names' own intrinsic existence. I am saying that as we say the names, we go inside the columns as inside their conscience wrecked by enslavement, war, and death.

The *kaachi* sounds. Back to St. Thomas. To dogs and to Maas Brown. The widower and war veteran alone in the country of cane. You can envision the emptiness and sorrow of his life. The many losses. He had fought in a foreign war. He had come back to Jamaica. Whether that war was won or not, he had come back defeated, his name never to be memorialized anywhere. For him, there can't be any victory. To live as a charcoal burner, mostly unliked, haunted by the myth of child sacrifice. Not even his coal was praised, not even that, and *that* was his life. He had only his dogs. And yet he did the most surprising thing, the most un-Jamaican thing, to these mongrels, the most Adamic thing: he named them. Classical heritage and war and history gave Maas Brown language to name his mongrels. Naming them was his consolation. His voice half chantingly calling their names—"Virgil, Homer . . ."—rescued me and impressed in me what I can belatedly acknowledge as a memory locus, to forge in

In Memory of Jordan Russell Davis
In Memory of Eric Garner
In Memory of John Crawford
In Memory of Michael Brown
In Memory of Akai Gurley
In Memory of Tamir Rice
In Memory of Walter Scott
In Memory of Freddie Gray
In Memory
In Memory
In Memory
In Memory
In Memory
In Memory
In Memory
In Memory
In Memory
In Memory
In Memory
In Memory
In Memory
In Memory
In Memory
In Memory
In Memory
In Memory
In Memory
In Memory

poetry "piety with regard to the dead: to do everything for what does not exist."

Which is, in the first instance, naming.

Where Oswald opens her atmospheric translation of Homer's *Iliad* with a catalog of names of the dead killed in battle, Claudia Rankine creates, near the close of her 2014 collection, *Citizen*, a catalog of the names of African American men killed by police on American streets: Rankine's column differs—a significant difference—from Oswald's in that Rankine's carries the epitaph "In Memory of" before the listed names. This one formal, even formulaic, stroke signals that *Citizen* is a tragic elegy.

In memory of. In memoriam. Into memory. The term "in memory of" is possessive, a stance "so as to keep alive the remembrance of; as a memorial to; as a record of" the departed, according to the *OED*. Rankine's use of it intends a radical stance against the neutrality that threatens to reduce the events of these deaths to death alone. They are not. They are deaths encountering the existential horror of American life for black lives. They are deaths caused by the force peculiar but not exclusive to an American systemic power of extreme erasure, white supremacy. That existential horror of erasure began when the African enslaved were stripped of their names on board the slave ships. Slavers tended to keep impeccable records of voyages. Ships, crew, and stocks were named and labeled, but of the African bodies on board, or rather

List of Slave Vessels captured by H.M.S. Sybille & Tender from May 1827 to May 1829 under the hulls of the ships, the records registered only their numbers, their assumed ages, and their genders, often followed by "ditto man" and "ditto woman" and "ditto boy" and "ditto girl."

Rankine's ritualistic "in memory of" brings that past of violent erasure to notice. I write "to notice," because I want to bring into orbit what the late Toni Morrison said, that "to notice is to recognize an already discredited difference." This, to a great degree, is what Rankine's "in memory of," as both the repetition of history and the refutation of that history's violence, amounts to. Rankine notices and subtly protests the ever-present past—the continual racist violence—by memorializing black names. Each yoking together of the commonplace, predictable sentiment of grief, "in memory of," with an intimate, unpredictable name of a black victim, intensifies the intimacy intrinsic to each name, so each name testifies to its humanity and against what seeks to erase that humanity.

Rankine's conjoining of "in memory of" with names forms an antiphony of mourning and rage; stricken by grief, passivity interacts with activity, inertia with velocity, and so her poem not only pronounces what Geoffrey Hill calls "a sad and angry consolation" but creates a pillar of remembrance, and remembrance is justice.

Above are eight names from my 2014 edition of *Citizen*. You hear them, the wailing in the streets. After these eight names, the phrase "In Memory" continues without any name next to it until it fades into the whiteness of the page. This eerie technique alerts us to a terrible anticipation: more names will come. They have come. They keep coming. Each subsequent edition of *Citizen* prints new names, bodies stacked on bodies, the recent dead fading into whiteness ad infinitum. Seven hundred and nine as of October 14, 2019, at 4:54 p.m., when I last could bear to look up the statistics.

"For other men," Simone Weil writes in her essay about force in the *Iliad*, "death appears as a limit set in advance on the future; for the soldier death is the future, the future his profession assigns him." This to me illuminates, in a perverse reversed sense, the predicament of black male life in America. The knowledge, inconsolable, calls the poem to function beyond the statistical representation of memorializing black victims, even as it participates in this process of naming and memorializing. In other words, Rankine takes what the Victorian historian A. W. Kinglake calls "the strong vertical light of Homer's poetry" into a modern or postmodern form of witnessing, one that is at once documentary—names are named—and prophesying, making space to memorialize future death.

And yet, and this is crucial, the poet (or the poet's voice) does not function as a mediating force between what has happened and what will happen; her column, which is its triumph, bears the *fact*—and something other than the fact, not fiction, but something resembling the transcendental work of fiction, which saves the fact from the degradation of becoming no more than a statistical artifact like the logbook of a slave ship. This double bearing, so to speak, is what I am terming "justice as remembrance"; with this column of naming, Rankine inaugurates the just credence that history and the present have so far failed to achieve, and so the future remains a white fade-out of unknowing. Such justice, to be certain, is not mere poetic justice; even as the column is restricted by the material and formal limit of the poem—echoing as it does in a modernistic way the Homeric catalog—both matter and form unite precisely to create that felt change in consciousness that occurs when a serious and sensuous ethic supersedes a poem's concrete conceit, so these names of extrajudicial killings—their present and past and future—have become permanent record.

The news in Homer remains news. Naming is news, it is how news travels, and it is, finally, a homecoming. Telemachus at the courts of Nestor and Menelaus. His father with Alcinous. Helen on the walls of Troy. She names the warriors, the majority of whom never return home, yet in her voice, as here translated into English by Robert Fitzgerald, they live on:

> *the earth already held them fast,*
> *long dead in the life-giving earth of Lacedaemon,*
> *the dear land of their fathers.*

Rankine's voice is such an oral archive. In it, all times are fused in order to recall, through remembrance, these black deaths, lifting them out of the ontological pit of social death and injustice, where these names would have been lost, as so many were across the transatlantic passage.

The sirens will become as loud as the *kaachi* you cannot hear.

The classics reveal what we have done to ourselves. They are an inexpungible record that bears a "mysterious predestination" and "the creative lucidity of the poet" (to use two phrases of Rachel Bespaloff's) necessary for us to understand the persistence of the past within the future. The canonical sense of the classics, the sense that perpetuates Eurocentrism, is still pervasive. This is the sense established by T. S. Eliot, that great purveyor of Western culture, in his well-known lecture "What Is a Classic?," delivered to the Virgil Society of London in 1944. The Eurocentrism of Eliot's classicism animates his book *After Strange Gods*, which consists of three addresses delivered in 1933 at the University of Virginia.

After Strange Gods is subtitled *A Primer of Modern Heresy*. Eliot's modern is medieval, dogmatic, and anguished; his heresy less a dissension and more an orthodoxy, stridently validating twentieth-century imperialism. The preface of *After Strange Gods* opens this way:

> The three lectures which follow were not undertaken as exercises
> in literary criticism. If the reader insists upon considering them
> as such, I should like to guard against misunderstanding as far
> as possible. The lectures are not designed to set forth, even in
> the most summary form, my opinions of the work of contempo-
> rary writers: they are concerned with certain ideas in illustration
> of which I have drawn upon the work of some of the few modern
> writers whose work I know.

Not literary criticism, therefore. What then are these "certain ideas" Eliot wished to pose to his Virginia audience? Before I say, it is useful to see how Eliot himself arrived—physically, psychically—in Virginia. He traces his circuit from New England across the Potomac, at which point he writes, "to cross into Virginia is as definite an experience as to cross from England to Wales, almost as definite as to cross the English Channel." That definite. Eliot here sets up arriving in the state of Virginia, the jewel of the antebellum South, like an emperor visiting from his beloved, fabled Rome to shore up his loyal but crumbling province.

It is not a jewel the visiting emperor finds. He finds, in Virginia—and herein lies the thrust of Eliot's ideas—a civilization that has "had to survive the immense pressure towards monotony exerted by the industrial expansion of the latter part of the nineteenth and the first part of the twentieth century." The ruins are spiritual and psychological wounds. But the emperor has come to heal, to restore faith in the civilizing project. As such, Eliot surmises with these three sentences a blend of malaise and prophecy that, if he were not dead serious and the sentences had not taken far-reaching hold in certain factions of American society in the second part of the twentieth century up to this very moment, would have been laughable. Eliot writes,

> The Civil War was certainly the greatest disaster in the whole of American history; it is just as certainly a disaster from which the country has never recovered, and perhaps never will: we are always too ready to assume that the good effects of wars, if any, abide permanently while the ill-effects are obliterated by time. Yet I think that the chances for the re-establishment of a native culture are perhaps better here than in New England. You are farther away from New York; you have been less industrialised and less invaded by foreign races; and you have a more opulent soil.

The pitch of the nativist argument is even, for us in 2019, more discomfiting when we hear it in the voice of the highest office in Washington. The intelligent, the magisterial weighing of words Eliot here practices is obscured and reduced to a few alarmists keening on the airwaves: "disaster," "native culture," "invaded by foreign races."

Evoking our current political moment and alloying it to Eliot's political views as expressed in his lectures of 1933 and 1944 is, I trust, not frivolous. It is also instructive to see Eliot through what J. M. Coetzee calls "supra-national organisation," which, for Eliot, of course, means all of Western civilization, which has "its descent . . . from Rome via the Church of Rome," and "its originary classic must therefore be the epic of Rome, Virgil's *Aeneid*." From where we are now, the major change in this program of Western hegemony is the demotion of the Church of Rome as the centralizing power and the elevation of a plutocratic secular system of governance as practiced by European and American powers.

Here I must ask a redundant but difficult question: Do the classics function as a currency within this system? The answer is easy. Yes, exponentially, and within a peculiar form of discredit I wish to make clear.

To say what this discredit is, or rather how this discredit functions, let me refer again to Coetzee. Ever the mordant ironist, he gave his lecture in Graz, Austria, in 1991 the same title as Eliot's lecture, "What Is a Classic?" Coetzee quotes from Ezra Pound's poem *Hugh Selwyn Mauberley* the famous line, "born / In a half-savage country, out of date," which Coetzee glosses as the stock-in-trade of Eliot's work: the "attempt to understand this feeling or this fate" of being out of date as something "not uncommon," "particularly [among] young colonials struggling to match their inherited culture to their daily experience." "To such young people," Coetzee continues, "the high culture of the metropolis may arrive in the form of powerful experience which cannot, however, be embedded in their lives in any obvious way, and which seem therefore to have their existence in some transcendent realm." In other words, one has to pay a high price—in effect, suppressing one's "native" cultural inheritance—in order to enter the high precincts of Euro-classicism.

The transcendent realm is like credit. You have to have credit to get credit. But it is the vast population of the creditless who are exploited so that some, a powerful minority, may have credit, while those without credit keep striving for it, without much recourse to alternatives. Herein lies the perpetual, servile state of colonization. A clear declension of an economy that began with the extermination of Indigenous peoples, the enslavement of African peoples, through to the Civil War, which for Eliot is "the greatest disaster in the whole of American history," up to Reconstruction and Jim Crow, and on to the varying present-day disenfranchisements of black lives.

It must be said, however, the undeniable will of the colonized, displaced yet rooted within their inherited culture, rises up to explode the human discredit reinforced by the classics. Such creative action persists as a living form of renunciatory consolation in the work of some of the writers I have been referencing here: Walcott, Oswald, and Rankine. These works, as Geoffrey Hill expresses it in *The Orchards of Syon*,

> *are to console us*
> *with their own gift, which is like perfect pitch.*
> *Let us commit that to our dust. What*
> *ought a poem to be? Answer, a sad*
> *and angry consolation. What is*
> *the poem? What figures? Say,*
> *a sad and angry consolation. That's*
> *beautiful. Once more? A sad and angry*
> *consolation.*

Coetzee ends part one of his lecture with this portrait of Eliot as "a man trying to redefine the world around him—America, Europe— rather than confronting the reality of his not-so-grand position as a man whose narrowly academic, Eurocentric education had prepared him for little else but life as a mandarin in one of the New England ivory towers." The portrait is accurate as far as it goes. Possessing the classics—like good credit—ensured Eliot's ascendancy. Put emphatically: possessing the classics, like currency handed down as if by aristocratic fiat, ensured Eliot the ivory towers *forever*. Eliot's notion of the "mandarin"—a reactionary patrician—far outstrips the confines of the New England ivory towers.

Something crude has entered my trajectory. I originally wrote these words for an audience at Princeton, about something I can approach only glancingly and with the distant echoes of dogs barking in my ears. It might not be too rash to ask myself now the strange question: Do I feel empowered?

I feel an undoubted mass of gratitude, but I feel doubt nonetheless. It is a doubt I can qualify only by saying I feel Blakean. This has been an abiding feeling from the start, the kind of mental fight a mind forged in and by empire, and yet through imagination against it, must carry out.

The Blake I feel now is one who in one instance cries, "The Classics, it is the Classics! & not Goths nor Monks, that Desolate Europe with wars."

And I feel the Blake who cries at length this renegade note attached to the appendix of his prophetic books—crying specifically at Eliot's beloved Virgil:

Sacred Truth has pronounced that Greece & Rome as Babylon & Egypt: so far from being parents of Arts & Sciences as they pretend: were destroyers of all Art. Homer Virgil & Ovid confirm this opinion & make us reverence The Word of God, the only

light of antiquity that remains unperverted by War. Virgil in the
Eneid Book VI. line 848 says Let others study Art: Rome has
somewhat better to do, namely War & Dominion.

Rome & Greece swept Art into their maw & destroyd it a
Warlike State never can produce Art. It will Rob & Plunder &
accumulate into one place, & Translate & Copy & Buy & Sell
& Criticise, but not Make.

But where Blake cries, and where I feel acutely with him, most
acutely where I find courage in the wrestling match of and for
survival, the *pallaksch*, that agon of bitter ambivalence, is in his
1804 preface to his great epic in miniature, *Milton*, a poem that
pushes against Euro-classicism and closes the gap between utter-
ance and act.

The Stolen and Perverted Writings of Homer & Ovid: of Plato &
Cicero, which all Men ought to contemn: are set up by artifice
against the Sublime of the Bible. but when the New Age is at
leisure to Pronounce; all will be set right & those Grand Works
of the more ancient & consciously & professedly Inspired Men
will hold their proper rank & the Daughters of Memory shall
become the Daughters of Inspiration. Shakespeare & Milton
were both curb'd by the general malady & infection from the
silly Greek & Latin slaves of the Sword.

Rouze up O Young Men of the New Age! set your foreheads
against the ignorant Hirelings! For we have Hirelings in the
Camp, the Court, & the University: who would if they could,
for ever depress Mental & prolong Corporeal War. Painters! on
you I call! Sculptors! Architects! Suffer not the fashionable Fools
to depress your powers by the prices they pretend to give for
contemptible works or the expensive advertizing boasts that they
make of such works; believe Christ & his Apostles that there is

a Class of Men whose whole delight is in Destroying. We do not want either Greek or Roman Models if we are but just & true to our own Imaginations, those Worlds of Eternity in which we shall live for ever, in Jesus Our Lord.

Blake knows the classics are blood money. He rejects their economy. His polyphonic, sensuous, and volatile intelligence values inspiration and imagination, the natural storehouses of the creative will. Blake also knows, to borrow words from Iris Murdoch, that "art attacks art and thrives by doing so." Therefore, he values the natural creative will not simply to be against the classics; doing so would be schismatic. His superb defiance converts the economy of the classics into, to repeat Hill's dictum, "a sad and angry consolation."

Arrive now with me at the source of my essay's title, which I promised at the start. Some years after the Maas Brown incident and some miles away and at a great psychic distance from the *kaachi*, I read Derek Walcott's poem "Sea Grapes." This is the sound I wish to trail now:

That sail which leans on light,
tired of islands,
a schooner beating up the Caribbean

for home, could be Odysseus,
home-bound on the Aegean;
that father and husband's

longing, under gnarled sour grapes, is
like the adulterer hearing Nausicaa's name
in every gull's outcry.

This brings nobody peace. The ancient war
between obsession and responsibility
will never finish and has been the same

for the sea-wanderer or the one on shore
now wriggling on his sandals to walk home,
since Troy sighed its last flame,

and the blind giant's boulder heaved the trough
from whose groundswell the great hexameters come
to the conclusions of exhausted surf.

The classics can console. But not enough.

I am simultaneously the sea wanderer and the one onshore of the poem. I survive by being liminal, nomad, and still. "Sea Grapes" is an embattled poem for me in both a literal and a figurative sense. I read it first in the sixth form of Titchfield High School, its campus a seventeenth-century British military fort built on a peninsula into the Caribbean Sea. I read it not inside a classroom but outside, seated on one of the rusty cannons still pointing toward invisible French and Spanish armadas, coming for England's sugarcane profit. Any moment at all, when I lifted my eyes from the page, a sail of one of those French or Spanish fleets could have passed by. On the ruins of the old fort: the coexistence of futility and hope.

The figurative sense in which "Sea Grapes" is an embattled poem is the way it works through classical textual allusion—to Homer's *Odyssey*—with a classical structural allusion—the terza rima of Dante's *Divine Comedy*—to become a tragic elegy, rather than a merely sensuous, merely postcolonial classic-lyric hybrid. The mutual contamination of its textual and its structural allusions is as radical as Blake's preface to his *Milton*. The poet suffers the dual allusion, resisting both as template even as he surrenders to them to achieve the aesthetic-political statement the poem ends with. "The classics can console. But not enough."

"The classics can console. But not enough": There you have the pitch of an embattled love that seems to be saying, "Though they can please beyond all pleasing, we turn to the classics not for aesthetic joy, but for the power of ontological disclosure." The process of mutual contamination in "Sea Grapes," in which the Homeric goes into the Dantean and into the Caribbean, creates a collective remembrance, a borderless cemetery in which all are recognized, none more than the other.

Further, the intertwining of the double allusion is a powerful consolidation of poetry's inner contradiction. It is a contradiction, like love, that never ceases to do everything for what does not exist. This love, writes Gillian Rose in *Love's Work*, is not "a love of suffering, but the work, the power of love, which may curse, but abides." Walcott's poem abides by noting a discredited difference, of which Maas Brown

is a part, as is the boy bitten by his dogs, and a consolation that is, to end with Rose's words, the "power to be able *to attend*, powerful or powerless; [with a] love to laugh bitterly, purgatively, purgatorially, and then to be quiet."

A quiet like the sea into which I now fall.

A ROOM IN AUGUST TOWN

■

THE MAN WHO WAS TO BECOME MY LANDLORD SHOWED ME
the yellow room in August Town just a couple of weeks before the first
semester of my second year began. The day was extremely hot. I recall
appreciating the cool of the house, a cool I thought might have been
coming from an air conditioner. Perhaps I even commented on it as I
followed him down a dark, narrow passageway to the room that was
for rent. If I did say something, he didn't respond; he spoke only after
I was inside the room, and again when we returned to the veranda
where I had met him, and on both occasions his voice had the clipped
reticence of someone who preferred, perhaps demanded, to be left
alone. He opened the door to the room and stood aside to let me in.

No more than ten by ten feet of wall-to-wall concrete, it was a
sealed-off, windowless closet—one so small it didn't have a closet of
its own. Pushed into the corner facing the door was a low bed with
a stripped twin-size mattress. Above the bed burned a single naked
bulb. I walked in and pressed my hand down on the mattress. No
spring. I pressed again, and that was when the man spoke from the
threshold, to say that the bed came with the room, and, he added,
pointing with lips pursed to the small table at its foot, "That, too."

There was no other furniture, nothing on which to sit besides the bed, nowhere to store anything but under the bed. The only other thing in the room, to the left of the door, was a picture in a frame. I decided to save looking at it until the room was mine; maybe the frame was this anchorite's secret window offering a miniature prospect of heaven. I could see myself pretending it was. The man cleared his throat. The tour was over.

I followed him back out to the veranda and the fresh air. I had noticed the faint smell of Dettol or some other cleaning agent—so different from the room's frowsy scent—emanating from elsewhere in the house, which made me wonder about the other tenants. Where were they now?

The man wore a heavy red windbreaker, odd, though not completely unusual for the scorching Kingston heat, and aviator-style sunglasses, even inside the house. He never removed them, not then, when I forked over the first month's rent and security deposit, nor the other times, after I had moved in, when I found him seated on the veranda's battered floral sofa—his business perch, for it was there that I would pay the rent at the start of each month. I would have assumed he was blind had he not seemed to return such an implacable, stony stare.

I signed the lease, a smudged brown piece of paper that looked like a Jamaican birth certificate of my parents' generation. He handed me a ring with three keys: one to the padlock on the veranda grille, one to the front door, and another, the smallest, to my room. It was a veritable Raskolnikov's garret, but I felt lucky. I had a room of my own.

I'd spent the previous year hauling my large army-green duffel bag from house to house across the city. Kingston—squalid, full of distemper—seemed worlds apart from my coastal hometown of Port Antonio, to which I returned every weekend I could, a journey of three hours by bus. I realized quickly just how small Kingston was. Places bumped up against one another, the lines that separated the haves from the have-nots so thin you'd think the disparity was a natural feature of the landscape.

My classmates at the University of the West Indies, Mona, came from all over the Caribbean, but most of the people I got to know were born Kingstonian. Quite a few of them lived uptown, in houses with maids and gardeners, in neighborhoods with names like Cherry Gardens, Mona Heights, and Norbrook. Their parents invariably worked in the "private sector"—doing what, I never understood. It was at their homes that I did my laundry, took hot showers—a novelty to me—and ate good meals, taking breaks from my studies to watch films in the "TV room."

Some of us off-campus students had become close during the two-week live-in orientation, a sort of sleepover cadet camp: we woke at five every morning to do exercise drills led by the dorm wardens while we sang ribald songs. There were light hazing rituals—carrying a backpack full of rocks around while mooing like a cow, or eating six whole Scotch bonnet peppers, fiery hot, without water. The only time we left the campus as a group was for a seven- or eight-hour hike up Blue Mountain Peak. We headed out to the foothills in the late afternoon and reached the summit, where we set up camp, in the pitch-black night. We woke at daybreak, seized by amazement when the sun flamed over the sea and moved slowly toward the valley.

According to university policy, once those two weeks were over, off-campus students were not permitted to stay the night in the dorms. "Squatting"—which required an on-campus boarder to sneak you past security—was prohibited. When you got inside, you had to find a room with an extra mattress: many had one or two stashed under a bed. Squatting was so common that none of this was done with any great sense of pity or awkwardness. "Me can squat at your room tonight?" you would ask, and often the answer came back, "Yea, man, forward in." It was a question I asked many nights, and I was caught many times, woken by water thrown in my face by a dorm warden who would march me to the exit gate in whatever state of dress I happened to be in.

When I wasn't squatting or staying with a friend, I spent weeks on end in the close-quartered one-bedroom my eldest brother was renting in Duhaney Park, a neighborhood I thought of as normal, in the sense of being for regular people: the have-a-bits. The houses were prefab, and you could see from the undulations of the walls that they were made in waffle molds. My brother, born to a different father nine years before me, had left high school in the tenth grade, when he was fifteen. Neither my mother—who was already living with my father in Port Antonio—nor my brother's father was able to afford the fees. Before moving to the city, he worked a fortnight for a factory in St. Thomas Parish, where he was living with our grandmother, cutting sugarcane with a machete in the field right across from the school he dropped out of, St. Thomas Technical.

"When it was lunch break, me could look over and see me friends them at school," he told me. So that they wouldn't recognize him, he wrapped his head with a piece of cloth and rubbed his face with black soot from the burnt sugarcane leaves. He told me this years later, when he was in his midtwenties, not all at once, but in pieces, when he started visiting me in Port Antonio. By that time I was already past the grade he had been in when he dropped out. There was no bitterness in this elder brother I only vaguely knew.

"Me used to sleep on cardboard box at Coronation Market," he said of his teenage years in the city.

"Really?" I marveled.

"True thing. 'Bout four years good I sleep at Coronation before me could afford a room, first in Denham Town and then all 'bout over West Kingston."

When he had free time, he would drive me around the western

flanks of Kingston in his rattling red Datsun 510, pointing out the neighborhoods where he'd resided, Rema or Tivoli Gardens, names I knew from the news and from dancehall music. He'd once had to flee Matches Lane in the trunk of a car because the house he was living in was firebombed. "But see how lucky you be to come from country to town and gone straight up a House a Parliament, eh, future P.J.?" P.J. were the initials of the prime minister at the time, P. J. Patterson, and Parliament, which he pronounced "par-lie-ment" as part of the joke, was the university.

My brother could put me up in his Duhaney Park room because he often worked the night shift at his security job, but that meant the lights were off in the evening, just when I needed to do homework. When he had the day shift, we slept head to toe, which felt to me like the fraternal intimacy I'd missed out on growing up, but for him meant not sharing the bed with his girlfriend, who eventually moved in. After that, I stayed for a month with my former English teacher, a man originally from Kingston who had returned to the city around the time I'd arrived, to live with his wife's family in a three-story house on a quiet cul-de-sac off Washington Boulevard. For the two years he'd taught me at Titchfield High School, we'd met at his run-down bungalow at the end of the school day to go over the writing exercises he would set for me—to describe the bay of Port Antonio; to write a twenty-line poem in blank verse about something I'd seen in the newspaper. He'd read what I had written back to me aloud, rarely giving feedback but occasionally pausing to ask me to explain my choice of word and sometimes pushing me to look for another. He was the first person I knew who'd gone to the UWI Mona, and he had encouraged me to apply.

Our meetings didn't continue in the city; in fact, we rarely saw each other at his wife's house, which was filled with four generations of her relatives. On any given night, it seemed, there was someone new sleeping over. When bedtime drew near, I'd look for a room that wasn't too crowded and, if no bed was available, spread a blanket on the floor, pull a sheet over my face, and drift off. Small talk went on throughout the night, and the building hummed with other sounds: a radio or a television set, the dull pedaling of a sewing machine, the duller, discreet sighs of trysting bodies. More often than not, I'd end up on the small terrace, piled with discarded clothing, newspapers, and flattened boxes that made me think of my brother in Coronation Market. I liked it on the terrace. The night air was always pleasant and cool, although sometimes a predawn rain would fall. I bore the wet, because it felt less daunting than looking for someplace else to sleep.

It was in the second semester of my first year, near the start of the exam study period in late April, that I'd started to crumble. I'd finished my final papers, except for one: a close reading of Hamlet's seven soliloquies. What madness led me to take on all seven?

Earlier that term, my professor had approved my proposal, and surely he would think me a time waster or worse if I changed the number to one or two: it was seven or nothing. With only a few days of school remaining, I went to ask for an extension.

The walk to my professor's office took me past the arched stone aqueduct from the university's plantation days and the stone chapel, a onetime rum storehouse flanked with royal palms. My professor and I had exchanged just a few words during seminars. He lectured without notes, and students instinctively stood up whenever he walked into or out of the lecture room, dressed the way he always dressed: in corduroy slacks and a guayabera, or "bush jacket." His wasn't a manner that promised second chances, so I was surprised to find myself pouring out my predicament to him, how unsettled I'd been in Kingston due to my precarious housing situation. As I spoke, I held back tears, conscious of how foolish I must have seemed. He listened without interrupting, then wrote down his home address in red ink.

"Bring it here at the end of July," he said. I had a 50 percent scholarship from the university, the rest of my tuition covered by a loan from the Students' Loan Bureau in Kingston. All other expenses were my own responsibility. The weight of my confounding worry over money made me wish I could live in a phalanstery, a word I'd learned from Razumikhin of *Crime and Punishment*, the novel that preoccupied me most that summer. Hell, I wouldn't have minded a nunnery. And so I got a summer job. In fact, I got two. At twenty-one, I had never had one before. When I was in high school, many of my friends had taken gigs in the summer to help buy back-to-school supplies and to secure pocket change, although the going term for that kind of work was less dignified: hustling. The hustle could range from washing cars at a roadside creek to cleaning hotels and villas to bagging groceries at the supermarket. Most popular was becoming a market boy (hustling was a boy's sport), doing anything to attract buyers to the stall or stalls you'd been commissioned to sell for. Many gave up on returning to school once the summer was over—which is in fact what my father had done, setting up shop in the market and secretly saving funds to try his luck in England; he'd left when I was six or seven and never returned. You'd see these boys idling in the main square of Port Antonio, sometimes, truth be told, up to no good. My mother and my father's mother did not want that fate for me, a good boy who did well at school and had a more than ordinary interest in books, novels I borrowed from the small public library in town (Dickens, Stevenson, Hemingway) or from my teacher (Baldwin, Joyce, Morrison). I would read them on the veranda of my grandmother's house, picking out individual words, clutching onto them, to look up their definitions later. There was nothing to explain the sense of purpose this reading gave me, other than that my unshakable faith in words led me to believe that they would take me on to the next thing. That next thing, logically, was university, which I began to talk about at home. All the while, my mother and grandmother protected me from the hustle with hustles of their own (my grandmother's baked goods; my mother's far less successful tourist trade of handmade jewelry, crocheted hats, and knit belts in Rasta colors).

I didn't go home that summer, not once. Anguished as the Danish prince, I saved almost all I made, spending only on my basic needs. From eight in the morning to one in the afternoon, I wrote ads for a tourist agency in the basement of a house in Beverly Hills, a ridge named for the one in Los Angeles; with its multilevel houses, sloping, sprinkler-watered lawns, bougainvillea-spilling fences, and wrought-iron gates through which you often caught glimpses of classic Benzes, it could play the part. The boredom of the job, each ad more inane than the last, made the hours move slowly. I was the youngest in a group of five or six but the most opinionated, and the others, ostensibly professional writers, resented me for chortling at their touristy adjectives. "It is to be touristy, little boy," the boss would say.

Then I'd take a half-hour bus ride to serve as the guide for a photography exhibition at Devon House, an old Georgian-style mansion built by George Stiebel, Jamaica's first black millionaire, which was set back from the road behind palms and fruit trees. The hours moved slowly there as well, with a kind of nineteenth-century languor. Because there were so few visitors, I could sit and read my *Crime and Punishment*, riffing on words in the margins and later transferring the marginalia to my notebook. When someone did arrive, I was alerted to their presence by heel strikes on the dark wood floors.

Each day, I left the exhibition at six, to work on my Hamlet paper in the air-conditioned library on campus. As I annotated Hamlet's soliloquies—a more systematic version of the kinds of notes I would jot down at the exhibition, flitting between the dictionary, the thesaurus, and a concordance to Shakespeare—I inhabited his language so intensely that Kingston dissolved and I was in the slate gray of Elsinore. Pate, contumely, unkennel, cerements. Sifting the words down to their roots, words that I would never use in conversation and often couldn't even pronounce, each gradually grew familiar. Nemean, pernicious, cellarage, paragon.

Those evenings were the times I felt closest to any kind of ease in the city. Sometimes, at midnight—the summer closing hour—a library worker had to tap me on the shoulder, waking me to an empty room. This presented the dilemma of finding, at that hour, a bus or a taxi. And the graver dilemma: A bus or a taxi to where? Many nights, leaning my head on the blue-and-white telephone booth near the library—my old Nokia 3310 hardly ever had credit—I trembled as I dialed number after number, hoping for a Good Samaritan.

I'd found the room in August Town in the classifieds section of the *Gleaner*. The house, with its "rooms for rent," was nestled among properties far above its value and offered rentals for a single semester (all that my summer savings would allow) rather than the standard term of a year. True, the neighborhood was as infamous as any of the West Kingston ghettos my brother had lived in, but I reminded myself of how a friend had assured me, somewhat puzzlingly, that the vigilantes and the police there tended to leave students alone. Plus the room was so close to the university that I'd be able to save on commuting and use the money to get home more often. I could walk to Papine Square, with its large, open-air produce market, and to the Hope Royal Botanical Gardens, where the buttery yellow blooms of the cassia trees could ease the worst of my homesickness.

I had secured the room for September, and summer ended with a second triumph. I finished my paper and delivered it, only two weeks later than I'd been told to, at my professor's home in Hope Pastures. The sun shone on the clipped zoysia grass—as neat, I thought, as my professor's red handwriting in my pocket—making his lawn look emerald and artificial. Everything I could see was immaculate: the black-and-white-tiled lettering and house number on the gate, the miniature oxblood Royal Mail–style pillar box, and the gleaming bronze doorbell, which I rang.

Shockingly, my professor was wearing a T-shirt and a pair of cargo shorts, out of which appeared two spindly legs. When he got closer, I saw that his face was set in the same weary half scowl I knew from class. He opened the gate but didn't invite me inside. I apologized for bringing the essay past the deadline and he waved it off, stretching out a hand for the paper. I grasped for something to say.

"How all occasions do inform against me." But that was only the voice in my head. It seemed to muffle something my professor had said as he walked back into his house. A season and an eternity passed before the spindly legs returned. He handed me a small plastic bag. "Here you go. Walk good," he said, and turned back again. I didn't peer into the bag until I was well out of view. Inside were four sets of CDs: recordings of Bach, Sibelius, Mahler, and Chopin. He must have prepared them for me. What had made him give me these discs? The exchange had an illicit air, as if I had just accepted contraband on a bright summer morning in Hope Pastures.

One evening two weeks later, a taxi dropped me and my things in front of the house in August Town. It was a single-floor box unit built in the typical "scheme" style of the mid-1970s, with a flat concrete roof; it was very long, as if three or four units had been added on to it over the years. An awning of blue-and-white aluminum loomed over the straggly, stunted croton trees lining the front steps. The veranda was enclosed by iron bars, mostly painted red; others, in white, were twisted into surprisingly delicate shapes of flowers. On both sides were barred aluminum-framed windows, and though I never went to check (Jamaicans can be particular about even people they know wandering around their yards), I was sure there were similar windows on the other side of the house—none of them, sadly, belonging to the room the landlord had shown me. Back in the room again, with my duffel bag of clothes, an oversize suitcase of books, and an ancient CD player with a digital clock (a gift from my brother), I wondered if anyone else was home. In all my time living there, I neither saw nor heard another tenant, and I never saw my landlord inside the house, except for on one awful occasion toward the end of my stay.

The walls of the yellow room weren't exactly yellow. They were painted a dull, sickly beige, a color I thought of as dirty desert sand. It gave off a deceptive softness, which was intensified by the magnesium-like flare of the E26 lightbulb hanging above the bed. The light had been on when the landlord first showed me the room, and it was on when I returned to move in. I sat for a moment, then got up and flipped the switch. The room was plunged into a dark as thick as tar. I opened the door, and the dark extended outward, joining the dark of the narrow corridor. The room, I saw then, was an abysmal cave. I flipped the switch back. The yellow jumped back into the room, causing me to blink. To my memory, in my four months in the room, I never again turned off the light. I glanced down the corridor; its darkness came right up to the threshold where I stood, and then stopped. I closed the door—it was the cheap kind, made from plyboard and filled with bagasse, and, I noticed, there were tiny, strangely uniform scratch marks on its brown surface—and sat back down on the bed to contemplate the picture frame.

It contained a painting of a bird. The picture appeared old and the pigments were faded, so the exact colors were hard to determine, but the reds and browns were still bright enough. Much later, I came to believe that the image was in fact made with crayons on matte paper. The bird was in profile, suspended in the air. There was no landscape in the background, not even sky; it was just a flightless bird on a pink-ish surface. This absence gave the painting a desolate feel, one that felt weirdly concentrated in the bird's single inscrutable eye, a black dot beneath a tiny oval flick of—good God—a human eyebrow.

What kind of bird was it? I decided it was a sparrow, for no reason other than that was the first word that came to me. Perhaps I had in the recesses of my mind Hamlet's wry line, spoken to Horatio: "There is special providence in the fall of a sparrow." And didn't Raskolnikov call someone a sparrow in *Crime and Punishment*? I picked a CD at random from the bag at the foot of the bed and put the disc in the player. Soon the swelling chorus of Bach's *St. Matthew Passion*— "Kommt, ihr Töchter, helft mir klagen"—was flooding the room.

Most Jamaicans associate the word "August" with the proclamation that legally ended British slavery on the island on August 1, 1834. The first of the month has been observed as a holiday in Jamaica ever since. Many so-called free villages sprang up in the wake of emancipation, and August Town was one of the earliest, founded by people recently freed from the Hope, Papine, and Mona plantations—the latter two later becoming the grounds of the university campus.

After emancipation, the struggle to complete full freedom from colonial rule took both political and spiritual forms. One of the best-remembered agitators is a black preacher of August Town named Alexander Bedward, whom I first learned about in primary school. Sometimes referred to as the Shepherd, he founded the esoteric, millenarian Jamaica Native Baptist Free Church in the 1880s. The congregation grew yearly, and since Bedward's rhetoric of black redemption didn't shy away from violent revolt against the colonial government, the local authorities were nervous.

When I was a child, Bedward seemed to me like one of those "madmen" I'd see on the streets in rural Jamaica—men looked upon with a mixture of revulsion and reverence. It seemed to me that their open displays of mental disturbance served a purpose, providing them with a sort of freedom. There was method in their madness. These men resembled contemporary incarnations of characters from the folk traditions that had surrounded me as a child—lore in which *guzu* men stole people's souls by laying traps or putting curses on people's shoes, and bodies performed impossible feats like shape-shifting. Bedward's thing was flying. As the story goes, one day when he was in his seventies, he tied a chair to a tree at the site along the banks of the Hope River where he gave his sermons and baptized his faithful. He had often told his followers, then some thirty thousand strong, that he would fly back to Africa, the earthly paradise of black people. At ten in the morning, he said, he would ascend from the chair into heaven like a latter-day Elijah, to prove that he was God's newly anointed prophet. But the designated hour kept changing, and Bedward remained seated in the tree. He descended after nightfall, and a few months later was arrested on charges of vagrancy and taken to a mental asylum. He died there in 1930.

When I first heard Bedward's story, it touched me personally. According to rarely spoken-of family legend, my father's father had died in a Kingston asylum when my father was still a boy. He had taken flight to the city, leaving my grandmother with seven children, supposedly to make a better life for his family. He, like my father, never came back. I once heard from an aunt that before my grandfather was institutionalized, his legs had been amputated, the result of having been run over by a truck. His death in the asylum seemed to me a coda to his more tragic end—being almost entirely forgotten at home.

I knew, as a student, that there was a still-active Bedwardite Revival church in Kingston, and friends had visited Bedward's grave in August Town, on a field trip for one of the many Jamaican literature courses on offer that brought in an element of "cultural studies," part of the effort to promote a new Caribbean identity for the university. These classes attempted to reclaim forgotten history—arguing, for instance, that the roots of dancehall culture could be found in the folk songs and dances of Bedward's congregations. True, maybe, yet to a country boy like me—the first of my family to attend a university—this was not what higher education was for. Looking back, I wonder whether I felt that studying Bedward would have seemed a betrayal—as if I were using my newfound privilege as a university student in the city to gaze back anthropologically upon a country uncle. I made a point of opting for the most traditional classes in Western and Caribbean literature, as I believed any English major should. I never visited Bedward's grave, or the church. But sometime in the middle of my stay in the yellow room, lying on my back with my eyes riveted to the ceiling, I heard a halting, childlike voice breaking into the quiet from somewhere in the house, singing a song I half remembered:

Dip dem, Bedward, dip dem
Dip dem in the healing stream
Dip dem sweet, but not too deep
Dip dem fi cure bad feeling.

That first semester of my second year, I took four classes: another on Shakespeare, this one taught by a professor visiting from England, a man the literature department seemed to regret hiring because of his long pirate earrings and the far worse crime of wearing short shorts to class; British Romantic Poetry; Victorian Poetry; and American Novels of the South. Most days, I'd attend three or four lectures, and seminars in between, for which I'd prepare by spending hours in the library reading secondary material, overthinking and getting tied up in my own notes. The previous semester, I'd formed a group of literature majors with an interest in creative writing that met weekly. We spent the time reading and discussing books not assigned in class— Aimé Césaire's *Notebook of a Return to the Native Land*, Erna Brodber's *Myal*—and giving ourselves exercises, the results of which we'd share in long and disorganized sessions that mainly felt like "liming," the Trinidadian term for idling with friends.

One evening, after which classes I don't recall, in my first week or two of staying in the room, a slip into bad feeling—what else to call it?—happened while I was looking at the bird. I was seated on the edge of the bed, staring at the black dot of the eye and the ironically raised eyebrow, when suddenly I felt faint. The sensation was so new that I stood up as if surprised by a knock at the door. I had to sit right back down again so as not to collapse on the floor. I waited, taking deep breaths. I was exhausted, bitterly so. Still, I told myself, it would pass; I just had to lie down for a couple of minutes and then go find food before it got late. I closed my eyes. When I opened them again, my breath caught in my throat. The stippled surface of the ceiling resembled a beehive, reflecting a waxy, vitelline membrane. The bulb seemed to be pulsating. As I stared at its glow, I grew heavy with sleep; maybe this was what hypnosis felt like. I tried to refuse the pressure I felt bearing down on me, half raising my body into a sitting position.

Two days later, at around 6:00 p.m., I left the room. I knew the hour from the clock on my CD player, but not whether it was morning or night until I emerged. How I got out I could remember only—after some time, from the safety of the library—in hazy, tiny bits. I had come to, shivering, my head hurting horribly. Then I had passed out again. When I came to the second time, I was on the floor, my back against the wall. How long I had stayed in this position I didn't know, but I did remember the great, painful effort it took to pull myself up by holding on to the doorknob, and then the intense, discombobulating walk through the dark corridor, encountering torn shards of yellow in the passageway to the veranda.

I recalled how these shards had melted like snow flurries on the vinyl tiles under my feet. That was how I thought of them, not as something more familiar, like raindrops—it would be another three years before I saw and felt snow—but as flurries turned to slush on the tiles, wet in some areas and frozen hard as rime in others. I had slipped and my hands had shot out to the sides in search of support from the walls, but I'd found none. When I got to the veranda, I felt somewhere on the outer edge of myself, and desperately cold. After a moment I realized I was soaked in sweat, my clothes stuck to my skin. I had soiled my pants. I lay down on the sofa, folded my body into a C, and wept.

I hadn't eaten, not for real, for forty-eight hours. My stomach groaned and cramped. Let the gunmen or the police of August Town kill me; I was going to find food and drink. Taking tentative steps, I walked up the hill toward campus, sticking to the shadows of the buildings. Fear kept me at the library until after midnight, replenishing myself with water and snacks—a spiced bun, banana chips, and nuts—in a secluded spot on the bottom floor. I had made up my mind to spend the night there. My head was throbbing, but as I ate, the rest of me seemed to snap back to normal. Had I been in a state of dehydration, one that coincided with a drop in my blood sugar levels? That could have explained my hallucinations. The weird thing, I told myself then, was not the room at all; it was that I was sitting in a library brooding in filthy clothes, having allowed myself to be spooked by a badly drawn bird and a lightbulb on the verge of being blown. I got up angrily—angry at myself especially for waiting so long before heading back. I headed south in the dark, which became even darker after I passed through the back gates of the campus and onto the shortcut, across an overgrown field, that led to the broken asphalt of the road down into August Town. Against the dark sky I could make out the silhouette, darker still, of the range of the Blue Mountains, rising steeply behind the town, as they did behind my grandmother's house in Port Antonio. They were becoming more familiar to me, those foothills—the strongholds of maroonage and the places of sanctuary where Bedward and his followers must have gone to gather strength before returning to August Town to carry on the unfinished business of freedom.

*   *   *

In the four months I spent in the yellow room, I went home to Port Antonio for only one weekend. A lethargy had crept over me, and as if in solitary confinement I spent countless hours lying on the bed, my mind blank, staring at the bulb. In my lectures, I listened listlessly, then crept back to the room, avoiding friends. I stopped attending the writing group. Sometimes I didn't make it to my classes, because I overslept and got to campus too late; on two occasions, I stumbled outside before dawn, fell asleep on the veranda's sofa, and didn't wake until noon. When I did, groggy and in tears, I shuffled back through the dark, narrow passage to the room. I lay back down in bed, waiting for sleep.

There were times when it seemed as though I got up from the bed only to go to the bathroom, feeling pains in my feet and legs. Some weeks, the most I did was take my bag of dirty clothes, late in the evening, to a public Laundromat beside one of the dorms. I'd sit and watch the washing and then the drying cycle, hardly ever taking my eyes off the machines, then head back to the room, praying sleep would claim me.

Once, a friend from Cherry Gardens saw me at the kiosk in front of the library. "Long time I haven't seen you. But stop, what a way you *mawga* down!" *Mawga* is the patois for "meager," but she meant something more than skinny: skeletal, emaciated. "You on fast or you bulimic?"

I went to the university hospital and got blood work and other exams done. The doctor told me I didn't have a *medical* problem. I feared I knew what he meant. Many nights, as I played *St. Matthew Passion* back in the yellow room in August Town, I believed I heard "Dip dem, Bedward" above Bach's chorus, and the chirping of birds in my ears.

I hadn't seen home sea in more than three months, and as the bus rounded the bend of the coastal road leading into Port Antonio, I shut my eyes to trap that first glimpse of the skyish water. ("Skyish" I'd picked up from *Hamlet*, and it seemed the only right word for that blue.) Half an hour later, I was seated on my grandmother's veranda. I fell asleep looking at the sea. I recall her telling me that I looked tired and thin, and not being able to tell her about what was preoccupying me. It had occurred to me that my landlord was likely a *guzu* man. I knew about them from staying with my mother's family in St. Thomas, where every evening I'd visited Miss Mona—ninety years old, blind, foulmouthed—in her yard. She would pat me down, reciting the Kumina words for my body parts until she reached my privates, which she would pinch, laughing as I squirmed. In her youth she had been a Kumina queen leading Nine Nights ceremonies of singing and drumming for the dead, with whom she communicated in their own language.

"*Guzu* come from Africa to right here in St. Thomas," Miss Mona told me once, hocking phlegm into her yard. "Is since slavery it up in them hill and bush. When me a girl child me see plenty people who *guzu* man catch them shadow and then crack up them bone like pottery." Touching or even glancing at a *guzu* trap could be fatal. "You see the *guzu* turn you into coconut husk, weak you down so duppy can tear open your body and haunt your soul."

My grandmother was disdainful of such superstitions; she would have been horrified if she'd known that, as a child, I'd attended Kumina ceremonies or Nine Nights with my cousins. How would I have explained to her that my landlord, sitting on his old sofa in his ever-present aviators, seemingly relaxed, was using obeah to bring about my demise? She would have been concerned about other things. Was I getting in with the wrong crowd in Kingston? Or, more frightening, was I descending into a madness that, though we never spoke of it, was in fact hereditary? I promised I'd eat more.

One evening I opened the door to my room in August Town and saw a pair of large black rubber rain boots. I froze. What was it Miss Mona had said about shoes? They were placed confidently in the middle of the room, toes turned toward the bed. Somehow, I grabbed a T-shirt off the bed, threw it over the boots, picked them up, and flung them into the hallway.

I started pacing the room, slowly, then faster, muttering to myself. Then I lost control and, like someone possessed, ran hollering through the house. I broke into room after room, and after I had entered what felt like dozens of them, each empty and unlit, I burst into a room where my landlord sat dozing in a chair in front of a television set. When he turned toward me, he didn't have his sunglasses on. His oblong face, black as a rubber tube, shone with sweat. It looked ordinary enough. But one eye was a bulbous scar and the other was a milky pearl staring unblinkingly at me. I fled his room and locked myself in mine. On the mattress, my eyes fixed on the bulb, I waited and waited and no one came.

Someone called my name. I was walking near the ruins of the stone aqueduct. I turned and saw a boy from Trinidad, a member of my writing group whom I hadn't talked to since our only session at the beginning of the semester. Had it been after that meeting that the bad feeling came over me?

"Dread, you don't hear me calling you? Long time don't see. What's the scene, man?" I stared at him as if trying to remember who he was. He spoke again. "I walking to back gate to go home. You want trod?"

We strolled through one of the high arches of the aqueduct, the cracks in the rain-battered pink bricks sprouting grass. He talked about plans for the group's next meeting, once exams were over. I didn't always follow what he was saying, but as we passed through the gate, I caught, "That's why I don't worry up myself over them things." They were the most comforting words I'd heard in months.

* * *

At first, I'd alternated between the CDs my professor had given me, but eventually I kept only *St. Matthew Passion* in the player, sometimes leaving it on as I stepped out toward the veranda with the feeling of treading slush, sometimes lying flat on my back, until sleep covered me again. Always, when I woke, I was bewildered for a moment. Where was I? What was this rhythm I could hang a tune on? "Kommt, ihr Töchter, helft mir klagen." "Dip dem, Bedward, dip dem." And this yellow viscous light—from where was it pouring?

It was out of the sludge of this confusion that I woke, certain that I was being buried alive. In my sleep I had heard a digging sound. As I opened my eyes, the sound grew sharper, a rasping noise of metal thrust into dirt, and with my eyes open the image of a black bent blade going into the black ground flashed in my mind. A clump of dirt hit my face. I tried to move and was unable. My legs were naked, clean, but they felt weighed down by semi-wet hillocks of earth.

I heard the spade again, digging. When I opened my mouth to scream, I tasted what smelled like horse shit and felt like horse shit, and I realized with terror that I was being force-fed dirt. I began to cough and choke and spit, trying to rid myself of what wasn't there. I wanted to throw up. I wanted to brush it off my face, but my hands were lifeless at my sides. I heard the shoveling begin again and closed my eyes, whimpering. With my eyes shut, I felt a kind of relief. Then another spade of dirt hit my face.

Would this dirt be my death? Strangely, something in the smell of it was beautiful. Was there a word for that smell? I grasped for a name for it, as though, if only I could summon it, a word perhaps I knew as a boy, I could begin to put myself together. "Skyish." "Cellarage." My mind cast about, reaching for a word that time had taken from me. The tears I was crying now were for that boy. Take him and take me back to Port Antonio, for the right and proper word.

ROUGH WATER: A SENEGAL DIARY

ROUGH WATER AT A DISTANCE. DARK BLUE BUT NOT TOO dark. It looks frigid. That this water could be anything but warm had never crossed my mind. And down on the shore, I recoil, startled, when the first waves touch my toes. I think of tears gone stale as the waves thin out and pool languidly around my ankles. A feeling of grief grows and grows inside me. This is ancestral water. My first time touching the Atlantic from the coast of West Africa. I walk calmly in, jeans and all, until the water is up to my waist.

Then a wave explodes in my face, the force knocking me back into the surf and leaving me soaked through. A second, stronger wave sucks me into the sea; another spits me back on to the sand. I land with such an impact that my mouth falls open, and all that cold-as-tears Atlantic rushes down my throat. Another wave drags me again out into the deep. I struggle to get to shore, but the water holds me back, pulls me under, and that is when I cry, "Jesus." But a wave punches me to shore again. I scramble away from the tide, breathing rapidly to calm my heaving chest. I sit for a while on the sand, staring into the distance at the rough water. My breath evens out. I stand and with a sigh turn left and begin to walk along the shoreline, staying away from the foaming waves. I walk for about a mile, my wet clothes feeling heavier as I go, before I can trust walking into the wake of the waves, ignoring the cold of the water gnawing at my ankles. Flecks of it like spittle fly into my face. Some time later I come up to an area of hundreds of black rocks, most of them long and flat, but here and there are a few large, round boulders. I climb to the top of one, slick with green algae and litter at its bottom. An exhaustion I have never felt before comes over me, and suddenly I begin to shake uncontrollably, my teeth chattering. I take my shirt and jeans off and sit holding my ankles. My eyes burn, whether from my own tears or from the salt of the sea I can't tell. I can't tell either what, or why, words begin to tumble from my gnashing teeth. They might be not words but a keening, repeated over and over until the rattling in my body slows and finally stops. I open my eyes: dark rough water. I slide down the boulder and pick up a little plastic bottle from the litter and wade into the water up to my chest. The waves toss me about as I hold the bottle down in the ocean, filling it to the brim.

Hours later that evening, I drink half the bottle while sitting in the half-darkened room of my villa. I don't know why, the same way I don't know what caused me to take the bottle into the raging Atlantic. The remaining half, I tell myself, is the veritable jar of tears I will take across the sea, back home with me.

The port of Dakar. I arrive early for the 10:00 a.m. ferry to Île de Gorée, but at the ticket window I'm told that the next boat will not depart until midday. I sit on one of the blue benches next to an old woman in the waiting area. She is dressed in a green-and-orange skirt with slashes of dark red stripes in the front. She strings colorful beads on a long thread. Every time a bead is strung, she clicks her tongue. She works fast, the belly of the thread distending from the weight of the beads as they pile on. I begin to count the beads, watching her hands so close that after a while I believe I can hear the silent abacus music of beads touching. I am so absorbed in her work that I jump at the sound of a ferry horn, forgetting for a moment where I am or where it is that I am going. People rise and I rise, too, causing an emaciated black-and-white kitten I hadn't noticed under my seat to scamper along the wall of the ticket office. It then darts back between the feet of the crowd rushing to queue for the boat. An old man, wearing a white kufi cap and dressed in a long white gown, kicks the kitten clear out of the way. Purity and such. We inch slowly up the plank of the boat; the mild morning cool is now almost gone. Yet when I look up at the sky I see some dark clouds, same as the last three mornings since I have been here. There will be no rain; I will see Gorée in scorching heat. *I will see Gorée*, I think as we inch farther up the plank. To go to Gorée, I carry a tremendous singing.

Bougainvillea bursts out of every crevice and corner of the island, all the way up to the slave fort. Their paper-thin ruby blossoms are the first thing I touch, plucking a few from a wall near the dock as soon as I disembark from the ferry. I keep them in my palm the entire long day I spend walking back and forth from the dock to the slave fort. In that merciless heat, the petals stick to my palms like flayed scabs of skin. Inside the slave fort I consider releasing them through the narrow frame of the Door of No Return into the sea, but instead I jam my hands in my pockets, afraid. I stare at the water calmly lapping the ledge and splashing over the sill onto the dark dirt of the slave fort. Here is a door with no door; here I am here and yet no return. Outside I blink to adjust my eyes to the sun, not because inside the fort is void of light—plenty of light streams through the Door of No Return—but because shadows appear in dense jumbles wherever they fall. Reknotting around my neck an old scarf of my grandmother's I have brought with me, I stroll to the dock. At the dock I turn around and stroll back to the slave fort. I do this a few times, but only once more do I have the courage to go back inside of the slave fort.

There is a crowd inside. People mill about in small batches, talking in hushed tones. I realize I can't make out a single accent much less a single language that I can speak as I strain to hear what's been said. Should I say something, add my voice to the babble? But to whom do I speak? To no one here, I think. As that thought crosses my mind, I see someone, a young boy in a blue shirt, who feigns diving from off the ledge through the Door of No Return into the sea. I jerk toward him, but he walks away, laughing into the shadows and leaving me alone in front of the door. Here is a door with no door. I am here. Then as if arranged by a set manager, a huge container ship glides slowly past, mere distance from the Door of No Return. Behind me I hear oohs and aahs and other cries as if at something amazing. Not until the voices leave can I turn around and exit. I walk to the dock and back up to the slave fort a few more times. On one of these circuits the heat forces me to seek shade under a cluster of almond trees by the shore adjacent to the dock. The container ship is gone, the water glitters in its ancient repose as if it has never been disturbed.

I arrive on a Friday at the beach in Popenguine, a small village about forty-five minutes by car outside Dakar. The beach is three miles of rough pink, reddish, and white sand. A cliff dominates the far eastern corner and offers enough shade for me to lie down and read and write while keeping the sea in full view. I have been naked since I arrived on the beach three hours ago. Except once when a group of three or four boys passed in the far distance, the beach stays empty. Not since I was a child in Port Antonio have I been fully naked on a beach. It calls to the boy in me, this beach: it awakens in me something I recognize as that gleam of alienated majesty Emerson talks about somewhere, that luminous thing that is love. It is past noon now. The sun is at its fiercest, but occasionally a light breeze off the sea ruffles the pages of my notebook. I can smell salt on the air when it blows, and when it does,

I play in my mind which of the water's three gradations of blue the breeze blows from, the cerulean (first), the cobalt (second), or the indigo (third)? Another hour passes. The beach remains empty, not a single pirogue at sea. When I stand, the sun cleanses me of my shadow.

I explore, bringing back shells and stones to my station under the cliff, making little piles of them that become overrun by red ants. A sound rumbles overhead behind me, and I turn, expecting to see a small plane, perhaps a drone, but there is nothing but the cliff and sky. Some time passes before I hear the rumble again. I get up to look more closely at the cliff and see that under the belly of the very top is a jagged hole the size of two basketball hoops. Breeze threading through the hole makes that groan-like rumble. A breeze blows and I hear it, not as loud as before, but distinct and constant. Strange that I didn't hear it earlier in all the hours I had been sitting almost directly under the cliff. Now that hollow roar blends with the incessant *shush* and *whoosh* of waves.

I wade in the cerulean part of the water, up to my waist, and stare out at the vast indigo: Beyond that, what? Gorée lies somewhere not far off; therefore, nearby are the currents that the slave ships navigated with relative ease to the Caribbean. How to even grasp the fact that there, right there, the currents of centuries of African pain still move? There are no markers on the sea to indicate those routes; I am reduced to the frail logic of intuition, to wonder as I gaze in another direction of the indigo, thinking this time now of my grandmother's house, my childhood home, above the Caribbean Sea. I turn my back to the indigo and wade to shore, where I crouch in the surf, feeling the splash of waves in my buttocks; the sun drums down on my back and water hits my chest and face. Thoughts sieve through my mind at each splash, too fast for me to make sense of, except for one: I am here, in *a now*. There has been no other time than now. Suddenly an overwhelming desire to climb the cliff comes over me.

Except for a patch of grass and a single thorn tree, the top of the cliff is bare of vegetation. The crumbly red dirt of the surface is spotted with white manna-like blotches like the sand below. The soil reminds me of Stokes Hall, a red dirt district in St. Thomas not too far from where my mother grew up. Like many of the districts in St. Thomas, Stokes Hall is named after a former sugar plantation owner, the ruin of whose great house still sits on a hill there. I know Stokes Hall only from car windows. As a kid I would drive through it to get to my high school, Happy Grove, situated on the border between St. Thomas and Portland. Mornings and evenings the red dirt on the stretch of main road would cloud behind the car, and if I was in the back of a pickup truck, as was sometimes the case, the dirt would lightly powder my khaki uniform, my hair, and my face, so light the dust would disappear in an instant. I loved the sight of that billowing red dust each school day, and looking down now at the red dirt of the cliff in Popenguine between my toes, I think how much that red dirt of Stokes Hall, banks of which you could see on the side of the road for several miles, defined that period of my life. Yet, but for the faintest patina that fell on me those school days, I have never touched the red dirt of home. I pat my palms on the ground, patting over and over and leaving my handprints everywhere on the cliff. Perhaps I am trying to find the location above the hole in the cliff where the breeze passes through and leaves a dry rumble. I put my ear to the ground and hear silence. Standing, I take up a handful of dirt and ball my hand into a fist, rubbing the brittle, warm texture with my fingers as it trails through them into the breeze. When the dirt is all gone, I smell my palm; then I lick the remaining red marks away.

The day ends with this miracle: a meeting with Ayi Kwei Armah. It is extraordinary how that happened, a sort of epiphanic encounter that explanation flattens. When I was going to Popenguine, a friend from Dakar mentioned that a famous old Ghanaian writer whom I should meet lives near the beach there. So excited I was about the prospect of visiting another of Senegal's sea-town villages that I didn't register the name of the old Ghanaian writer, nor did I bother to have it clarified. I was open to the meeting, whoever the writer happened to be; all I wished for was to get to the sea. Through a friend of my friend who lives in Popenguine, a meeting was arranged. I met my friend's friend, herself a writer, at her place first thing when I arrived early in Popenguine. She told me that after I had spent some time at the beach to walk back to her place and then together we would go over to the house of the old Ghanaian writer. I am sure she said his name, but again, somehow, it didn't ring. What rang was the sea, which I could see from her house, purplish blue from afar. I agreed with the plan and left for the sea.

On my walk to the beach through the main road of the village, I remember passing a man who was dressed in a faded lilac jumpsuit, a perfect halo of white hair framing his small, dark face. The jumpsuit, I thought when I passed him, looked like an astronaut's outfit. He nodded greetings and went his way. The stay at the water and the cliff, abiding in their healing, kept me overtime, and so I was late in rushing back to the village to meet up with my friend's friend to go to the old Ghanaian writer's house. But even as I rushed back, I stopped at an artisan's shop at the side of the road, an old corrugated-zinc shack with masks made of refuse—iron, bottle stoppers, carton boxes— hanging on the side walls of the shack. I called for the owner. A man, fiftyish, emerged from the inside. He said that the artist who owns the shop, Mussa, was presently at home. Mussa's house was a short walk up the dusty and craggy hill behind the shack.

Late to meet the old Ghanaian writer, I went in search of Mussa instead, climbing the hill and arriving at Mussa's yard, which resembled his art shack: litter everywhere, but because of the paintings and masks hanging from the little house and the trees, the yard, like the shack, took on the quasi-sacred feeling I recognized from the yards of obeah men or witch doctors from home.

Mussa was sleeping in a low rugged hammock in front of the house. Cooking utensils were strewn around him; wisps of smoke rose from a fire recently gone out. A puppy was tied on a string next to Mussa. I had to call several times to wake him; when he did wake, he literally unfolded his limbs out of the hammock, so the man who had seemed so small lying down stood as tall as a palm tree in front of me, with the biggest smile on his face. Mussa spoke some English and invited me into the house, a one-room box structure that had a dirty mattress in a corner and scrap material all over the floor, the stuff Mussa turned into art. He told me he worked in this room by a candle at night.

"Only at nights?" I asked.

"Only at nights," Mussa said.

I wondered why and if his art can only be made by the light of a candle. But there wasn't enough language in common between us to discuss it. Mussa showed me the mask he was making the night before. It was laden with rusty keys and coins and bent nails in the mouth holes.

"Beautiful," I said.

Mussa touched his chest and said thanks in English.

We left the room and walked down to Mussa's art shack. He opened the door and windows and showed me around. Besides several masks, there were many painted canvases on the walls, some of which were embellished with Mussa's signature use of metal scraps and other materials. One canvas was particularly arresting. It was painted a stark pink orange, evocative of the Lompoul desert, Mussa explained to me, where he was from. Stitched to the middle of the desert was a raft-like structure made from cowrie shells. Mussa told me to rub my fingers on the shells. I did and I was surprised to feel not a smooth hardness but the rubbery elasticity of keloid scars, which I was about to say to Mussa when my friend's friend showed up in a panic at the shop's entrance: she had gone searching for me at the beach and got worried when I was nowhere to be found. We were two hours late to meet with the old Ghanaian writer. Apologizing to Mussa and promising to return for the raft piece, we left the shop.

As we climbed a small hill to the writer's house, she told me a heartbreaking story. That morning one of her friends, an aspiring writer from Ghana, had taken his own life. It was a heavy thing to hear amid the bougainvillea in the sunlight. His death, sadly, was one in a recent series of suicides committed by African artists all over the continent. "And all so young," she said. I said, "I am sorry to hear that," unsure of what else to say. I thought of a young Kenyan photographer I had met in Berlin in the summer of 2013 who, not long after he went back to Kenya, took his own life. We walked on in deep silence, each thinking of loss, and it is in silence we arrived at the old writer's yard. The main house was a rambling ranch-style building in front of which sat an empty concrete pool, several feet long and deep and made in the shape of an Egyptian ankh. It was a commanding sight, and standing above it at the entrance to the house was the cloud-hair man in the lilac suit from several hours ago! I apologized to him for keeping "island time," and he waved me off with a smile and showed us into a large, airy, bright room, lined with low shelves of books along the walls. Books were also laid out for browsing on a table-tennis table in the center of the room.

I chose some books from the dozen or so stacks, which had about four or five books per pile. Issued by the same publishing house, the books had green laminate covers and black texts printed on bright white pages, which were bound in a way that resembled xeroxed reproductions. They were in several languages, the ones I held were in English, French, and Arabic. I started to notice that quite a lot of the books bore the name Ayi Kwei Armah. I picked up more, and they, too, had the name Ayi Kwei Armah. I looked at the old man in the lilac suit across the table, and that was when it finally struck me: he was Ayi Kwei Armah. Yet foolishly I said, "Are you Mr. Armah? Am I in Mr. Armah's house?"

Armah nodded, as surprised as I was. I walked over and took his hands: the myth made flesh, the hands of the very first African writer I ever read, at Happy Grove, and the hands of the man who deepened my love of literature, whose writing haunted me in those early days of becoming a reader. After reading *The Beautyful Ones Are Not Yet Born*, I refused to touch the railings of stairs and doorknobs for months, so powerfully, and lastingly, Armah conveyed human disgust. *The Beautyful Ones Are Not Yet Born* was my first African book; the first time I lived with African characters that were not *National Geographic* loincloth-clad hunter-gatherer forest dwellers. The book had opened in me, in those very young years of reading, the sense or knowledge that one of the worst crimes brought about in the aftermath of colonialism was the state of apathy. It infected everything, it existed on every scale, subjecting lives to carry on with disgust as if it were a seminatural condition, commonplace in Africa and the African diaspora. Reading that book as a boy was an awakening. I said as much to him while I shook his hands.

And so, in a village by the sea, I met the old man of my early glimmering of self-consciousness, and it was truly moving.

Naturally, the conversation was about the man himself. His coming to Senegal ("snared by a beautiful woman"), and how before that he had decided, when very young, to develop his knowledge of Africa, to, in fact, become African, he said, by traveling throughout the continent and residing long-term in different countries. That peripatetic life has made him fluent in several African languages.

The knowledge, of Africa, his knowledge and great passion, began in Egypt. The books lining the walls were mostly about Egypt, ranging from its language to its culture and history. "No country in Africa," he said, "studies in their institutions the knowledge of Egypt. They don't see that Egypt is the source knowledge of all of Africa." He spoke sadly and slowly. I could see the young man he was in the old man he had become, the singular determination to possess something difficult and far larger than could be grasped in one lifetime: that was the drive, to submit to that impossibility and write a way into it.

He had lived many lives in that personal search. Now in his twilight years, his restlessness has taken on another form. His home in Popenguine was a kind of informal cultural center, a place where schoolchildren from the village visited to do, he said, "play workshops" in which they learn about Egyptian hieroglyphics. It was here, too, that he had founded his own printing house. Alongside publishing multi-genre books on Egypt, including Egyptian-themed children's books, the press reissues out-of-print Egyptology books, thick as phone books, in a multilingual format of seven or more languages, including African languages in which only a handful of published works exist. The labor seemed extensive and demanding. Even so, there was something arcane about it given that countless web pages exist, some with language translation hyperlinks, to the books he has printed on glossy, colorful pages. If he knew this, he seemed unbothered. "Success," not even in the sense of widespread reach, was not what he was after. It was hard to say what that was, but he returned again and again to the point that African people should have easy access to the literature on Egypt. "It is our African legacy," he said. His work in Popenguine, and before Popenguine, is its own extension of that legacy.

I sat in the low-slung canvas chair, looking at him. "I am in Ayi Kwei Armah's house" still ran through my head. There he was before me, the head of cloud, the lilac jumpsuit (like an astronaut's uniform), the affable expression that remained present even when he voiced his disappointments at things he did that didn't come to fruition. "It is so large an issue," he said, "to do service to the cradle of knowledge of an entire continent and the world." When he said this, I looked around the room, at the books on the table and those on the walls, wondering how many people will see a bit of the "service" he has done. I hadn't spoken, not much beyond the occasional "yes" to some of the things he said. Then, drawing his chair closer to mine, he said, "Now, tell me about your life and your work."

My mouth went dry. Had we been alone, I am sure I would have wept. I didn't know what to say. Then I started to speak to him about home, especially, to my surprise, the rivers of Port Antonio.

Îles de la Madeleine at dark. The sea at night is basalt. It gleams like a dance floor, foaming with occasional white lights cutting thin and broad, horizontal and vertical, so that one feels, standing before the waves, ready to plunge into a parallel universe of happiness.

The night sea wears a light-feather coat and a scent so dangerous planets cover their noses, but still they bow to the sea. Sea night music: What is the music?

That music is the underbelly of leaves flashing in slight breeze so that the sound is much more in sight: I can hear an acute sound like razor blades thrown on ice, and I can hear the mountains taking small steps backward and forward, rocking in place, repeating and repeating.

The sea at night. I am here, Îles de la Madeleine, but I am also there, Port Antonio. I am somewhere between the two. In Îles de la Madeleine lie four never-inhabited islets with rock pools of shallow water that looks black and greenish but is as see-through as mirrors, as tears. Many of the rocks are whitened by the shit of cormorants that looks like icing sugar plastered on the fluted scallop of pilgrims' shells, indelible Proustian madeleines. I breathe in the pure scent of ancient and renewed bird shit, of the salt of the sea, of myself.

Now I know something else, something about the composition of the sea at night, the dance that lasts into the shimmer of morning when all is full of a settled, coral joy.

* * *

Dusk. Soft light falls through the bougainvillea on the wall of the villa, their petals brighter than rubies. I think of coals dying in a stove, that roseate last gasp of life. Sounds fill the soft dusk. I can hear the movements of things, and I register them as familiar. Not familiar but intimate. Right now I hear the clatter of utensils from the building next door: in the clatter I can see a hand pulling out a kitchen drawer and grabbing the well-used silverware. For no other reason but the sheer delight of their sound, the hand jiggles the forks and spoons and knives, coupling and uncoupling them, letting an old silver trill fill the house. I hear voices. Bubbling up, wavering, their tones overlap and coax carefree around each other. I think of light glinting off a dark river. Then a woman's voice cuts sharply above the rest, silencing them. The silence stretches a long moment before it breaks and the voices erupt into a loud laughter, easing back into the carefree, overlapping chatter. Perhaps there is a party, old friends gathering for evening drinks and sitting, I imagine, at a low table, hands reaching for glasses and peanuts. I am writing this at the villa, in a lounge chair by the blue-and-white-tiled pool, in which a single swimmer treads the cloudy chlorine water, moving waddlingly without haste, sort of like the slow filtering of dusk. From somewhere a radio blares a jingle peppered with the English phrase "Magic touch!" Elsewhere a door slams shut twice.

The light is cool; the dusk is light as breeze. I can touch the light the way I would the breeze, and it touches me. The light wavers and I see that it is about to sink into extinction. My heart beats faster because the dark—look, the petals of the bougainvillea are going out—is spreading its cloak. More petals vanish, the entire top wall above the pool gone. I will miss this light terribly; already I do. Light, substance I can touch. Touching light. *Is then a touch, quivering me to a new identity?*

I sit here in all that's happening, all that has happened and all that will happen when I am gone from this gentle dusk. This dusk: if I had to trivialize and risk giving it a painter's name, right now I would say Constable, his happily melancholic light like alchemized hay, but here, right now, this light at dusk of low-wattage bruised peach has no parallel. I strain my eyes in the light so as not to see but to feel who is touching me. *Is then a touch, quivering me to a new identity?* My grandmother's eyes are the color of this dusk.

A change of swimmer. A man in his early sixties, brisker than the previous, younger, swimmer, splashing as he does laps, diving to the bottom of the pool, resurfacing, and spurting out water.

Lights are coming on in apartment windows. The dusk has reached its final moment. Another thought comes to me: the soft light of dusk could be so soft or is softened because the extraordinary swirl of dust in the heat of the day, tempestuous and unrelenting, has quieted and transformed into dusk. Dust to dusk. One is being touched by luminous dust particles. The final moment of dusk! Exactly now the evening's call to prayer is struck up. And that is like the sound of what the light emits: pay attention, give thanks.

I will go pick a few bougainvillea petals from the bottom of the wall by the pool and put them on the table in my room, next to the bottle of Atlantic water, the jar of tears I filled nearly a week ago, now half-empty.

OF JOAL, ONLY THE ROAD TO JOAL. NOT THE SEA. NOT A GLINT of cerulean, or cobalt, or indigo. Of Joal, only the road to Joal.

Early waking and quickly packing for St.-Louis. Morning is made tropical by the various sounds of birds in the mango tree in the courtyard of the villa. The mango tree has the broadest leaves I have ever seen on a mango tree, almost the size of the leaves of a breadfruit tree, only waxier and of a denser green. I sip coffee. Few guests are about.

Those I have met come from nearby countries south of Senegal, like the Gambia and Guinea-Bissau, almost all invariably visiting for one conference or another. Yesterday I met a guest, a newspaper worker from the Gambia, here for an editorial conference being held at a hotel in Dakar. He had seen me writing at breakfast and took from the inner pocket of his dark suit a business card, which he gave me with an expression that said, "From one writer to another." Breakfast: baguette with tomato and cheddar and goat cheese. I eat little of it. My food is the morning and the journey to come.

Garbage lined the shore. In the town, garbage spilled out of every nook and cranny. Garbage was in the open spaces; in fields and squares garbage bubbled up in great heaps. Garbage in alleyways and on the side streets. The stench of garbage. The smell was of dead things, commingling. The smell wasn't everywhere, but it was in many places. The smell was also of horse shit, mounds of it littered the roads and was splattered against the side of buildings by cars. My heart ached that first evening in St.-Louis. I went to bed early to begin early, refreshed, to see the city in a different light.

And I did. I woke early and walked to the edge of the oldest part of the town, the traditional quarter for fishermen. I could see gray cinder-block apartment buildings behind jumbled lines of innumerable pirogues that were beached and left to rot on wooden jetties. A jetty took me down to the seawalls dividing the ocean from the land. There I stood in the cool of the morning, looking at the sea, when an old fisherman came up beside me. He smiled and greeted me in Wolof. I returned the standard Wolof greeting, and the fisherman immediately realized I was a visitor and didn't speak any of the local languages. He said he spoke enough English for us to get on and would accompany me through the fishermen's quarter. "You see through my eyes," he said, walking off, and I followed.

I had crossed over an iron bridge to arrive at the fishermen's quarter. This bridge connects the old colonial artery of St.-Louis, where I was staying, to where the fishermen lived. It took me a few days to realize that the iron bridge was less a connector and more a marker of the deep division between the area of the fishermen's quarter, black and poor, and the other side, touristy with strong vestiges of French colonial attitudes. I noticed on both sides of the bridge innumerable children scavenging and playing in the squalor, fishing things out of bilge water. I saw a boy piss and then scoop up the murky water and wash his penis with it. The previous evening on a walk I had seen a man doing the same thing near my villa. Rotten pirogues were beached on both sides of the bridge. In the guts of these discarded pirogues was trash, filth beyond comprehension. Across the bridge, on the side of the fishermen's quarter, were market streets: tumbledown shacks streaming with people and goods. There was a monument at the small roundabout to World War I soldiers. Two figures whose race I couldn't tell faced each other. There was an inscription in French.

Past the monument was the seawall. The strong, unremitting smell of urine and filth at odds with the strong, healing smell of the ocean reached me. I stood on the wall and looked down at the muddy black water foaming with trash below. I looked away out to the sea; the waves were large and rough. The water was pure turquoise. In the distance there were some pirogues, barely visible, moving in a lovely symmetrical line on the great waves. Yet, momentarily, I thought I could make out the bright-color effigies painted on the pirogues that brought to my mind the art on Indigenous American canoes. As I was thinking this, the old fisherman appeared next to me. I put him at around eighty. Only much later, after we had passed through the fishermen's quarter and beyond, did I figure out that the fisherman was not that old, actually, and was probably about sixty but had been retired for some years now from the sea. It was retirement, he said, that made him an old man. "With no work," he said with a wink, "I do nothing but survive."

He first took me through a network of narrow lanes filled with cinder-block houses closely crammed together. I felt at some moments as if we were wandering inside a honeycomb. I could glimpse open spaces, little courtyards in between some of the buildings. A few of these little courtyards had a waterpipe in the middle with a trough where animals, mostly sheep, were tethered on pegs. People were doing morning chores: women washing in tubs at front doors and other women cooking on blackened iron stoves in the narrow passages. Food peels, chopped-up vegetables, and parts of fish were thrown in heaps on the pathways. The ground made a squelchy sound with each step I took. Children were everywhere; they came running out of the dark passages, dragging bewildered animals behind them, or I could see them gathered in groups of three or more, sitting and talking on concrete steps of the buildings. Later I found out from the owner of my villa that five years ago a tidal wave had destroyed the main public school and other municipal buildings, including the main clinic in the fishermen's quarter, and that was partly why so many kids were about during the daytime.

We turned into a much wider passageway, this one almost clogged with animals, mostly sheep again, and mongrels being driven by shaved-headed young boys in dirty shifts. The tumult dazed me. I thought of blood sacrifice, of wide, frightened eyes going dim. We exited the passage into another, even larger one, and there I saw, wondrously, an old man in a splendid light blue gown sitting on a crate with a gigantic pelican in front of him. The pelican, spotlessly white, was pecking food from the old man's palm. After every mouthful or so the bird cleansed its great yellow beak on a black cloth hanging on the old man's shoulder. The retired fisherman told me that the pelican was the man's guard. "Like a watchdog?" I asked, and the retired fisherman said, "No, like a spiritual guard. A gris-gris." This surprised me, for I knew that a gris-gris in West Africa was usually a small talisman worn around the neck or somewhere else on the body.

The retired fisherman explained brokenly at length that the pelican could never leave the old man's side until the old man dies, that the pelican would always be with the old man everywhere right up to that moment of death, and the care that the old man gives to the pelican would ensure that the pelican carries the old man's soul safely to the next realm. "It is always with him," he repeated, and winked as he added, "even in bed."

We continued through the rows of houses. The deeper we went, the narrower the lanes and the more buildings looked like rubble. The cries of humans and animals grew louder. My mind flashed back to the old sugarcane barracks I knew in St. Thomas. Though I had only ever walked through the lanes of those former slave barracks once or twice, the sensation I felt never left me. I felt that sensation now. From those walks in the barracks, I remembered the soft squelch of the gray-black ground under my feet. It was the sound of the spongy mixture of cane ash, marl, and mud. I was still a boy, no older than thirteen, and I had felt a sadness and a grief in my chest I couldn't comprehend. It was not the derelict condition of the barrack buildings or the destitution of the people that triggered those feelings; those conditions were familiar enough in my daily life. In those barracks lanes, exposed, naked, and festering on the ground were the open wounds of the colonial past that I was spared from seeing, but there was its ugliness, which made me physically ill, on the tumbledown wooden houses, in the stunted garden plots, and on the mashed-mouth faces of people.

And here it was again, that same barrack feeling that sickened. It was there in the shadowy inside of entryways crowded with people, whose faces would briefly turn to us and then turn away as if to avert their gaze from the stranger peering into their private sorrow. The retired fisherman took me inside one of these buildings with a large, cavernous entryway. It turned out to be a maternity clinic. Inside I saw heavily pregnant women moaning in terrible pain, rolling on beds and stretchers pulled up to the walls of the passages. The strong scent of disinfectant filled the corridors, and there were blobs of thick liquid matter running on the floor, which I didn't want to look down at too much. I could hear the sea above the groans of the women, and I asked the retired fisherman if we could please go to the water.

We cut behind the maternity ward and strolled down a white sand trail, passing by the shambles of a medium-size mosque: it, too, like the main school, was half-destroyed by the tidal wave of five years ago. We walked toward the sea. The fresh air cleared my nausea. We walked in silence on the sand. I was happy, quite glad to find such a clean stretch of beach. The retired fisherman pointed out to the sea and explained that Mauritania was that way, and that way was Spain, and that way the currents took you straight to Brazil. Boyish glee filled his face as he pointed these out. "Have you gone to Brazil?" I asked, and he said no, only to Mauritania, and pointed again in that direction, adding, "Good fishing there." This was true, and later I heard that the fishing water was the cause for much tension between Senegal and Mauritania; Senegalese fishermen, apparently, routinely broke offseason fishing laws in Mauritanian territory.

The retired fisherman began to talk about his fishing days, first in English but, growing excited, slipping almost exclusively into Wolof, gesturing nonstop at the sea. The gestures, the voice being ripped by the breeze, all of it was an intense, moving pleasure for me to listen to, though I did not always understand what he was saying. Then, suddenly, fueled by the excited talk, he grasped my shoulder and said, in English, "I take you to meet my amigos for tea." I thought "amigos" was a strange word and wondered if he was perhaps referring to friends from Spain. "My amigos is a good, good man, a big man of pirogues, my amigos," he said. I then understood "amigos" might be referring to one person. I agreed to meet the "amigos," and we moved side by side in silence on the clean sand.

*　　*　　*

It began with a smell and the beach started to change. We were a mile and a half from the clinic. Then I saw it, a dead, bloated sheep on the pathway. With the decomposing body, the air was suddenly rancid. But the terrible scent wasn't just because of the dead sheep: immediately on the opposite side of its body was a veritable slum yard, miles upon miles of garbage stretching along the shore. The sand was hardly visible. Where was all this garbage coming from? The beach was choked with every type of debris imaginable. Did currents bring it from the ocean, therefore from anywhere or everywhere? Or was this area an informal dump site for the fishermen's quarter we had passed through? I wanted to ask the retired fisherman but didn't know how to put such a question to him. It would've been arrogant to ask. He wasn't responsible for this municipal nightmare. We picked our way in silence through the cyclonic spread of garbage.

After twenty minutes we came to an area that was mostly cleared.

On a raised hill from the beach, I could see the low whitewashed wall of a Muslim cemetery. We started going up the hill toward the cemetery when I saw not too far down the surf an old man, bowing in prayer toward the sea. We stopped to watch. The old man wore a dark wrap around his privates, which rippled around his frail body in the wind, and snatches of his chants could be heard carrying on the wind. Standing at the foreshore, only the fading parts of the run-ups of waves reached where the old man stood in a large, dark wet circle in the sand; it was as if he were standing in his own radiance. He then fell to his knees and stretched flat on his belly with his head toward the sea and began to crawl into the surf: the water rushed up and covered his body, momentarily making his dark form gauzy white as if wrapped in ceremonial cerement. Chanting louder, the old man then sprang to his feet. He tightened the wrap around his waistline and walked into the sea, the waves pounding against his thin frame. When he was waist-deep in the roiling blue, he paused and raised his hands, his chants intense and loud on the wind; then in one smooth, age-defying motion, he leaped in the air and dove into the water without making a splash. He was gone for several moments, an eternity to us watching from a dune in front of the cemetery. I looked wildly around for him, the moments stretching. Just when I began to fear the worst, he surfaced some distance from where he had dived into the water. He swam calmly to shore, the dark wrap clinging to his wizened figure. Once onshore he walked back to the same spot where he had left his radiance on the wet sand, chanting and spinning around in the circle a few times before stopping abruptly, and began to walk on the dry sand toward the township.

We climbed up to the sea-blasted cemetery and walked in between the rows of headstones, most of which were plain small slabs of concrete lying flat or put standing in the sand. Some of the headstones were covered with pieces of old fishing net. Those headstones that were bleached extra white looked like skulls peering out from under the tattered brown nets. There was something solemn about passing through the haphazard rows of graves, just the two of us, the retired fisherman mumbling to himself, perhaps lines of suras for the departed. I wondered if he had loved ones buried here. I didn't ask. We walked quietly until there were no more graves. The solemnity of the walk through the cemetery, the near sea without garbage, the old man muttering prayers—I took it all in and prayed in my own way.

Set on top of a series of leveled dunes, made from scrap material and wood, weatherworn and blackened, were rows of shacks. As we drew near, a horrific scent filled my nose, a stench far worse than before. I saw the source of it: beneath the shacks were rotten wooden racks, hundreds of them, on top of which were innumerable piles of fish. The fish were sardines, I was soon to find out. The ground in and around the shacks was completely covered with the guts and other parts of the fish, a swirling mass of red and black hardening into a muddy mixture of both. Several women were standing in this putrid blend and bent over the racks. They were wearing bright head wraps of blue, green, orange; some had thinner strips of pastel cloths wrapped around the bottom of their faces. I quickened my pace to go inside the shacks, but the retired fisherman gently pulled me back and said no. For a moment I hesitated; maybe men—I couldn't make out any male bodies present inside—were not allowed to go inside the shacks, but already a few women, looking up from their work, waved greetings to us. That was invitation enough, and I grasped the retired fisherman's hand and climbed the last grating into the shacks.

If the smell was terrible outside the shacks, inside the stench was vile beyond words. My nostrils burned. At the feet of the women were fresh heaps of sardine heads; the dead eyes of the fish shone where sunlight through the gaps in the roof hit them; on the long-slatted tables were the bodies of the fish, spread open and flattened for salting. And that was the work they did by hand, an assembly line of women salting sardines, their clothes and foreheads splattered with the guts and blood of the fish. As we walked down the middle aisle of their workstation, some of the women working in silent clusters of three and four would look up and greet us with a smile. I would mechanically raise my hand, mechanically smile back, and then pass on to the next group, each looking just like the other, their faces made almost featureless in this satanic mill of unbearable smell.

But as I approached another group at what seemed like the midpoint of the shacks, I stopped dead in my tracks and nearly passed out. There was my mother, waving at me. I was visibly shaking as I gave the Wolof greeting to her, and perhaps because I was shaking so hard, she walked over to me. Tears filled my eyes when she stood in front of me. Despite her face crusted in grime and almost obscure, I could clearly see the spitting image of my mother in her face. I didn't know what to do; she spoke, in Wolof, staring into my eyes. The retired fisherman was translating what she said, but I was too dazed to follow, so I embraced her, weeping. She held me for a moment; then after I was able to speak, I asked the retired fisherman to tell her that she looks exactly like my mother. The retired fisherman did. Keeping her hands on my shoulders, she again spoke directly to my eyes. I heard the retired fisherman say, "She says to you that she is your mother and you're welcome here." In her own voice what was translated was much longer, and only after she had finished speaking did she take her hands from my shoulders. I tottered forward when she moved off, returning to the mound of sardines waiting at her station, which she immediately began salting. I realized I didn't get a chance to ask her her name. Down the line beyond her the shacks seemed to extend out of sight. I looked down and all began to appear blurry, even what was right before my eyes, even my own mother. I knew that it was an attack of vertigo. I was too shaken to continue farther down the salting line. Without saying anything, the retired fisherman took my arm and led me out of the shack, over the dune, and back to the beach.

I walked in the surf this time, carrying my sandals in my hand as the retired fisherman, his sneakers on, skirted waves that came up too close. The sea cleared my head. I kept my eyes on it, lost in thoughts. "That woman," I kept thinking, "that woman, that woman, that woman." The retired fisherman's voice broke into my thoughts; he was calling out and pointing to a range of unpainted cinder-block buildings, the beachside of a township, in the near distance. "There my amigos," he said, and we walked up to the town where many new and old pirogues were beached at the edge of the sand before it thinned into several rutted asphalt streets.

Little corner shops, where men gathered talking or standing in their shade, dotted the streets, which were crossed frequently by pedestrians and people on bicycles. There seemed to be nothing else in the area except for these corner shops. The place had a desolate feel but with a general sense of calm, unlike the traditional fishermen's quarter, which suggested it might be a place of upward mobility. Gesturing to me to sit on a rock under an almond tree next to a brand-new pirogue, the paint still wet on its side, the retired fisherman said he would tell the amigos to expect a "foreign" (it was the first time he used the word) visitor. The sea was to my back. I sat on the rock, leaned against the tree, and immediately dozed off.

A boy in a long white tunic, pulling my hair, woke me. He was touching his own head, which was shaved close and seemed to have fresh nicks on the skull. I greeted him and he smiled and said nothing as he continued to touch my hair, tugging to pull a coil from the knot holding up my dreadlocks. I took a long dread from the knot, and the boy pulled it, still silent. Just for fun I said, touching my hair, "Rasta," and the boy said it back and paused before saying, "Burna Boy." I laughed at that, the name of the dreadlocked Nigerian Afrobeats star whose music I had heard playing everywhere in Dakar. The ice broken, I smiled and said one of the few Wolof phrases I have memorized, "Naka-nga sant?" "What is your name?" But before the boy could say anything, the retired fisherman returned, and the boy strolled off.

The retired fisherman had a marked happy look on his face. In a somewhat stiffly formal tone, he said that the amigos would see me now. We walked through a dusty narrow lane crammed with midrise cinder-block apartments before turning down a wide road, notable for having plane trees standing in front of colorfully painted two-story houses. After a couple of blocks, the retired fisherman repeating that the amigos would see us now (I couldn't tell anymore if he was excited or anxious), we entered the yard of one of those colorful houses. The spacious ground floor had large white tiles and several water drums in one corner. A woman in a long, shimmery blue-and-white frock escorted us into a sitting room, surprisingly small given how large the house seemed from the outside. Part of the room's smallness had to do with the fact that it was stuffed with two oversize sofas, large and dark and still wrapped in cracking laminate plastic, and in the corners and along the walls were several cardboard drums, on top of which sat a flat-screen TV playing with the volume turned low. The woman pointed at a sofa for us to sit down; she then called out to the adjacent room. Two teenage girls dressed in similar crinkly rose-colored gowns came in, the woman whispered something to them, and the girls went out of the room. Two boys, also young teenagers, entered; they greeted me first and then greeted the retired fisherman, who had opted to sit on the floor. Both boys sat next to me on the sofa and immediately started to play with their mobile phones. I crouched down to ask the retired fisherman who these people were. He explained that the woman was the second wife of the amigos, and the girls and boys were the amigos's youngest children.

But where was the amigos? I asked the retired fisherman, and he turned to talk with the boys, their exchange going on for a few minutes, after which the retired fisherman said to me, "My amigos is sleeping." Then he added, by way of consolation, that the amigos was busy all day seeing to the making of new pirogues for the large fleet he owned. I gave him a confused look, and he continued explaining that the amigos gets tired from . . . and here he cast about for a word in English that would serve and came up with "operation," which he pronounced by spreading his arms wide to demonstrate the indelible point that the amigos was a man of great importance, a man who didn't have a lot of time to spare for social calls even if he had agreed on one just fifteen minutes ago. The amigos then was something in the manner of a *patrón* or jefe, the retired fisherman's former boss.

I suggested, rising up from the sofa, that we should leave and not intrude on the amigos's rest, but the retired fisherman said, "My amigos only sleep short and will come soon. We wait." We did, the boys playing on their mobile phones, the retired fisherman's eyes fixed on a locked amber vinyl door to the left side of the room. Directing his voice at this door, the retired fisherman then began to speak loudly, then said in English, "My amigos is good to me," and then in Wolof directed his voice back at the door, undoubtedly speaking about the goodness of his amigos. I began to wonder if there was a caste complex to their relationship, for it seemed that the retired fisherman was performing some sort of abasement. He didn't stop speaking, his voice rising almost to the pitch of ululation, until the vinyl door opened and an extremely tall man in a long, resplendent white tunic entered the room. The retired fisherman rose instantly and clutched the man's hand, bowing as he did.

The amigos had a lean, very black face and small, groggy eyes. He seemed indeed a man carrying the weariness of big operations. His face struck me as familiar, but I was blanking on where I knew it from. The retired fisherman pointed to me and spoke in Wolof at length to the amigos, who nodded while looking at me and then after a moment smiled and said, in English, "You're welcome here." His voice was reedy and low. I thanked him and he held out his hand to me, which I took, and he repeated the phrase, "You're welcome here." That turned out to be the extent of his English, so everything said between us was communicated through the rapid tapestry of simplified French, English, Wolof, and the gestures of the retired fisherman. He then covered my hand with both of his palms and scrutinized my face, his eyes staring almost unblinkingly into mine. I held his stare, and after a moment it came to me where I thought I had seen his face before: his face looked very much like that of the cart driver in Ousmane Sembène's great short film *Borom Sarret*. For many years I was obsessed with that film, watching it sometimes up to four times per day to the point that the poor, nameless cart driver entered into my dreams. And now here he was, I fooled myself, in the flesh.

We sat down. His daughters immediately reentered the room with a tray of tea things that they placed on the floor and left, and then the boys made the dark brew and handed it out to us in frothy shot glasses. Only the retired fisherman spoke. The amigos smiled placidly at him and then at me. When we had our first sip, the amigos spoke. The retired fisherman translated: we would finish this round and then leave for the amigos's fishing hut on the sea. The room was very hot. The boys were sent ahead to get the hut ready.

Two gulps later we exited the house, going the same route back to the beach the retired fisherman and I had taken. As we passed again one of the freshly painted pirogues, the retired fisherman told me it was a new one for the amigos's fleet. The retired fisherman and I circled it; he rapped his knuckles against the prow, which had "Zola" blazoned in red on the tip. The amigos stood back, smiling, arms folded behind his back. The new pirogue conveyed more of his status. He said nothing, but the retired fisherman explained that this pirogue was for the youngest son of the amigos, a boy destined to soon have his own fleet of pirogues at sea like all the elder sons of the amigos who were bosses of big fleets. It was unclear how many elder sons the amigos had, but it seemed as if he had quite a few. Yet with so many sons plowing the sea,

the retired fisherman continued, the amigos still had his own boats and many other men working for him. The retired fisherman used to be one of these men. In bits and parts I learned later that the retired fisherman depended on the amigos for handouts and that was his only means of survival. I learned later, too, that the retired fisherman had a nineteen-year-old daughter who works at the same dreadful sardine-salting mine we had walked through an hour ago. She might have been there when we were, something I didn't know when we stood in that abominable stench.

The sea hut was one very large room with old carpets laid on the sand a few meters from the sea. It seemed the boys had swept it before we arrived, but already sand was coming back inside. Attached to the back of the hut, away from the sea, was an animal pen but with no animals currently. Inside the hut was quite pleasant. Light filtered through the wooden slats and green canvas tarpaulin of the ceiling; on the carpet were piled several stoles and pillows. The retired fisherman began to unroll them and arranged them into a space for us to lounge. Once the space was created, the amigos reclined his full length, like a pasha, in the swarm of fabric. The smile never changed from his face when, comfortably stretched out, he began to speak to me. He wanted to hear about Jamaica, about America. I answered briefly and asked him about his life. He spoke about growing up poor in a big family of fishermen, about Allah's grace making him a good fisherman early, about becoming "a man over men" (I was surprised when the retired fisherman spoke the words), and now he was better off than when he started decades ago, now soon to retire. Even through glitches of language, his life came so clear to me. It was clear he was a man who was precise and decisive. At some point in the narrative, he got up and walked over to a large wooden box, out of which he took things to make tea: a little coal stove, a water jug, a box of loose-leaf tea, and tea glasses. As he took out these things, the retired fisherman began to busy himself with getting the tea ready. The amigos, meanwhile, dragged out more pillows from another large box and bunched them up behind my back. He reclined back where he was, the smile still playing on his face. His smile, I began to realize, was because he was shy.

Just as he was about to talk again, a faint cry like a kitten's came from the back of the sea hut. The cry got louder and louder. They seemed unbothered by it, but I asked if we could check. The amigos nodded to the retired fisherman, who went, and I followed him to the back of the hut. Indeed, it was a scrawny kitten, tangled up in strands of an old net in the fencing of the animal pen. The retired fisherman hissed. I said we must get it out. He hissed more and went back into the hut. He returned with a small scissors and a mirror, for what I didn't know. I held up the net as he cut until we got the kitten free.

He brought the kitten inside the hut to the amigos, who, reclining in the same position, reached out his hands for it. When the retired fisherman gave him the kitten, he held it to his chest, gently stroking its neck. I stared at this show of affection, which went on for several minutes before he handed the kitten back to the retired fisherman, who took it outside and released it at the front of the hut. The kitten stood still, shaking in one spot. The retired fisherman hissed; then he clapped. The kitten didn't move.

That was when the retired fisherman brought out the mirror, aimed it at the sun, and reflected the ray on the kitten. It stood still. I stood still. After a moment, the kitten yelped and tottered away toward the sea. I stared after it, puzzled. When I turned toward the doorway, the amigos was standing there, the water jug in his hand, with the retired fisherman standing beside him. I couldn't shape any words; the retired fisherman said that the amigos had to fetch water from his house for tea because the jug was empty and would be right back and that I should come back into the hut. The amigos strolled off; the retired fisherman and I went back inside the hut. He continued to do more preparation for the tea and repeated again how good the amigos was. Finally I spoke; I told the retired fisherman I'd like to sit outside and watch the sea. He grabbed a small carpet and took it outside and spread it on the sand. I sat down and looked out at the sea.

A boat had just come in, and a small crowd had gathered around to help the fishermen come to shore. To the right of me, horses and cows were eating garbage. The sun was high; the heat was intense. I took it all in, my gaze coming back to the sea. I wondered where the kitten was and looked but didn't see it. My eyes returned to the sea. Something heavy began to lift as I looked. Then the amigos returned, the jug in his hand filled with water and four or five men with him, all dressed, like him, in beautiful white gowns. They greeted me and invited me back into the hut. And there we were, a collective of old African fishermen and me, a Jamaican, half their age and from a world away. Their faces glowed with a congeniality that was hard to describe. They said the same word in English, "welcome"; the grace in it rang with something more than a benign affectation. I felt such luck to be in their presence on the carpet, their voices bending around the hut into a chorus I could only follow by the gentle pulse of kindness I heard in it, punctuated by the single English word they used over and over, "welcome."

The retired fisherman then told me that the fishermen wanted to pray for me after lunch. I told him to tell them that I was very grateful. After a silence they started to talk among themselves again, slowly at first and then rapidly. I was forgotten, and after a while I managed to tell the retired fisherman to let us step outside. We did. I realized that lunch was going to be a very slow affair, and because it was already 2:00 p.m. or later and I had been out since early morning, I needed to get back to my villa. He understood and we went back into the hut and he explained to the collective as he blew the coal stove fire and put on the kettle for the tea. They regretted I had to leave so soon but said again that I am welcome and they'll pray for me after tea. The retired fisherman sat back and began to clip his fingernails with a large clipper. There was silence again, except for the snipping of nails. I smiled at them, and they smiled at me. Then the amigos's two daughters arrived with two covered steel bowls of food. The amigos was happy, because at least now I could eat. But when he uncovered the bowls, they contained meat stews poured over macaroni. I told him, apologizing, that I didn't eat meat. He said no problem, smiling, and covered back the bowls. They will eat after tea, after I am gone. Tea was soon ready, a dark brew the retired fisherman dropped several cubes of granulated sugar into, which he then poured into a shot glass, swirled around, and drank half of. Satisfied, he filled the remainder of the glass with tea and handed it to me. It was a very dirty glass. I wanted a fresh glass but felt bad asking him for one, and so as he turned to serve the other fishermen, I poured out the tea he gave me and grabbed an unused glass out of the clean pile. When he came back around to me, he filled my glass, and I drank the strong, sweet brew in one swallow. Seconds of tea were served; I reminded the retired fisherman I must go. He told the others and they rose and came over to where I was seated. Before I could stand, they each put a hand on my shoulders and began to chant. I bowed my head. They prayed. When they were done, I got up and said my thanks, my cheeks wet, and wished them well and left with the retired fisherman.

We took the direction back to St.-Louis that was by a harbor where most pirogues returned from the sea to the main fishery depot. I watched fish by the thousands being brought back and forth in shallow plastic bins from the hundreds of pirogues docked, nodding, at the wooden jetties. We watched a while the haggling, the passing of cash for fish, newspapers of fish in black hands, fish in clear plastic bags on top of bright head wraps, fish thrown in the sand and trampled on the ground. Halfway past the fisheries, the retired fisherman pointed out to me where I needed to walk to get back to my villa. He asked me for some money. I was planning on giving him some; what he asked for I would've given to him, but I simply didn't have that amount with me, which I tried to explain. I gave him all I had. He was for a moment disappointed, but then he walked me a little way farther through the rush of fishmongers on the squelchy ground, saying I am welcome and should return. I said I am glad and that I will.

I was chained to one or more strangers in a brightly lit room. I was forced to smoke something. I choked and clamped my mouth shut. The person forcing me to smoke tore my mouth open. Someone next to him, one of the people I was chained to, said he would do the smoking and blew the smoke in my face. He said it quite calmly, and the person forcing me to smoke left me alone. A gust of smoke blew in my face. My mouth tasted like gunpowder. My eyes watered, and through them, hazily, I saw a woman walk into the room. She wore a tight-fitting yellow dress. She smiled. She kept smiling as a voice started to shout questions from somewhere. I felt it belonged to the person who was forcing me to smoke, but I was unsure because that person didn't speak. The person I was chained to, who blew smoke into my face, was gone. The questions seemed to be about, relentlessly, the name of a person or of a place. My eyes searched wildly for the voice as I pulled at my chains and screamed, "I don't know. I don't know any name." The woman came closer. There was an intense heat coming off her body. I saw in her hand a steel pan that resembled, so I thought, an animal's feeding bowl. She was still smiling. As I was about to scream again, she smashed the pan over my head, and that was when I jumped out of my sleep. I woke to the before-dawn darkness of the room. Lying still on my back, I breathed heavily as objects took shape and I was certain where I was, that I had escaped that bright room. I didn't move until I heard the call to morning prayer.

One evening near sunset while walking along a quiet side of the quay, I came upon a beautiful large red building with yellow louver windows. I was drawn to it, and as I circled from its back to the front, my breath caught to see the name painted above the wide entrance: Lycée d'Excellence Privé Aimé Césaire. Just seeing the name of the great Martinican poet, this brilliant Antillean mind I have loved since my student days in Jamaica, touched me with something inexplicable. Compelled to, I sat on the wall of the quay across from the building.

The sun began to set. For a while no one passed; as I was about to head off and continue down the quay, a group of joggers emerged. I decided to watch and waited until they passed. There were about eight of them, all dressed in the same black shorts and green tops, except for one, the only girl in the group, dressed in running pants, black headdress, and the green top. Could they be a sports team from the lycée? As they jogged in a half sprint past me, I noticed the girl was straggling. One of the boys slowed and reached back a hand to her. The others jogged on past me, and then, hand in hand, the boy and the girl jogged past me, too. I could hear that he was saying something to her. Her laugh in response was cheerful as it carried on the sunset breeze.

Joal. This time Joal. Joal: at once like Port Antonio in its expanse of sea light and like St. Thomas with its thick mangroves and roadsides lined with thorn trees. These parallels of home in Joal made being there a deeply sensual homecoming. Even the road to Joal from Dakar through the town of M'bour, a long esplanade dotted with markets on both sides, shacks hanging with fruits, clothing, and housewares, strongly resembled the main roads in Jamaica going east from St. Thomas to Portland or south from Portland to Kingston. A portion of the red road to Joal so evoked the arid red dirt road of Stokes Hall in St. Thomas that along its stretch I swore I was back home, on my way to Happy Grove, my school on the cliff.

I took a slender canoe, made from a single tree, out into shallow marsh water to a large mangrove where I saw women half-submerged in the murky water, fishing for oysters. As the canoe passed them, they lifted their heads from the water, shielded their eyes from the sun, and waved to us. I waved back. The canoe passed on, and they bowed back to the water.

The canoe cut through the mangrove and arrived at an island made completely of oyster shells: shells shucked for centuries until accumulated into a landmass between the grooves of the mangrove. On this shell island, rice and sorghum were grown, two of the most ancient food sources: ancient land, ancient food. Still standing in some areas of the shell islands were the traditional tiny huts of brown thatch on long stilts. They seemed like cranes about to lift off to the sky. I walked past them, shells crunching beneath my feet, toward the "mixed" cemetery on the island. My guide explained to me that Muslims and Christians, for centuries, have been buried there, each playing a role in the different sects' burial rituals. He explained that the two religions have shared an intimate closeness for as long as forever in Joal: a typical family from Joal, like his, was made up of both faiths. The cemetery seemed to have more crosses, however, which were skewed in directions that appeared consistent enough to suggest a pattern. I asked why the crosses were laid out in these different ways, and he told me this was due to the different Christian denominations on the island, four I believe, the majority being Catholic. Later, indeed, I got to see the main Catholic church, which was in the center of the island, the altar laden with fruit offerings to various saints, all represented by white figurines.

We left the cemetery, crossing by foot the beautiful long bridge, recently built, of the shell island from Joal into Fadiout. Fadiout is a large island of about six thousand people. An extraordinarily beautiful place that reminded me of the rugged terrain of the parish of St. Elizabeth on the southern coast of Jamaica. I brushed my hand on the dusty, pebbly ground. Tufts of grass grew in sparse bursts all over the marl-like earth. I put the dust in my pocket and we walked on. My guide took me to the four public meeting spaces, all big gazebos built in a small square surrounded by flat-roofed residential houses. In the meeting spaces were men of different ages, broken up into small groups talking or playing checkers. Some looked up from their conversation or game and greeted us.

After the last meeting place, the guide said now he would take me to the King of the Sea.

*   *   *

The King of the Sea was ninety years old. He could be a hundred or over a hundred, depending on whom you asked. He was a very old man, one eye sunken so deep into his skull and congealed into a smooth lump of skin, the other, opened, small and clouded over with glaucoma. I was told about him before going to Joal and that I had to meet him. From all accounts he was an amazing man. I didn't ask a lot of questions about him in Dakar, where I first heard about him; I loved the fact or idea of his title, King of the Sea. It was not a title, as was explained to me, but a calling, and I wanted to meet him on the terms of just that detail.

My guide and I arrived at the King of the Sea's house, a small raw concrete structure crowded in by other houses nearby, nondescript and plain. A woman who seemed to be in her thirties took us to the living room, where we sat on a sofa and waited for the King of the Sea. Shortly, the old man came out of his bedroom to the living room, brushing his hands on the furnishings as he made his way to the large sofa, where he sat on one of the cushions in a far corner by the curtained window. The sofa seemed to envelop his small form like quicksand. He was dressed in white cotton pajama pants and a loose T-shirt with a thin gold chain with a cross pendant over the shirt's collar. Above his head was a calendar with an image of Christ of the Sacred Heart, the same one ubiquitous in Caribbean homes: my grandmother's house had one of these calendars, and I started to wonder if I had ever seen my grandmother sit directly beneath her calendar Jesus. A TV blared loudly from another room.

I stared from the sofa in front of him at the large white tiles on the floor, then back at the King of the Sea; I did again and realized I could see him reflected in the tiles. His shaved head had sprinklings of white on it. Then he began to speak. He lifted his head slightly up and down as if nodding and raised his right hand in the same rhythm to match his speech. His voice was husky but not deep. I listened intently to it as my guide translated softly, directly into my ear. He told me that the King of the Sea has welcomed me, that I'm not a stranger to him. Though by now various people have said this to me all over Senegal, to the point that it has become commonplace, here it moved me so much as I listened to the cadence of his voice, which, the more I listened, the more I'm convinced was like sea waves on a calm day.

I wish I could've thanked him in a shared language, but I asked my guide to tell him that I'm grateful to be in his home. He welcomed me again and said I'm free to ask him any question. I asked my guide to ask him to tell me, what is the work of the King of the Sea? His cloudy eye blinked, and then he began to speak at length, so much so my guide wasn't able to keep up with translating and began to do something I hadn't noticed since we met: he clicked his tongue to signal he was listening. The King of the Sea spoke for a long time. The guide clicked and I listened. After a while the King of the Sea fell silent. The guide then summarized for me.

The King of the Sea says prayers for fishermen before they go out to sea; he prays for a good catch and for the sea to be kind to the fishermen on their journey. If the catch is bad, the King of the Sea goes to the sea and makes sacrifice and prayers to the sea for a better catch next time. He repeats this ritual of sacrifice and prayers until the sea answers with good catches. The King of the Sea cannot—can never—spend a night away from the village; wherever he is during the day, he must be back to the village by nightfall. The consequences of staying away from the village for a night seemed dire, but I wasn't told what they were.

After the guide explained this to me, I asked him to ask the King of the Sea how he became the King of the Sea and if he always wanted to be king. Again, the King of the Sea spoke for a long time, much longer than before. My eyes strayed from him, down to the white tiles and then outside to the window behind his head: the large light behind him framing his head was as magnificent as that in the print of Christ above his head. When he stopped speaking, the guide gave a rough summary.

One day the elders of the village came and said to him that since he was such a good boy who went to church and was a good son to his father, he would make a good King of the Sea. He was selected because he belonged to a particular ethnic group that was the minority in his village, which all Kings of the Sea came from. No, he didn't want to be the king. But then regular people, his friends and family, first in jest, began to call him King of the Sea. That bothered him and he spoke to his father about his discomfort with the whole matter. His father reassured him that the matter was his choice and that he was free to say no to becoming the king. He didn't say no then to his father after they spoke, neither did he say yes. One day after that talk with his father, he was leaving the hospital, whether as a visitor or as a patient was unclear, and he met an old friend about to enter the hospital—again it was unclear whether as a visitor or as a patient—who called him King of the Sea, and right then and there in front of the hospital he decided he wanted to become the King of the Sea. He spoke again to his father. His father was happy about his choice. The rites were performed, many decades ago, and ever since he has been the King of the Sea.

Was he a fisherman before he became the King of the Sea? I asked. No, not in any serious way. He was a farmer. He said this, and for the first time I heard him laugh.

■

THE SUN IS FADING. A SEAGULL SKIMS THE ROILING WATER. The breeze is slightly cold. The sun is like a moon that Basho or someone might have called an "ice wheel," but without any of the frigidity of that image. Now the sun is like doused fire. No color but dust particles, ocher fused with orange. I dig my heels in the cool sand. I rub my palms over shells and gritty pebbles. The sound of the sea is a massive, self-leafing tome. Leafing and leafing and leafing and leafing.

The sea is a vast gray-blue curtain as far as the eye can see. The sky is similar but more of a pale gray. Leafing and leafing. God, the sun, an ice wheel again. Has it gotten lower? I feel an alarm of joy ringing in me. Again, the empty beach in Popenguine: nobody but myself here, the breeze riffling my shirtsleeves, and when I sigh or just breathe, I'm astonished to think I'm the only one in creation adding my breath to this breeze. I look to where the sun is, and there's now a moon. High up, bone white. I can't believe I'm beneath this moon, which moments ago was a sun. I stand up only to confirm that, yes, I'm on the earth still.

Rougher sea this morning. One small pirogue with one fisherman in a bright orange life jacket, close to shore. He is casting lines. Otherwise, again, the beach is empty. On the walk here I passed a woman with a colossal load on her head. She seems over fifty years old, dressed in a long, curtain-like yellow dress. She balances her burden by swinging her arms at her sides. Her walk certain on the damp, craggy sand. A wave, a smile, as we passed each other. Then I look back to see her, arms akimbo, resting a bit as she looked out to the sea. Did my grandmother ever stop like that with her double-*bankra* basket every Saturday morning for most of her life as she went to sell in the market in Port Antonio? She had to.

A small airplane flies low in the near distance. Other than that sound, which is brief before it is gone, all I can hear is the steady rise and fall of the waves all along the long stretch of beach. I sit in the shade underneath the cliff. The waves break on the great black boulders at the sea's edge with a sound like thunder then receding softly as rain. I strip myself again. I bite into a mango. I eat it, sucking all the juice from the hole I've bitten in its bottom. I throw the seed into the sea, running after it and sinking my whole body under the water.

By early afternoon the day changes to its proper self: fierce heat but pleasant. The sea waves beat at the same tempo: fierce but pleasant. In all this time since I've been here, except for the woman with the basket from about two hours ago, not a soul has passed. Translucent crabs scuttle on the sand. The only shade is under the cliff's overhang with the hole like two conjoined basketball hoops. I go to it. But soon the sun chases away that shade and there's nothing but the naked sun on my naked back. In which direction is Gorée? I try to imagine and decide that it is to the east and turn my face to the east. Before I leave Senegal, I tell myself, I will return to Gorée, to write about the bougainvillea jostling over the slave castle where twice, inside, I had stood in front of the Door of No Return and saw myself shimmering in the water a mere step off the ledge. I can hear no call to prayer from here. Still, pray.

ACKNOWLEDGMENTS

Original versions of these essays appeared in *Agni, The American Reader, The Common*, FSG's *Work in Progress, Granta, Gropius Bau, The Happy Reader, Harper's Magazine, The New Yorker, The New York Review of Books, The Paris Review, The Poetry Review, The Sewanee Review, Tate Etc.*, and *The Yale Review*.

"An Exquisite Simulacrum: Remembering Philip Levine" first appeared in *Coming Close: Forty Essays on Philip Levine* (2013).

"The Trauma of Joy: Wilson Harris's *Guyana Quartet*" first appeared as a foreword to the 2021 edition of *The Guyana Quartet* by Wilson Harris.

"Bottle Torches: A Fantasia on Nari Ward" was first delivered at the Outside the Box Gallery Talks on the occasion of the exhibition *Nari Ward: We the People* at the New Museum in 2019.

"The Fire Thus Kindled, May Be Kindled Again: The Figure of Frederick Douglass" was first delivered as a lecture at the Newcastle Poetry Festival in 2019 and subsequently published in pamphlet form by Newcastle University.

"The Bearings of the Island" was first delivered as a lecture at the Oslo Poesifestival in 2016.

"The Classics Can Console?" was first delivered as the Robert Fagles Lecture at Princeton University in 2019.

I would like to thank Sarah Chalfant at Wylie and Jonathan Galassi at Farrar, Straus and Giroux. I am indebted to Valzhyna Mort, Colin Channer, Teju Cole, and Rowan Ricardo Phillips for their thoughtful feedback that helped me to realize this book. My deepest gratitude to all my friends and family.

Illustration Credits

198 *Sketchbook number 41. Sketch of a splash of blood and text.* 1995. Donald Rodney. Tate. © Estate of Donald Rodney. Photograph: Tate.

199 *Sketchbook number 41. Sketch titled 'a nigger splash.'* 1995. Donald Rodney. Tate. © Estate of Donald Rodney. Photograph: Tate.

200 Photograph by EG Schempf.

202 "Nari Ward: We the People," 2019. Exhibition view: New Museum, New York. Photograph: Maris Hutchinson / EPW Studio.

207 Photograph by EG Schempf.

211 "Nari Ward: We the People," 2019. Exhibition view: New Museum, New York. Photograph: Maris Hutchinson / EPW Studio.

214 Courtesy National Park Service, Museum Management Program, and Frederick Douglass National Historic Site.

217 Courtesy National Park Service, Museum Management Program, and Frederick Douglass National Historic Site.

231 Courtesy National Park Service, Museum Management Program, and Frederick Douglass National Historic Site.

277 "Boy on Plaza" by Valzhyna Mort.

282 Photograph by Ishion Hutchinson.

285 Photograph by Ishion Hutchinson.

286 Photograph by Ishion Hutchinson.

289 Slave Ship Log. © National Maritime Museum, Greenwich, London.

300 Photograph by Ishion Hutchinson.

336 Photograph by Ishion Hutchinson.

337 Photograph by Ishion Hutchinson.

342 Photograph by Ishion Hutchinson.

350 Photograph by Ishion Hutchinson.

362 Photograph by Ishion Hutchinson.